Mobile Context Awareness

Tom Lovett · Eamonn O'Neill
Editors

Mobile Context Awareness

Foreword by David Pollington

 Springer

Editors
Tom Lovett
Department of Computer Science
University of Bath/Vodafone Group R&D
Bath, UK

Eamonn O'Neill
Department of Computer Science
University of Bath
Bath, UK

ISBN 978-1-4471-5999-5   ISBN 978-0-85729-625-2 (eBook)
DOI 10.1007/978-0-85729-625-2
Springer London Dordrecht Heidelberg New York

Springer is part of Springer Science+Business Media (www.springer.com)

Foreword

Over the 15 years+ I've spent in the mobile industry, I've seen the mobile phone evolve through a number of innovation cycles. In its humble beginnings the focus was understandably around communications (voice and SMS) but with the introduction of Multimedia Messaging (MMS) at the turn of the new Millennium the focus shifted to generating new revenues around content, the mobile phone evolving to become a music player and perhaps even a portable TV player.

As phones (and networks) evolved over the next 5 years to support multimedia (larger displays, faster processors, higher bandwidth) it was realised that the mobile phone could be more than just a communications device or a portable media player: it could become a multi-purpose portable computer. What followed was the exploration of open operating systems, application environments and enhanced brows-ing capabilities that delivered a new breed of mobile phone that could truly herald the start of a new post-PC era—the smart-phone. With the introduction of enhanced sensors, AI and machine learning we're now witnessing the next evolutionary step, one in which the mobile phone becomes much more contextually aware and able not only to personalise the services it provides but potentially anticipate the needs of its owner; truly exciting times.

Mobile phones have already evolved to enable us to navigate our surroundings but such insight will become more fine grained as technology evolves, opening up the ability to infer intent in addition to place and thereby unlocking elements of contextual awareness that will make future mobile services more intelligent and useful to the end-user. This book pulls together research that explores the art of the possible in contextual awareness via mobile phones, the opportunities it presents and the challenges that will need to be overcome to deliver on the vision.

Newbury, UK
David Pollington

Preface

This book originated from a workshop at *UbiComp 2010* in Copenhagen, Denmark, in which both academic and industrial researchers presented their work in the field of mobile context awareness. The work addressed common challenges and problems encountered when using mobile devices to enable context-aware computing; from low-level sensing to middleware and applications. It is this range that forms the scope of this edited volume.

The purpose of the book is to present this work to a wider audience, particularly researchers and practitioners in the field of context-aware computing. The authors have expanded considerably on their work from the workshop, and the chapters present an overview of the capabilities, challenges and applications of mobile context-aware systems. The book is a collection of research, so it is primarily aimed at an audience of human computer interaction (HCI) researchers in both industry and academia. However, those interested in designing and implementing mobile context aware applications may find the content useful to their work.

We are grateful to our authors for their hard work in contributing the book's chapters, and our thanks to Ben Bishop and Beverley Ford at Springer for their assistance.

Bath, UK   Tom Lovett
                                                                    Eamonn O'Neill

Contents

Contributors

Alessio Agneessens University of Genova, Genova, Italy

Sherif G. Aly Department of Computer Science and Engineering, The American University in Cairo, Cairo, Egypt

Gustavo Baptista Laboratory for Advanced Collaboration (LAC), Pontifícia Universidade Católica do Rio de Janeiro, Rio de Janeiro, RJ, Brazil

Igor Bisio University of Genova, Genova, Italy

Kenta Cho Corporate Research & Development Center, Toshiba Corporation, Tokyo, Japan

Jon Crowcroft Computer Lab, University of Cambridge, Cambridge, UK

Lincoln David Laboratory for Advanced Collaboration (LAC), Pontifícia Universidade Católica do Rio de Janeiro, Rio de Janeiro, RJ, Brazil

Jakob Eg Larsen DTU Informatics, Cognitive Systems Section, Technical University of Denmark, Copenhagen, Denmark

Markus Endler Laboratory for Advanced Collaboration (LAC), Pontifícia Universidade Católica do Rio de Janeiro, Rio de Janeiro, RJ, Brazil

Salvador Faria Madeira Interactive Technologies Institute, University of Madeira, Madeira, Portugal

Hubert Fonseca Laboratory for Advanced Collaboration (LAC), Pontifícia Universidade Católica do Rio de Janeiro, Rio de Janeiro, RJ, Brazil

Cristina Frà Telecom Italia S.p.A., Turin, Italy

Ahmed M. Hamza Department of Computer Science and Engineering, The American University in Cairo, Cairo, Egypt

Masanori Hattori Corporate Research & Development Center, Toshiba Corporation, Tokyo, Japan

Naoki Iketani Corporate Research & Development Center, Toshiba Corporation, Tokyo, Japan

Henry Kautz Department of Computer Science, University of Rochester, Rochester, NY, USA

Takahiro Kawamura Corporate Research & Development Center, Toshiba Corporation, Tokyo, Japan

Vassilis Kostakos Department of Computer Science and Engineering, University of Oulu, Oulu, Finland

Fabio Lavagetto University of Genova, Genova, Italy

Tom Lovett Department of Computer Science, University of Bath/Vodafone Group R&D, Bath, UK

Marcelo Malcher Laboratory for Advanced Collaboration (LAC), Pontifícia Universidade Católica do Rio de Janeiro, Rio de Janeiro, RJ, Brazil

Cecilia Mascolo Computer Laboratory, University of Cambridge, Cambridge, UK

Roderick Murray-Smith School of Computing Science, University of Glasgow, Glasgow, Scotland, UK

Mirco Musolesi School of Computer Science, University of Birmingham, Birmingham, UK

Eamonn O'Neill Department of Computer Science, University of Bath, Bath, UK

Yuzo Okamoto Corporate Research & Development Center, Toshiba Corporation, Tokyo, Japan

Kiran K. Rachuri Computer Laboratory, University of Cambridge, Cambridge, UK

Adam Sadilek Department of Computer Science, University of Rochester, Rochester, NY, USA

Hisao Setoguchi Corporate Research & Development Center, Toshiba Corporation, Tokyo, Japan

Massimo Valla Telecom Italia S.p.A., Turin, Italy

Narseo Vallina-Rodriguez Computer Lab, University of Cambridge, Cambridge, UK

José Viterbo Instituto de Computação, Universidade Federal Fluminense, Niterói, RJ, Brazil

Esben von Buchwald DTU Informatics, Technical University of Denmark, Copenhagen, Denmark

Chapter 1
Introduction

Tom Lovett and Eamonn O'Neill

Abstract The importance of context in computer science has increased in recent decades as computers have become ever more pervasive in everyday life. Context awareness—the idea that computers can sense and react to a user's situation—has been a popular research topic for a number of years. One of the most ubiquitous tools in the progress of context awareness has been the mobile device; its enormous popularity and permeation into daily life—coupled with increasingly sophisticated hardware—has greatly improved the potential for context awareness in the world. This chapter introduces the concepts of context and context awareness, as well as their integration with mobility. Current mobile context awareness research is summarised and a brief introduction of each chapter is presented.

1.1 Context

This book explores the concept of *context*. Context has been described as "information that can be used to characterise the situation of an entity" [7], and its importance in computer science has increased in recent decades as computers have become ever more pervasive in everyday life.

Context has no strict definition, and its interpretation can vary depending on application. In computer science, the definition by Dey [7] in the opening paragraph is sometimes regarded as a *de facto* standard, although sub-categories such as location, activity, identity or time [8] are often used in reference to context.

Following Dey's definition, there is a myriad of information that could be used to describe a user's situation, e.g. their location, what they're doing (the activity), whom they're doing it with, when they're doing it, what they're using to do it, where they're intending to go next, where they've been, etc. Each of these somewhat abstract categories can be further described by more concrete data, e.g. location may

T. Lovett (✉)
Department of Computer Science, University of Bath/Vodafone Group R&D, Bath, UK
e-mail: tom.lovett@vodafone.com

E. O'Neill
Department of Computer Science, University of Bath, Bath, UK
e-mail: eamonn@cs.bath.ac.uk

T. Lovett, E. O'Neill (eds.), *Mobile Context Awareness*,
DOI 10.1007/978-0-85729-625-2_1, © Springer-Verlag London Limited 2012

1

be described by degrees latitude and longitude or by user-defined interpretations (e.g. 'home' or 'work'); activity may be described generally (e.g. "travelling") or specifically, as relevant to the user (e.g. "walking to work").

As these examples illustrate, users may interpret their context differently from others, who in turn may describe their own context in a different manner. An apparently objective description of the same context may differ again, e.g. the user describes her location as "the office"; her friend, referring to the same location, may describe it as "in London"; and a GPS sensor might describe it as 51.5049672, −0.0197931.

There are challenges, therefore, when it comes to using context in computer science. Being useful to the user is a key objective in HCI, and making use of context can be advantageous if implemented effectively from the user's perspective. To do this requires the system accurately to sense and to interpret context and to provide a useful 'reaction' to the sensed context. The ability of a system to do this is known as *context awareness*.

1.2 Context Awareness

Context awareness—the idea that computers can sense and react to a user's situation—has been a popular research topic for a number of years, featuring regularly in computer science conferences and journals and occasionally in commercial products. Its appeal lies in a number of areas, notably through making users' lives easier by relieving task burden, e.g. searching for nearby shops, restaurants or transportation links. The vision of pervasive computing integrating into the environment—functioning only when necessary and without obstructing or annoying the end user—is certainly not a reality yet, but technology is moving incrementally closer to a world of "computing everywhere".

Context awareness intersects many other fields in computer science and engineering. For example, some of the key ideas behind artificial intelligence—agents sensing and reacting to environments, knowledge representation, inference, reasoning, learning and planning—interweave with the desirable traits of a context-aware system. Relations to other fields include: HCI (ubiquitous computing, user interfaces and user-centred design); telecommunications (sensors and wireless sensor networks); and mathematics (statistics, inference, data structures and algorithm design).

For implementation, context awareness requires a computing device to both sense and react to its user's situation. These devices could be desktop or laptop PCs (as they were during the genesis of context-awareness research); wireless sensor networks, e.g. smart homes that contain multiple autonomous sensors; or—as is becoming ever more common—mobile devices such as smartphones or tablet PCs.

1.3 Mobile Context Awareness

One of the most ubiquitous tools in the progress of context awareness has been the mobile device. Its enormous popularity and permeation into daily life—coupled with increasingly sophisticated hardware—has greatly increased the potential for context awareness in the world. The very mobility of these devices is key to the idea of *mobile context awareness*, where the sensing and reacting is enabled by— and even conducted upon—the device itself. It is both a sensing platform and a computer, and the relentless increase in mobile computing power and sensing capability—motion sensors, light sensors and multiple radio sensors come as standard in the modern smart-phone—allow for a whole new area of mobile context awareness research and development.

In the contemporary technological environment, mobile device users are becoming used to "always on" network connectivity; taking advantage of faster connections to use services such as push email, synchronised calendars and online application programmable interfaces (APIs) into social media services, e.g. Facebook. These 'virtual' sensors can expose the mobile device to additional data sources such as social networks, user preferences, tagged photographs and music playlists. Fusion of these sources with traditional 'physical' sensors, e.g. GPS, can allow for better context inference and, subsequently, a wider range of mobile applications. Furthermore, software developers are turning to mobile devices for application development. The soaring popularity of services such as Apple's App Store and the Android Marketplace means the mobile application business is predicted to be worth $17.5 billion by 2012 [18].

Many of the currently available context aware mobile services are limited to being "location-based services"; they focus primarily on the device's location, the user's interaction with the device and the services that the location-aware capability can enable, e.g. navigation. As we discussed in the initial section, location is a key feature of context, but it is not the only one; and this is even more apparent with the increasing range and diversity of data available to the typical mobile device.

The potential for mobile context-awareness is encouraging—the mobility of the device offers an enabler for sensing and reacting to users' everyday situations with little or no specialist hardware and relatively simple system architectures. This mobility comes at a price however: mobile devices are typically resource constrained— battery power, CPU limitations and network connectivity must be traded off against the demand for accurate and usable context aware applications. These trade-offs, coupled with the potential applications of—and improvements to—mobile context aware computing methods, offer many challenges to the research community.

This book introduces a selection of current research around the subject of mobile context awareness. Before introducing the book's motivation and contents, we provide a brief overview of some important mobile context awareness research to date. This research forms a basis for the field of mobile context awareness and the work described in the chapters of this book.

1.3.1 Mobile Context-Awareness Research

There has been a substantial amount of research on the underlying enabling technology for context awareness, e.g. sensing, sensor fusion and inference, but not so much on the practical application of these enablers [11]. With variables such as sensor availability, connection speed and processing power constraining performance, it is difficult to maintain context awareness at such a level that services remain usable in the face of sensing or inference failure.

Mobile device based context aware systems and applications are active research areas [3]. Work by Anagnostopoulos *et al.* [1] uses historical mobile context with a supervised machine learning method in order to predict the location of the mobile user. This illustrates the capability of using contextual data to predict user actions and estimate future context parameters. Other learning approaches include Krause *et al.* [12], who have shown that mobile devices can be used for online context inference. In a series of studies using their SenSay system, the authors demonstrate the capabilities of mobility when applied to real-time inference of user context.

ContextPhone [15] is a mobile platform built to enable context-aware technology such as the ContextContacts application that lets users represent and exchange presence information with their mobile device contacts. More recent work within the field of mobile social context-awareness includes EmotionSense [14]: a programmable mobile context-aware system that uses mobile devices to sense emotions, activities and various activities within proximate social groups. Other social applications include the Friendlee application by HP Labs [2], which uses call records and contextual data to infer the user's immediate social network, before reordering the device contacts accordingly.

Further examples of mobile context-aware application research include Microsoft's Virtual Compass [4], a peer-to-peer indoor localisation system for mobile phones. To establish relative location, the application uses data on the relative spatial relationships between proximate devices through short range radio sensors. Privacy applications are also being developed; including the TreasurePhone application [17] that uses a context sensitive security model for privacy protection on mobile devices.

To encourage physical activity for mobile device users, the UbiFit Garden application was developed [6]. UbiFit Garden is a mobile context-aware application that infers the device user's activity using online sensing and machine learning techniques. The application uses the information gained from context inference to communicate the healthiness of each activity the user performs by way of a novel "garden" interface.

Extensive data collection is possible with mobile devices, as demonstrated by both MyExperience [10] and the mobile sensing platform [5]. These systems collect extensive context data about their users, and the mobile sensing platform performs activity recognition using specialist embedded hardware. Both of these systems demonstrate the capability of the mobile device to enable context-awareness without architectural complexity.

At the user level, advances have been made to better communicate the context-awareness process to the user through their own device. Lim and Dey's toolkit

[13] supports intelligibility in context-aware applications by generating explanations about context-related decisions to the user. Through a mobile interface, the user is able to view the system's state (with quantified certainty), why the system is in that state, why it's not in other states and how to take action given the state. Recommendation systems are a popular application for mobile context-awareness, e.g., [20], with complex inferences made from mobile data leading to suggestions for the user in areas such as restaurants, films and products. Perhaps the most notable implementation of mobile context-awareness (and commercial AI) is Apple's Siri [19]—a mobile personal assistant that uses a multitude of AI techniques and context data from the mobile device to help with its user's daily tasks.

Finally, the field of activity recognition is using mobile devices to advance its research. COSAR [16] uses statistical and ontological reasoning with mobile devices to classify a user's activity at a given time, and Figo *et al.* [9] use a mobile device's accelerometer sensor to process motion features for inference of the user's activity.

1.4 Book Motivation

The motivation behind this book is threefold: to explore the capabilities, challenges and applications of mobile context awareness. In addition to the very mobility that smartphones and similar devices bring to context awareness, we are interested in the capabilities that these mobile devices bring, the problems or challenges that they might introduce, and the applications and use cases for which mobile devices play a key part.

Each chapter within the book focuses on one or more of these areas, and the book serves as a collection of research around these important topics, which we hope will provide an interesting, informative and broad overview of current mobile context awareness.

1.5 Book Structure

"Modeling Success, Failure, and Intent of Multi-Agent Activities Under Severe Noise", by Adam Salidek and Henry Kautz, describes their extensive work in using mobile context-awareness to perform intelligent reasoning about complex human intentions. Using a real-world game—capture the flag—as a case study, the chapter outlines how raw sensor data can be used for learning an activity model, which can subsequently reason successfully about the intent of multiple agents, given the rules of the game. This chapter emphasises how the notion of mobility can lead to complex context scenarios, and the data obtained from mobile devices can be used for surprisingly sophisticated inference about a characteristically complex area of reasoning: human intent.

"Energy-Accuracy Trade-offs of Sensor Sampling in Smart Phone based Sensing Systems" by Kiran Rachuri, Cecilia Mascolo and Mirco Musolesi addresses the important issue of energy management in mobile devices, and effects on accuracy requirements in mobile context aware systems. The chapter outlines a series of trade-offs between energy demand and sensor data accuracy, using the accelerometer, Bluetooth and microphone sensors on a mobile device. Furthermore, the authors present a range of sampling methods that aim to optimise the energy-accuracy trade-off in practical applications. This work has wide-reaching applications in mobile context awareness: performance is paramount for usable systems, but the mobility aspect of mobile context awareness carries a series of unique resource constraints—most notably that of the device's energy resources.

"Acceleration Noise Correction for Transfer Inference Using Accelerometers on Mobile Devices", by Hisao Setoguchi, Yuzo Okamoto, Naoki Iketani, Kenta Cho, Masanori Hattori and Takahiro Kawamura, discusses a practical method to reduce motion noise in mobile devices caused by 'unimportant' events, e.g. removing the device from a pocket. These events can mask more important events, e.g. boarding transportation, and affect the performance of context inference in mobile devices. This chapter focuses on the sources of low-level motion noise and presents an algorithm to reduce its effects, allowing more important events to be inferred from the same sensor source. Many modern devices are equipped with accelerometers and, while they are useful data sources for inferring users' activities, they are noisy and typically ill positioned. This chapter addresses the challenge of inference from a single noisy mobile data source, and highlights the difficulties associated with stochastic 'noise' obfuscating more important 'signal' data.

"Mobile Sensing of User's Motion and Position Context for Automatic Check-in Suggestion and Validation", by Cristina Frà, Massimo Valla, Alessio Agneessens, Igor Bisio and Fabio Lavagetto, addresses a useful application of mobile context awareness: the check-in service. Many services exist that allow users to 'check-in' or tag their context, and establishments that are frequented by these users can offer rewards or discounts for loyalty. This chapter is concerned with problem of check-in validation, i.e. how can the check-in be authorised for the establishment with minimal disruption to the user? The chapter presents a method to do this using mobile device sensors and real-time decision algorithms, and the implications are important for real-world applications that utilise mobile context awareness.

"The case for context aware resource management in mobile operating systems", by Narseo Vallina-Rodriguez and Jon Crowcroft, also addresses the issue of resource management in mobile devices. The authors argue that mobile device design is driven by usability rather than resource optimisation, and they present an interesting overview of how users' context affects resource consumption in mobile devices. Furthermore, they show how awareness of this context can help to optimise the consumption of various resources, including: power; device CPU; device sensors, e.g. GPS and cellular connections; and wireless interfaces. This work has important implications for mobile device design, and presents the case for 'context-driven' mobile devices—an interesting alternative to 'context aware' mobile devices.

"A scalable sensor middleware for social end user programming", by Salvador Faria and Vassilis Kostakos, focuses on the social element of mobile context awareness. Using a sensor-based middleware comprising of multiple 'physical' and 'virtual' sensors, the middleware brings together mobile context awareness and social media. Through a series of case studies, the authors show how the data from large numbers of sensors can be aggregated and interfaced with actuators, which has important implications for deployable mobile context aware systems. Indeed, the authors go beyond the typical mobile smart-phone, and integrate a diverse range of mobile sensors with a social element. The ability for different users to utilise sensor sets depending on their context is addressed, and raises interesting questions about the potential for context aware resource sharing.

"Mobile Context-Aware Support for Public Transportation Users", by Esben von Buchwald, Jakob Eg Larsen and Roderick Murray-Smith, discusses another application of mobile context awareness: transportation support. Acquiring information about public transport can be problematic, especially when using it *ad hoc* or in an unfamiliar location. This chapter addresses these issues using a context aware mobile device and gestural recognition. From a case study conducted in Copenhagen, Denmark, the chapter shows how timetabling information and services such as ticket purchasing can be integrated into the device to relieve the burden of public transportation for the user. The authors show how mobile context awareness can really aid users' experiences in a real world scenario.

"Quality Sensitive Web Service Profiling and Discovery: In support of Mobile and Pervasive Applications", by Sherif G. Aly and Ahmed M. Hamza, uses the idea of web services to aid mobile context aware applications. The popularity of web-based mobile applications is increasing as network connectivity becomes more available, and this offers an opportunity to address the challenge of sensor and service quality. By applying a Quality of Service (QoS) framework to mobile web services, the chapter shows how services can be selected based on the user's current context, as well as a quality criterion.

"A Middleware Supporting Adaptive and Context-aware Mobile Applications" by Lincoln David, José Viterbo, Marcelo Malcher, Hubert Fonseca, Gustavo Baptista and Markus Endler presents a system for collaborative mobile context aware application design. The authors address the issue of developing mobile context aware applications from scratch, and avoid needless repetition through a framework of common context components. Focusing on collaborative context awareness, i.e. users sharing context data such as location at a particular time, examples of applications built using this framework are presented, including: the mapping of Trekking routes from users' location data; managing collaborative meetings; travel services for the visually impaired; and instant messaging based on motion data.

References

1. Anagnostopoulos, T., Anagnostopoulos, C., Hadjiefthymiades, S., Kyriakakos, M., & Kalousis, A. (2009). Predicting the location of mobile users: a machine learning approach. In *ICPS '09: Proceedings of the 2009 international conference on pervasive services*, London, UK (pp. 65–72). New York: ACM.
2. Ankolekar, A., Szabo, G., Luon, Y., Huberman, B. A., & Wilkinson, D. (2009). Friendlee: A mobile application for your social life. In *MobileHCI '09: Proceedings of the 11th international conference on human-computer interaction with mobile devices and services*, Bonn, Germany (pp. 1–4). New York: ACM.

3. Baldauf, M., Dustdar, S., & Rosenberg, F. (2007). A survey on context-aware systems. *International Journal of Ad Hoc and Ubiquitous Computing, 2*(4), 263–277.
4. Banerjee, N., Agarwal, S., Bahl, P., Chandra, R., Wolman, A., & Corner, M. (2010). Virtual Compass: relative positioning to sense mobile social interactions. In P. Floréen, A. Krüger, & M. Spasojevic (Eds.), *Pervasive computing* (pp. 1–21). Berlin: Springer.
5. Choudhury, T., Borriello, G., Consolvo, S., Haehnel, D., Harrison, B., Hemingway, B., & Hightower, J. (2008). Others: The mobile sensing platform: An embedded activity recognition system. *IEEE Pervasive Computing, 7*(2), 32–41.
6. Consolvo, S., Mcdonald, D. W., Toscos, T., Chen, M. Y., Froehlich, J., Harrison, B., Klasnja, P., Lamarca, A., Legrand, L., Libby, R., Smith, I., & Landay, J. A. (2008). Activity sensing in the wild: A field trial of UbiFit garden. In *Proceedings of the twenty-sixth annual SIGCHI conference on Human factors in computing systems*, Florence, Italy (pp. 1797–1806).
7. Dey, A. (2001). Understanding and using context. *Personal and Ubiquitous Computing, 5*(1), 4–7.
8. Dey, A. K., & Abowd, G. D. (2000). Towards a better understanding of context and context-awareness. In *CHI'2000 workshop on the what, who, where, when, and how of context-awareness.*
9. Figo, D., Diniz, P. C., Ferreira, D. R., & Cardoso, J.a.M.P. (2010). Preprocessing techniques for context recognition from accelerometer data. *Personal and Ubiquitous Computing, 14*(7), 645–662.
10. Froehlich, J., Chen, M., & Consolvo, S. (2007). MyExperience: a system for in situ tracing and capturing of user feedback on mobile phones. In *Proceedings of the 5th international conference on mobile systems, applications and services* (pp. 57–70).
11. Hong, J. Y., Suh, E. H., & Kim, S. J. (2009). Context-aware systems: A literature review and classification. *Expert Systems With Applications, 36*(4), 8509–8522.
12. Krause, A., Smailagic, A., & Siewiorek, D. (2006). Context-aware mobile computing: learning context- dependent personal preferences from a wearable sensor array. *IEEE Transactions on Mobile Computing, 5*(2), 113–127.
13. Lim, B., & Dey, A. (2010). Toolkit to support intelligibility in context-aware applications. In *Proceedings of the 12th ACM international conference on ubiquitous computing* (pp. 13–22). New York: ACM.
14. Rachuri, K., Musolesi, M., & Mascolo, C. (2010). EmotionSense: a mobile phones based adaptive platform for experimental social psychology research. In *Proceedings of the 12th ACM international conference on ubiquitous computing* (pp. 281–290).
15. Raento, M., Oulasvirta, A., Petit, R., & Toivonen, H. (2005). ContextPhone: A prototyping platform for context-aware mobile applications. *IEEE Pervasive Computing, 4*(2), 51–59.
16. Riboni, D., & Bettini, C. (2011). COSAR: hybrid reasoning for context-aware activity recognition. *Personal and Ubiquitous Computing, 15*(3), 271–289.
17. Seifert, J., De Luca, A., & Conradi, B. (2009). A context-sensitive security model for privacy protection on mobile phones. In *MobileHCI '09: Proceedings of the 11th international conference on human-computer interaction with mobile devices and services*, Bonn, Germany (pp. 1–2). New York: ACM.
18. Shiels, M. Mobile application sales to reach '$17.5bn by 2012' (2010). http://news.bbc.co.uk/1/hi/technology/8571210.stm.
19. Siri. Your wish is its command (2011). http://www.apple.com/iphone/features/siri.html.
20. Zhuang, J., Mei, T., Hoi, S., & Xu, Y. (2011). When recommendation meets mobile: contextual and personalized recommendation on the go. In *Proceedings of the 13th international conference on ubiquitous computing* (pp. 153–162).

Chapter 2
Modeling Success, Failure, and Intent of Multi-Agent Activities Under Severe Noise

Adam Sadilek and Henry Kautz

Abstract This chapter takes on the task of understanding human interactions, attempted interactions, and intentions from noisy sensor data in a fully relational multi-agent setting. We use a real-world game of capture the flag to illustrate our approach in a well-defined domain that involves many distinct cooperative and competitive joint activities. We model the domain using Markov logic, a statistical-relational language, and learn a theory that jointly denoises the data and infers occurrences of high-level activities, such as a player capturing an enemy. We show that while it may be impossible to directly detect a multi-agent activity due to sensor noise or malfunction, the occurrence of the activity can still be inferred by considering its impact on the behavior of the people involved. Further, we show that given a model of successfully performed multi-agent activities, along with a set of examples of failed attempts at the same activities, our system automatically learns an augmented model that is capable of recognizing success and failure, as well as goals of people's actions with high accuracy. We compare our approach with other alternatives and show that our unified model, which takes into account not only relationships among individual players, but also relationships among activities over the entire length of a game, although more computationally costly, is significantly more accurate. Finally, we demonstrate that interesting game segments and key players can be efficiently identified in an automated fashion. Our system exhibits a strong agreement with human judgement about the game situations at hand.

2.1 Introduction

Our society is founded on the interplay of human relationships and interactions. Since every person is tightly embedded in our social structure, the vast majority of human behavior can be fully understood only in the context of the actions of

A. Sadilek (✉) · H. Kautz
Department of Computer Science, University of Rochester, Rochester, NY 14627, USA
e-mail: sadilek@cs.rochester.edu

H. Kautz
e-mail: kautz@cs.rochester.edu

T. Lovett, E. O'Neill (eds.), *Mobile Context Awareness*,
DOI 10.1007/978-0-85729-625-2_2, © Springer-Verlag London Limited 2012

others. Thus, not surprisingly, more and more evidence is emerging from social networks research showing that when we want to model behavior of a person, the single best predictor is often the behavior of people in her social network. For instance, behavioral patterns of people taking taxis, rating movies, choosing a cell phone provider, or sharing music are best explained and predicted by the habits of related people, rather than by all the "single person" attributes such as age, race, or education [10, 67].

In contrast to these observations, most research effort on activity recognition to date has concentrated on modeling single individuals [13, 50, 51], or statistical properties of aggregate groups of individuals [1, 35], or combinations of both [24]. Notable exceptions to this "isolated individuals" approach include Kamar and Horvitz [40] and Gupta, Srinivasan, Shi, and Davis [31], where simple relationships among people are just starting to be explicitly considered and leveraged. For instance, Eagle and Pentland [24] elegantly model the location of individuals from multi-modal sensory data, but their approach is oblivious to the explicit effects of one's friends, relatives, *etc.* on one's behavior. The isolated individuals approximations are often made for the sake of tractability and representational convenience. While considering individuals independently of each other is sufficient for some constrained tasks, in many interesting domains it discards a wealth of important information or results in an inefficient and unnatural data representation. On the other hand, decomposing a domain into a set of entities (representing for instance people, objects in their environment, or activities) that are linked by various relationships (*e.g.*, is-a, has-a, is-involved-in) is a natural and clear way of representing data.

To address the shortcomings of nonrelational behavior modeling, we introduce the capture the flag domain (described below), and argue for a statistical-relational approach to learning models of multi-agent behavior from raw GPS data. The CTF dataset is on one hand quite complex and recorded by real-world sensors, but at the same time it is well-defined (as per the rules of the game), thereby allowing for an unambiguous evaluation of the results.

Being able to recognize people's activities and reason about their behavior is a necessary precondition for having intelligent and helpful machines that are aware of "what is going on" in the human-machine as well as human-human relationships. There are many exciting practical applications of activity recognition that have the potential to fundamentally change people's lives. For example, cognitive assistants that help people and teams be more productive, or provide support to (groups of) disabled individuals, or efficiently summarize a long complex event to a busy person without leaving out essential information. Other important applications include intelligent navigation, traffic prediction, optimal traffic lights timing, and mass transit scheduling. All these applications and a myriad of others build on top of multi-agent activity recognition and therefore require it as a necessary stepping stone. Furthermore, as a consequence of the anthropocentrism of our technology, modeling human behavior plays—perhaps surprisingly—a significant role even in applications that do not directly involve people (*e.g.*, unmanned space probes).

Furthermore, reasoning about human *intentions* is an essential element of activity recognition, since if we can recognize what a person (or a group of people) *wants* to do, we can proactively try to help them (or—in adversarial situations—hinder them). Intent is notoriously problematic to quantify (*e.g.*, Baldwin and Baird [8]), but we show that in the capture the flag domain, the notion is naturally captured in the process of learning the structure of failed activities. We all know perhaps too well that a successful action is often preceded—and unfortunately sometimes also followed—by multiple failed attempts. Therefore, reasoning about attempts typically entails high practical utility, but not just for their relatively high frequency. Consider, for example, a task of real-time analysis of a security video system. There, detecting that a person or a group of people (again, relations) *intend* to steal something is much more important and useful than recognizing that a theft has taken (or even is taking) place, because then it is certainly too late to entirely *prevent* the incident and it may also be too late or harder to merely stop it. We believe that recognition of attempts in people's activities is a severely underrepresented topic in artificial intelligence that needs to be explored more since it opens a new realm of interesting possibilities.

Before we delve into the details of our approach in Sects. 2.5 and 2.6, we briefly introduce the CTF dataset (Sect. 2.2), highlight the main contributions of our work (Sect. 2.3), and review background material (Sect. 2.4). We discuss related work, conclude, and outline future work in Sects. 2.7, 2.8 and 2.9 respectively.

2.2 Capture The Flag Domain

Imagine two teams—seven players each—playing capture the flag (CTF) on a university campus, where each player carries a consumer-grade global positioning system (GPS) that logs its location (plus noise) every second (see Fig. 2.1). The primary goal is to enter the opponent's flag area. Players can be captured only while on enemy territory by being tagged by the enemy. Upon being captured, they must remain in place until freed (tagged by a teammate) or the game ends. The games involve many competitive and cooperative activities, but here we focus on (both successful and attempted) capturing and freeing. Visualization of the games is available from the first author's website.

We collected four games of CTF on a portion of the University of Rochester campus (about 23 acres) with Columbus V-900 GPS loggers (one per player) with 1 GB memory card each that were set to a sampling rate of 1 Hz. The durations of the games ranged approximately from 4 to 15 minutes.

Our work is not primarily motivated by the problem of annotating strategy games, although there are obvious applications of our results to sports and combat situations. We are, more generally, exploring relational learning and inference methods for recognizing *multi-agent activities* from location data. We accept the fact that the GPS data at our disposal is inherently unreliable and ambiguous for any one individual. We therefore focus on methods that *jointly and simultaneously* localize and recognize the high-level activities of groups of individuals.

Although the CTF domain doesn't capture all the intricacies of life, it contains many complex, interesting, and yet well-defined (multi-agent) activities. Moreover,

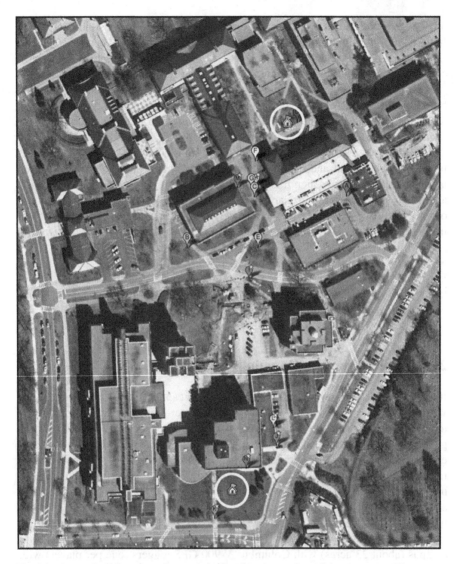

Fig. 2.1 A snapshot of a game of capture the flag that shows most of the game area. Players are represented by pins with letters. In our version of CTF, the two "flags" are stationary and are shown as *white circles* near the top and the bottom of the figure. The horizontal road in the middle of the image is the territory boundary. The data is shown prior to any denoising or corrections for map errors. Videos of the games are available at http://www.cs.rochester.edu/u/sadilek/

it is based on extensive real-world GPS data (total of 40,000+ data points). Thus most of the problems that we are addressing here clearly have direct analogs in everyday-life situations that ubiquitous computing needs to address—imagine people going about their daily lives in a city instead of CTF players, and their own smart phones instead of GPS loggers.

One of the main challenges we have to overcome if we are to successfully model CTF is the severe noise present in the data. Accuracy of the GPS data varies from 1 to more than 10 meters. In open areas, readings are typically off by 3 meters, but the discrepancy is much higher in locations with tall buildings (which are present within the game area) or other obstructions. Compare the scale of the error with the granularity of the activities we concern ourselves with: both capturing and freeing involves players that are within reaching distance (less than 1 meter) apart. Therefore, the signal to noise ratio in this domain is daunting.

The error has a systematic component as well as a significant stochastic component. Errors between devices are poorly correlated, because subtle differences between players, such as the angle at which the device sits in the player's pocket, can dramatically affect accuracy. Moreover, since we consider multi-agent scenarios, the errors in individual players' readings can add up, thereby creating a large discrepancy between the reality and the recorded dataset. Because players can move freely through open areas, we cannot reduce the data error by assuming that the players move along road or walkways, as is done in much work on GPS-based activity recognition (*e.g.*, Liao, Fox, and Kautz [50]). Finally, traditional techniques for denoising GPS data, such as Kalman filtering, are of little help, due to the low data rate (1 sample per second) relative to the small amount of time required for a player to completely change her speed or direction.

If we are to reliably recognize events that happen in these games in the presence of such severe noise, we need to consider not only each player, but also the relationships among them and their actions over extended periods of time (possibly the whole length of the game). Consider a concrete task of inferring the individual and joint activities and intentions of the CTF players from their GPS traces. For example, suppose the GPS data shows player A running toward a stationary teammate B, then moving away. What occurred? Possibly player A has just "freed" player B, but GPS error has hidden the fact that player A actually *reached* B. Another possibility is that player A had the *intention* of freeing player B, but was scared off by an opponent at the last second. Yet another possibility is that no freeing occurred nor was even intended, because player B had not been previously captured.

Understanding a game thus consists of inferring a complex set of interactions among the various players as well as the players' intentions. The conclusions drawn about what occurs at one point in time affect and are affected by inferences about past and future events. In the example just given, recognizing that player B is moving in the future reinforces the conclusion that player A is freeing player B, while failing to recognize a past event of player B being captured decreases confidence in that conclusion. The game of CTF also illustrates that understanding a situation is as much or more about recognizing attempts and intentions as about recognizing successfully executed actions. For example, in course of a 15 minute game, only a handful of capture or freeing events occur. However, there are dozens of cases where one player unsuccessfully tries to capture an opponent or to free a teammate. A description of a game that was restricted to what actually occurred would be only a pale reflection of the original.

As a concrete example, consider a real game situation illustrated in Figure 2.2. There we see three snapshots of a game projected over a map of the campus before

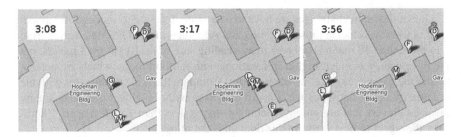

Fig. 2.2 Three snapshots of a game situation where both successful and failed capturing occur. This example also illustrates the need for an approach that exploits both the relational and the far reaching temporal structure of our domain. (See text for explanation)

any modification of the GPS data. The game time is shown on each snapshot. Players D, F, and G are allies and are currently on their home territory near their flag, whereas players L and M are their enemies. In the first snapshot, players L and M head for the opponent's flag but then—in the second frame—they are intercepted by G. At this point it is unclear what is happening because of the substantial error in the GPS data—the three players appear to be very close to each other, but in actuality they could have been 20 or more meters apart. However, once we see the third snapshot (note that tens of seconds have passed) we realize that player G actually captured only player M and didn't capture L since G is evidently still chasing L. The fact that player M remains stationary coupled with the fact that neither D nor F attempt to capture him suggests that M has indeed been captured. We show that it is possible to infer occurrences of capturing events even for complex situations like these whereas limited approaches largely fail. However, we need to be able to recognize not just individual events, we also need to discover new activities, identify their respective goals, and also distinguish between events based on whether their outcomes are favorable or negative. For instance, in the second frame, player G tries to capture both L and M. Although he succeeded in the former case, he failed in the latter.

Many different kinds of cooperative and competitive multi-agent activities occur in the games. The lowest-level joint activities are based on location and movement, and include "approaching" and "being at the same location." Note, that noise in the GPS data often makes it difficult or impossible to directly detect these simple activities. At the next level come competitive multi-agent activities including capturing and attacking; cooperative activities include freeing; and there are activities, such as chasing and guarding, that may belong to either category or to both categories. There are also more abstract tactical activities, such as making a sacrifice, and overall strategies, such as playing defensively. In this paper, we concentrate on activities at the first two levels.

2.3 Our Contributions

The main contributions of this paper are as follows. We first present a novel method that simultaneously denoises positional data and learns a model of multi-agent activities that occur there. We subsequently evaluate the model on the CTF dataset and show that it achieves high accuracy in recognizing complex game events.

However, creating a model by manually writing down new rules or editing existing axioms is laborious and prone to introduction of errors or unnecessarily complex theories. Thus, we would like to automate this process by *learning* (or *inducing*) new axioms from training data. For people, it is much easier to provide or validate concrete examples than to directly modify a model. This leads us to our second contribution: We show how to automatically augment a preexisting model of (joint) activities so that it is capable of not only recognizing successful actions, but also identifies *failed attempts* at the same types of activities. This line of work also demonstrates that explicitly modeling attempted interactions in a unified way improves overall model performance.

As our third contribution, we demonstrate that the *difference* (defined below) between the newly learned definitions of a failed activity and the original definition of the corresponding successful activity directly corresponds to the *goal* of the given activity. For instance, as per the rules of the capture the flag game, a captured player cannot move until freed. When our system induces the definition of failed capture, the new theory does not contain such a constraint on the movement of the almost-captured player, thereby allowing him to move freely.

Finally, we show that interesting game segments and key players can be efficiently identified in an automated fashion. Our kernel-based convolution detects novel and dynamic sequences of events, and exhibits a strong agreement with human judgement about the game situations at hand.

2.4 Background

The cores of our models described below are implemented in Markov logic (ML), a statistical-relational language. In this section, we provide a brief overview of ML, which extends finite first-order logic (FOL) to a probabilistic setting. For a more detailed (and excellent) treatment of FOL, ML, and inductive logic programming see [79], [23], and [19] respectively.

In order to compare the Markov logic based models to alternative approaches, we consider a dynamic Bayesian network (DBN) model in the experiments below as one of our baselines. We therefore review relevant aspects of DBNs in this section as well.

2.4.1 Markov Logic

Given the inherent uncertainty involved in reasoning about real-world activities as observed through noisy sensor readings, we looked for a methodology that would provide an elegant combination of probabilistic reasoning with the expressive, relatively natural, and compact but unfortunately strictly true or false formulas of first-order logic. And that is exactly what Markov logic provides and thus allows us to elegantly model complex finite relational non-i.i.d. domains. A Markov logic network (MLN) consists of a set of constants $\mathscr{C}$ and of a set of pairs $\langle \mathscr{F}_i, w_i \rangle$ such that each FOL formula $\mathscr{F}_i$ has a weight $w_i \in \mathbb{R}$ associated with it. Optionally, each weight can be further scaled by a real-valued function of a subset of the variables that appear in the corresponding formula. Markov logic networks that contain such functions are called *hybrid* MLNs [86].

A MLN can be viewed as a template for a Markov network (MN) as follows: the MN contains one node for each possible ground atom of MLN. The value of the node is 0 if the corresponding atom is *false* and 1 otherwise. Two nodes are connected by an edge if the corresponding atoms appear in the same formula. Thus, the MN has a distinct clique corresponding to each grounding of each formula. By $\mathscr{F}_i^{g_j}$ we denote the j-th grounding of formula $\mathscr{F}_i$. The MN also has a clique factor $f_{i,j}$ for each $\mathscr{F}_i^{g_j}$ such that

$$f_{i,j} = \begin{cases} 1 & \text{if } \mathscr{F}_i^{g_j} \text{ is } true \\ 0 & \text{otherwise} \end{cases}$$

Each weight w_i intuitively represents the relative "importance" of satisfying (or violating, if the weight is negative) the corresponding formula $\mathscr{F}_i$. More formally, the weight scales the difference in log-probability between a world that satisfies n groundings of the corresponding formula and one that results in m true groundings of the formula, all else being equal (*cf.* Eq. (2.1)). Thus the problem of satisfiability is relaxed in MLNs. We no longer search for a satisfying truth assignment as in traditional FOL. Instead, we are looking for a truth assignment that maximizes the sum of the weights of all satisfied formulas.

The weights can be either specified by the knowledge base engineer or, as in our approach, learned from training data. That is, we provide the learning algorithm with labeled capture instances and pairs of raw and corresponding denoised trajectories along with labeled instances of game events and it finds an optimal set of weights that maximize the likelihood of the training data. Weight learning can be done in either generative or discriminative fashion. Generative training maximizes the joint probability of observed as well as hidden predicates, whereas discriminative learning directly maximizes the conditional likelihood of the hidden predicates given the observed predicates. Since prior work demonstrated that Markov network models learned discriminatively consistently outperform their generatively trained counterparts [80], we focus on discriminative learning in our activity recognition domain.

Once the knowledge base with weights has been specified, we can ask questions about the state of hidden atoms given the state of the observed atoms. Let X be a vector of random variables (one random variable for each possible ground atom in the MN) and let χ be the set of all possible instantiations of X. Then, each $x \in$

χ represents a possible world. If $(\forall x \in \chi)[\Pr(X = x) > 0]$ holds, the probability distribution over these worlds is defined by

$$\Pr(X = x) = \frac{1}{Z} \exp\left(\sum_i w_i n_i(x_{\{i\}})\right) \tag{2.1}$$

where $n_i(x_{\{i\}})$ is the number of true groundings of i-th formula with w_i as its weight in a world x and

$$Z = \sum_{x \in \chi} \exp\left(\sum_i w_i n_i(x_{\{i\}})\right) \tag{2.2}$$

Equation (2.1) can be viewed as assigning a "score" to each possible world and dividing each score by the sum of all scores over all possible worlds (the constant Z) in order to normalize.

Maximum *a posteriori* (MAP) inference in Markov logic given the state of the observed atoms reduces to finding a truth assignment for the hidden atoms such that the weighed sum of satisfied clauses is maximal. Even though this problem is in general #P-complete, we achieve reasonable run times by applying Cutting Plane MAP Inference (CPI) [71]. CPI can be thought of as a meta solver that incrementally grounds a Markov logic network, at each step creating a Markov network that is subsequently solved by any applicable method—such as MaxWalkSAT or via a reduction to an integer linear program. CPI refines the current solution by searching for additional groundings that could contribute to the objective function.

Up to this point, we have focused on *first-order* Markov logic. In first-order ML, each variable ranges over objects present the domain (*e.g.*, apples, players, or cars). On the other hand, in finite *second-order* Markov logic, we variabilize not only objects but also predicates (relations) themselves [45]. Our CTF model contains a predicate variable for each *type* of activity. For example, we have one variable *captureType* whose domain is

{capturing, failedCapturing}

and analogously for freeing events. When grounding the second-order ML, we ground all predicate variables as well as object variables.

Implementations of Markov logic include Alchemy[1] and theBeast.[2] Our experiments used a modified version of theBeast.

2.4.2 Dynamic Bayesian Networks

A Bayesian network (BN) is a directed probabilistic graphical model of data [39]. Nodes in the graph represent random variables and edges represent conditional de-

---

[1] http://alchemy.cs.washington.edu/.

[2] http://code.google.com/p/theBeast/.

pendencies. For a BN with n nodes, the joint probability distribution is given by

$$\Pr(X_1, \ldots, X_n) = \prod_{i=1}^{n} \Pr(X_i | \text{Pa}(X_i)), \qquad (2.3)$$

where $\text{Pa}(X_i)$ denotes the parents of node X_i. In a typical setting, a subset of the random variables is *observed* (we know their actual values), while the others are *hidden* and their values need to be inferred.

A dynamic Bayesian network (DBN) is a BN that models sequential data. A DBN is composed of *slices*—in our case each slice represents a one second time interval. In order to specify a DBN, we either write down or learn intra- and inter-slice conditional probability distributions (CPDs). The intra-slice CPDs typically constitute the observation model while the inter-slice CPDs model transitions between hidden states. For an extensive treatment of DBNs, see [62].

There are a number of parameter learning and inference techniques for DBNs. To match the Markov logic-based framework, in the experiments with the DBN model presented below, we focus on a supervised learning scenario, where the hidden labels are known at training time and therefore a maximum likelihood estimate can be calculated directly.

We find a set of parameters (discrete probability distributions) θ that maximize the log-likelihood of the training data. This is achieved by optimizing the following objective function.

$$\theta^{\star} = \underset{\theta}{\operatorname{argmax}} \log\big(\Pr(x_{1:t}, y_{1:t} | \theta)\big), \qquad (2.4)$$

where $x_{1:t}$ and $y_{1:t}$ represent the sequence of observed and hidden values, respectively, between times 1 and t, and $\theta^{\star}$ is the set of optimal model parameters. In our implementation, we represent probabilities and likelihoods with their log-counterparts to avoid arithmetic underflow.

At testing time, we are interested in the most likely explanation of the observed data. That is, we want to calculate the most likely assignment of states to all the hidden nodes (*i.e.*, Viterbi decoding of the DBN) given by

$$y_{1:t}^{\star} = \underset{y_{1:t}}{\operatorname{argmax}} \log\big(\Pr(y_{1:t} | x_{1:t})\big), \qquad (2.5)$$

where $\Pr(y_{1:t} | x_{1:t})$ is the conditional probability of a sequence of hidden states $y_{1:t}$ given a concrete sequence of observations $x_{1:t}$ between times 1 and t. We calculate the Viterbi decoding efficiently using dynamic programming [39].

2.5 Methodology

In this section, we describe the four major components of our approach. In short, we first manually construct a model of captures and freeings in CTF and optimize its parameters in a supervised learning framework (Sect. 2.5.1). This constitutes our "seed" theory that is used for denoising raw location data and recognition of successful multi-agent activities. We then show, in Sect. 2.5.2, how to automatically extend the seed theory by inducing the structure and learning the importance of failed captures and freeings as well as the relationships to their successful counterparts. Third, in Sect. 2.5.3, we use the augmented theory to recognize this richer set of multi-agent activities—both successful and failed attempts—and extract the goals of the activities. Finally, in Sect. 2.5.4, we concentrate on our method for detecting interesting game segments and key players.

Specifically, we investigate the following five research questions:

Q1. Can we reliably recognize complex multi-agent activities in the CTF dataset even in the presence of severe noise?

Q2. Can models of attempted activities be automatically learned by leveraging existing models of successfully performed actions?

Q3. Does modeling both success and failure allow us to infer the respective goals of the activities?

Q4. Does modeling failed attempts of activities improve the performance on recognizing the activities themselves?

Q5. Can we accurately identify interesting game situations and key actors?

We now elaborate on each of the four components of our system in turn, and subsequently discuss, in light of the experimental results and lessons learned, our answers to the above research questions.

2.5.1 Recognition of Successful Activities

In this section, we present our unified framework for intelligent relational denoising of the raw GPS data while simultaneously labeling instances of a player being captured by an enemy or freed by an ally. Both the denoising and the labeling are cast as a learning and inference problem in Markov logic. By denoising, we mean modifying the raw GPS trajectories of the players such that the final trajectories satisfy constraints imposed by the geometry of the game area, the motion model of the players, as well as by the rules and the dynamics of the game. In this paper, we refer to this trajectory modification as "snapping" since we tile the game area with 3 by 3 meter cells and snap each raw GPS reading to an appropriate cell. By creating cells only in unobstructed space, we ensure the final trajectory is consistent with the map of the area.

We begin by modeling the domain via a Markov logic theory, where we write the logical formulas that express the structure of the model by hand, and learn an optimal set of weights on the formulas from training data in a supervised discriminative fashion (details on the experimental set-up are in Sect. 2.6). In the following two subsections, we will show how to augment this seed Markov logic theory to recognize a richer set of events and extract the goals of players' multi-agent activities.

Thus, in order to perform data denoising and recognition of successful capturing and freeing, we model the game as weighted formulas in Markov logic. Some of the formulas are "hard," in the sense that we are only interested in solutions that satisfy all of them. Hard formulas capture basic physical constraints (*e.g.*, a player is only at one location at a time) and inviolable rules of the game (*e.g.*, a captured player must stand still until freed or the game ends).[3] The rest of the formulas are "soft," meaning there is a finite weight associated with each one. Some of the soft constraints correspond to a traditional low-level data filter, expressing preferences for smooth trajectories that are close to the raw GPS readings. Other soft constraints capture high-level constraints concerning when individual and multi-agent activities *are likely* to occur. For example, a soft constraint states that if a player encounters an enemy on the enemy's territory, the player is likely to be captured. The exact weights on the soft constraints are learned from labeled data, as described below.

We distinguish two types of atoms in our models: *observed* (*e.g.*, GPS(P_1, 4, 43.13°, −77.71°) and *hidden* (*e.g.*, freeing(P_1, P_8, 6)). The observed predicates in the CTF domain are: GPS, enemies, adjacent, onHomeTer, and onEnemyTer;[4] whereas capturing, freeing, isCaptured, isFree, samePlace, and snap are hidden. Additionally, the set of hidden predicates is expanded by the structure learning algorithm described below (see Table 2.1 for predicate semantics). In the training phase, our learning algorithm has access to the known truth assignment to *all* atoms. In the testing phase, it can still access the state of the observed atoms, but it has to infer the assignment to the hidden atoms.

Figure 2.3 gives an English description of our hard and soft rules for the low-level movement and player interactions within capture the flag.

We compare our unified approach with four alternative models. The first two models (**baseline** and **baseline with states**) are purely deterministic and they separate the denoising of the GPS data and the labeling of game events. We implemented both of them in Perl. They do not involve any training phase. The third alternative model is a **dynamic Bayesian network** shown in Fig. 2.4. Finally, we have two models cast in Markov logic: the **two-step ML model** and the **unified ML model** itself. The unified model handles the denoising and labeling in a joint fashion whereas the two-step approach first performs snapping given the geometric constraints and subsequently labels instances of capturing and freeing. The latter three models are evaluated using four-fold cross-validation where in order to test on a given game, we first train a model on the other three games. ML formulas for the hard and soft rules for movement and interactions in Fig. 2.3 are shown in Figs. 2.5 and 2.6.

All of our models can access the following observed data: raw GPS position of each player at any time and indication whether they are on enemy or home territory, location of each 3 by 3 meter cell, cell adjacency, and list of pairs of players that

---

[3]Cheating did not occur in our CTF games, but in principle could be accommodated by making the rules highly-weighted soft constraints rather than hard constraints.

[4]While the noise in the GPS data introduces some ambiguity to the last two observed predicates, we can still reliably generate them since the road that marks the boundary between territories constitutes a neutral zone.

Table 2.1 Summary of the logical predicates our models use. Predicate names containing the word "failed" are introduced by the Markov logic theory augmentation method described in Sect. 2.5.2.1

Predicate	Type	Meaning
capturing(a, b, t)	hidden	Player a is capturing b at time t
enemies(a, b)	observed	Players a and b are enemies
adjacent(c_1, c_2)	observed	Cells c_1 and c_2 are mutually adjacent
failedCapturing(a, b, t)	hidden	Player a is unsuccessfully capturing b at time t
failedFreeing(a, b, t)	hidden	Player a is unsuccessfully freeing b at time t
freeing(a, b, t)	hidden	Player a is freeing b at time t
isCaptured(a, t)	hidden	Player a is in captured state at time t
isFailedCaptured(a, t)	hidden	At time t, player a is in a state that follows an unsuccessful attempt at capturing a. a in this state has the same capabilities as when free
isFailedFree(a, t)	hidden	At time t, player a is in a state that follows an unsuccessful attempt at freeing a. a in this state has the same capabilities as when captured
isFree(a, t)	hidden	Player a is in free state at time t (isFree$(a, t) \equiv \neg$isCaptured(a, t))
onEnemyTer(a, t)	observed	Player a in on enemy territory at time t
onHomeTer(a, t)	observed	Player a in on home territory at time t
samePlace(a, b, t)	hidden	Players a and b are either snapped to a common cell or to two adjacent cells at time t
snap(a, c, t)	hidden	Player a is snapped to cell c at time t

are enemies. We tested all five models on the same observed data. The following describes each model in more detail.

- **Baseline Model (B)**

    This model has two separate stages. First we snap each reading to the nearest cell and afterward we label the instances of player a capturing player b. The labeling rule is simple: we loop over the whole discretized (via snapping) data set and output capturing(a, b, t) every time we encounter a pair of players a and b such that they were snapped (in the first step) to either the same cell or to two mutually adjacent cells at time t, they are enemies, and a is on its home territory while b is not. Freeing recognition is not considered in this simple model since we need to have a notion of persisting player states (captured or free) in order to model freeing in a meaningful way.

- **Baseline Model with States (B+S)**

    This second model builds on top of the previous one by introducing a notion that players have states. If player a captures player b at time t, b enters a captured state (in logic, isCaptured$(b, t + 1)$). Then b remains in captured state until he moves (is snapped to a different cell at a later time) or the game ends. As per rules of CTF, a player who is in captured state cannot be captured again.

Hard Rules:

H1. Each raw GPS reading is snapped to exactly one cell.

H2. a. When player a frees player b, then both involved players must be snapped to a common cell at that time.

    b. A player can only be freed by a free ally.

    c. A player can be freed only when he or she is currently captured.

    d. Immediately after a freeing event, the freed player transitions to a free state.

    e. A player can only be freed while on enemy territory.

H3. a. When player a captures player b, then both involved players must be snapped to a common cell at that time.

    b. A player can only be captured by a free enemy.

    c. A player can be captured only if he or she is currently free.

    d. Immediately after a capture event, the captured player transitions to a captured state.

    e. A player can be captured only when standing on enemy territory.

H4. All players are free at the beginning of the game.

H5. At any given time, a player is either captured or free but not both.

H6. A player transitions from a captured state to a free state only via a freeing event.

H7. A player transitions from a free state to a captured state only via a capture event.

H8. If a player is captured then he or she must remain in the same location.

Soft Rules:

S1. Minimize the distance between the raw GPS reading and the snapped-to cell.

S2. Minimize projection variance, *i.e.*, two consecutive "snappings" should be generally correlated.

S3. Maximize smoothness (both in terms of space and time) of the final player trajectories.

S4. If players a and b are enemies, a is on enemy territory and b is not, b is not captured already, and they are close to each other, then a *probably* captures b.

S5. If players a and b are allies, both are on enemy territory, b is currently captured and a is not, and they are close to each other, then a *probably* frees b.

S6. Capture events are generally rare, *i.e.*, there are typically only a few captures within a game.

S7. Freeing events are also generally rare.

Fig. 2.3 Descriptions of the hard and soft rules for capture the flag

Thus, this model works just like the previous one except whenever it is about to label a capturing event, it checks the states of the involved players and outputs capturing(a, b, t) only if both a and b are *not* in captured state.

Freeing recognition is implemented in an analogous way to capturing recognition. Namely, every time a captured player b is about to transition to a free state, we check if b has a free teammate a nearby (again, within the adjacent cells). If that is the case, we output freeing(a, b, t).

- **Dynamic Bayesian Network Model (DBN)**

The dynamic Bayesian network model can be viewed as a probabilistic generalization of the above baseline model with states. The structure of the DBN model for one player is shown in Fig. 2.4. In each time slice, we have one hidden node and four observed nodes, all of which represent binary random variables.

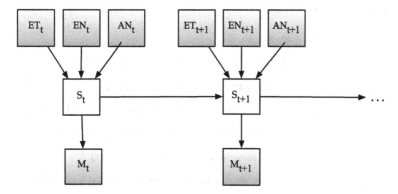

Fig. 2.4 Two consecutive time slices of our dynamic Bayesian network for modeling the state of an individual player P from observations. Shaded nodes represent observed random variables, unfilled denote hidden variables. All random variables are binary. ($ET_t = 1$ when P is on enemy territory at time t, $EN_t = 1$ when there is an enemy nearby at time t, $AN_t = 1$ when there is an ally nearby at time t, and finally $M_t = 1$ if P has moved between time $t - 1$ and t. The value of hidden state S_t is 1 if P is captured at time t and 0 when P is free)

We want to infer the most likely state S for each player at any given time t over the course of a game. The state is either free or captured and is hidden at testing time. There are four observed random variables per time step that model player's motion (M), presence or absence of at least one enemy (EN) and ally (AN) player nearby, and finally player's location on either home or enemy territory (ET). Each player is modeled by a separate DBN. Therefore, there are fourteen instantiated DBNs for each game, but within any one game, all the DBNs share the same set of parameters.

Note that the DBN model does not perform any GPS trajectory denoising itself. To make a fair comparison with the Markov logic models, we use the denoising component of the Markov logic theory using only constraints H1 and S1–S3 (in Fig. 2.3). This produces a denoised discretization of the data that is subsequently fed into the DBN model. The random variables within the DBN that capture the notion of player "movement" and players being "nearby" one another is defined on the occupancy grid of the game area, just like in the two deterministic baseline models. Namely, a player is said to be moving between time t and $t + 1$ when he or she is snapped to two different nonadjacent cells at those times. Similarly, two players are nearby if they are snapped either to the same cell or to two adjacent cells.

- **Two-Step ML Model (2SML)**

  In the two-step approach, we have two separate theories in Markov logic. The first theory is used to perform a preliminary snapping of each of the player trajectories individually using constraints H1 and S1–S3 (in Fig. 2.3). This theory is identical to the one used in the discretization step in the DBN model above.

  The second theory then takes this preliminary denoising as a list of observed atoms in the form preliminarySnap(a, c, t) (meaning player a is snapped to cell c at time t) and uses the remaining constraints to label instances of capturing and

Hard formulas:

$$\forall a, t \; \exists c : \text{snap}(a, c, t) \tag{H1}$$

$$\forall a, c, c', t : \big(\text{snap}(a, c, t) \wedge c \neq c'\big) \Rightarrow \neg\text{snap}\big(a, c', t\big)$$

$$\forall a_1, a_2, t : \text{freeing}(a_1, a_2, t) \Rightarrow \big(\text{samePlace}(a_1, a_2, t) \wedge \text{isFree}(a_1, t)$$
$$\wedge \neg\text{enemies}(a_1, a_2) \wedge \text{isCaptured}(a_2, t) \wedge \text{isFree}(a_2, t+1)$$
$$\wedge \text{onEnemyTer}(a_1, t) \wedge \text{onEnemyTer}(a_2, t)\big) \tag{H2}$$

$$\forall a_1, a_2, t : \text{capturing}(a_1, a_2, t) \Rightarrow \big(\text{samePlace}(a_1, a_2, t) \wedge \text{isFree}(a_1, t)$$
$$\wedge \text{enemies}(a_1, a_2) \wedge \text{isFree}(a_2, t) \wedge \text{isCaptured}(a_2, t+1)$$
$$\wedge \text{onHomeTer}(a_1, t) \wedge \text{onEnemyTer}(a_2, t)\big) \tag{H3}$$

$$\forall a_1, a_2, t : \text{samePlace}(a_1, a_2, t) \Rightarrow \big(\exists c_1, c_2 : \text{snap}(a_1, c_1, t) \wedge \text{snap}(a_2, c_2, t)$$
$$\wedge \text{adjacent}(c_1, c_2)\big)$$

$$\forall a, t : (t = 0) \Rightarrow \text{isFree}(a, t) \tag{H4}$$

$$\forall a, t : \text{isCaptured}(a, t) \oplus \text{isFree}(a, t) \tag{H5}$$

$$\forall a, t : \big(\text{isFree}(a, t) \wedge \text{isCaptured}(a, t+1)\big) \Rightarrow \big(\exists_{=1} a_1 : \text{capturing}(a_1, a, t)\big) \tag{H6}$$

$$\forall a, t : \big(\text{isCaptured}(a, t) \wedge \text{isFree}(a, t+1)\big) \Rightarrow \big(\exists_{=1} a_1 : \text{freeing}(a_1, a, t)\big) \tag{H7}$$

$$\forall a, t, c : \big(\text{isCaptured}(a, t) \wedge \text{isCaptured}(a, t+1) \wedge \text{snap}(a, c, t)\big) \Rightarrow \text{snap}(a, c, t+1) \tag{H8}$$

Fig. 2.5 Our hard formulas in Markov logic. See corresponding rules in Fig. 2.3 for an English description and Table 2.1 for explanation of the predicates. In our implementation, the actual rules are written in the syntax used by theBeast, a Markov logic toolkit. ($\exists_{=1}$ denotes unique existential quantification, $\oplus$ designates exclusive or)

freeing, while considering cell adjacency in the same manner as the previous three models. The two-step model constitutes a decomposition of the unified model (see below) and overall contains virtually the same formulas, except 2SML operates with an observed preliminarySnap predicate, whereas the unified model contains a hidden snap predicate instead. Thus we omit elaborating on it further here.

• **Unified ML Model (UML)**

In the unified approach, we express all the hard constraints H1–H8 and soft constraints S1–S7 (Fig. 2.3) in Markov logic as a single theory that jointly denoises the data and labels game events. Selected interesting formulas are shown in Fig. 2.6—their labels correspond to the listing in Fig. 2.3. Note that formulas S1–S3 contain real-valued functions d_1, d_2, and d_3 respectively. d_1 returns the distance between agent a and cell c at time t. Similarly, d_2 returns the dissimilarity of the two consecutive "snapping vectors"[5] given agent a's position at time

---

[5]The initial point of each snapping (projection) vector is a raw GPS reading and the terminal point is the center of the cell we snap that reading to.

Soft formulas:

$$\forall a, c, t : \big[\mathrm{snap}(a, c, t)\big] \cdot d_1(a, c, t) \cdot w_p \tag{S1}$$

$$\forall a, c_1, c_2, t : \big[\mathrm{snap}(a, c_1, t) \wedge \mathrm{snap}(a, c_2, t+1)\big] \cdot d_2(a, c_1, c_2, t) \cdot w_s \tag{S2}$$

$$\forall a, c_1, c_2, c_3, t : \big[\mathrm{snap}(a, c_1, t) \wedge \mathrm{snap}(a, c_2, t+1)$$
$$\wedge \mathrm{snap}(a, c_3, t+2)\big] \cdot d_3(a, c_1, c_2, c_3, t) \cdot w_t \tag{S3}$$

$$\forall a_1, a_2, t : \big[\big(\mathrm{enemies}(a_1, a_2) \wedge \mathrm{onHomeTer}(a_1, t)$$
$$\wedge \mathrm{onEnemyTer}(a_2, t) \wedge \mathrm{isFree}(a_2, t)$$
$$\wedge \mathrm{samePlace}(a_1, a_2, t)\big) \Rightarrow \mathrm{capturing}(a_1, a_2, t)\big] \cdot w_c \tag{S4}$$

$$\forall a_1, a_2, t : \big[\big(\neg\mathrm{enemies}(a_1, a_2) \wedge \mathrm{onEnemyTer}(a_1, t)$$
$$\wedge \mathrm{onEnemyTer}(a_2, t) \wedge \mathrm{samePlace}(a_1, a_2, t) \wedge \mathrm{isFree}(a_1, t)$$
$$\wedge \mathrm{isCaptured}(a_2, t)\big) \Rightarrow \mathrm{freeing}(a_1, a_2, t)\big] \cdot w_f \tag{S5}$$

$$\forall a, c, t : \big[\mathrm{capturing}(a, c, t)\big] \cdot w_{cb} \tag{S6}$$

$$\forall a, c, t : \big[\mathrm{freeing}(a, c, t)\big] \cdot w_{fb} \tag{S7}$$

Fig. 2.6 Soft formulas in Markov logic. See corresponding rules in Fig. 2.3 for an English description. Each soft formula is written as a traditional quantified finite first-order logic formula (e.g., $\forall a, c, t : [\mathrm{snap}(a, c, t)]$), followed by an optional function (e.g., $d_1(a, c, t)$), followed by the weight of the formula (e.g., w_p). This syntax denotes that at inference time, the instantiated logical part of each formula evaluates to either 1 (true) or 0 (false), which is then effectively multiplied by the product of corresponding function value and formula weight

t and $t+1$ and the location of the centers of two cells c_1 and c_2. Finally, since people prefer to move in straight lines, function d_3 quantifies the lack of smoothness of any three consecutive segments of the trajectory. Since w_p, w_s, and w_t are all assigned negative values during training, formulas S1–S3 effectively softly enforce the corresponding geometric constraints.

The presence of functions d_1 through d_3 renders formulas S1–S3 hybrid formulas. This means that at inference time, the instantiated logical part of each formula evaluates to either 1 (true) or 0 (false), which is in turn multiplied by the product of corresponding function value and formula weight.

We will see how we train, test, and evaluate these four models, and how they perform on the multi-agent activity recognition task in Sect. 2.6. Next, we turn to our supervised learning method for augmenting the unified ML model in order to recognize both successful and failed attempts at multi-agent activities.

2.5.2 Learning Models of Failed Attempts

In the work described above, we manually designed the structure of a Markov logic network that models the capture the flag domain and allows us to jointly denoise the raw GPS data and recognize instances of actual capturing and freeing. Now we show how to *automatically*—in a supervised learning setting—extend this theory to encompass and correctly label not only successful actions, but also failed attempts at those interactions. That is, given the raw GPS data that represent the CTF games, we want our new model to label instances where player *a* captures (or frees) player *b* as *successful captures* (*successful frees*) and instances where player *a* almost captures (or frees) player *b* as *failed captures* (*failed frees*). For instance, by "failed capturing" we mean an instance of players' interactions where—up to a point—it appeared that *a* is capturing *b*, but when we carefully consider the events that (potentially) preceded it as well as the impacts of the supposed capture on the future unfolding of the game, we conclude that it is a false alarm and no capture actually occurred. In other words, the conditions for a capture were right, but later on, there was a pivotal moment that foiled the capturing agent's attempt.

For both activities (capturing and freeing), our model jointly finds an optimal separation between success and failure. Note that since we cast our model in second-order Markov logic, we do not learn, *e.g.*, an *isolated* rule that separates successful freeing from a failed attempt at freeing. Rather—since capturing and freeing events (both actual and failed) are related and thus labeling an activity as, say, "successful capturing" has far-reaching impact on our past, present, and future labeling—we learn the separations in a joint and unified way. Namely, both the structure (logical form) and importance (weight) of each formula in our theory is considered with all its consequences and influence on other axioms in the theory. Our system thus finds an optimal balance between success and failure in capturing and freeing activities with respect to the training data.

2.5.2.1 The Theory Augmentation Algorithm

In what follows, we will describe our Markov logic theory augmentation algorithm (Algorithm 2.1). For clarity, we will explain how it works in concrete context of the ML models of capture the flag we discussed in previous sections. However, the underlying assumption that successful actions are in many ways similar to their failed counterparts, and that minor—but crucial—deviations cause the failure to occur, often hold beyond capture the flag. Therefore, the same algorithm is applicable to other domains with different activities, as long as they are modeled in Markov logic.

At a high-level, the augmentation algorithm belongs to the family of structure learning methods. Starting with a seed model of successful actions, it searches for new formulas that can be added to the seed theory in order to jointly model both successfully and unsuccessfully carried out actions. The declarative language bias—essentially rules for exploring the hypothesis space of candidate structures—is defined implicitly by the notion that for any given activity, the structure of unsuccessful attempts is similar to the successful attempts. Therefore, the augmentation algorithm goes through an "inflation" stage, where formulas in the seed theory are generalized, followed by a refinement stage, where superfluous and incompatible formulas in the inflated model are pruned away. The refinement step also optimizes

---

Algorithm 2.1 Extend a ML theory to model successful as well as failed activities

---

Input: A: set of activities

    $\mathscr{M}_S$: ML theory that models successful instances of activities in A

    S: set of examples of successful activities

    F: set of examples of failed activities

Output: $\mathscr{M}_{S+F}$: augmented ML model with learned weights that models both successful and attempted activities in A

    $\mathscr{I}$: intended goals of the activities

1: $\mathscr{M}_S^2 \Leftarrow \text{liftToSecondOrderML}(\mathscr{M}_S, A)$

2: $\mathscr{M}_S' \Leftarrow \text{instantiate}(\mathscr{M}_S^2, A)$

3: $\mathscr{I} \Leftarrow \text{findIncompatibleFormulas}(F, \mathscr{M}_S')$

4: $\mathscr{M}_{S+F} \Leftarrow \mathscr{M}_S' \setminus \mathscr{I}$

5: $\mathscr{M}_{S+F} \Leftarrow \text{learnWeights}(S, F, \mathscr{M}_{S+F})$

6: $\mathscr{M}_{S+F} \Leftarrow \text{removeZeroWeightedFormulas}(\mathscr{M}_{S+F})$

7: **return** $\mathscr{M}_{S+F}, \mathscr{I}$

---

the weights within the newly induced theory. We will now discuss this process in more detail.

The input of our theory augmentation algorithm consists of an initial first-order ML theory $\mathscr{M}_S$ that models successful capturing and freeing (such as the unified ML model defined in Sect. 2.5.1 that contains formulas shown in Figs. 2.5 and 2.6), a set of activities of interest A, and a set of examples of successful (S) as well as failed (F) captures and frees. $\mathscr{M}_S$ does not need to have weights for its soft formulas specified. In case they are missing, we will learn them from scratch in the final steps of the augmentation algorithm. If the weights are specified, the final weight learning step for $\mathscr{M}_{S+F}$ can leverage them to estimate the initial weight values. A can be specified as a set of predicate names, *e.g.*, {capturing, freeing}. Each example in sets S and F describes a game segment and constitutes a complete truth assignment to the appropriate literals instantiated from $\mathscr{M}_S$. Table 2.2 shows two toy examples of sets S and F for three time steps. Since the goal is to learn a model of failed (and successful) attempts in a supervised way, the example game segment in F contain activities labeled with predicates failedCapturing() and failedFreeing().

If $\mathscr{M}_S$ contains hybrid formulas (such our formulas S1–S3 in Fig. 2.6), the appropriate function definitions are provided as part of S and F as well. Each definition consists of implicit mapping from input arguments to function values. For instance, function d_1 in formula S1 quantifies the L2 distance between the agent a and cell c at time t in the projected Mercator space: $d_1(a, c, t) = \sqrt{(a.gpsX_t - c.gpsX)^2 + (a.gpsY_t - c.gpsY)^2}$.

Our system goes through the following process in order to induce a new theory $\mathscr{M}_{S+F}$ that augments $\mathscr{M}_S$ with a definition of failed attempts for each activity already defined in $\mathscr{M}_S$.

First we lift $\mathscr{M}_S$ to second-order Markov logic by variabilizing all predicates that correspond to the activities of interest (step 1 of Algorithm 2.1). This yields a lifted theory $\mathscr{M}_S^2$. More concretely, in order to apply this technique in

Table 2.2 Two examples of a logical representation of successful (S) as well as failed (F) capture events that are input to Algorithm 2.1. The closed-world assumption is applied, therefore all atoms not listed are assumed to be false. For clarity, we omit listing the adjacent() predicate

Set S: Successful Capture	Set F: Failed Capture
enemies(P_1, P_2)	enemies(P_4, P_5)
enemies(P_2, P_1)	enemies(P_5, P_4)
	onEnemyTer($P_5, 1$)
onEnemyTer($P_2, 2$)	onEnemyTer($P_5, 2$)
onEnemyTer($P_2, 3$)	onEnemyTer($P_5, 3$)
capturing($P_1, P_2, 2$)	failedCapturing($P_4, P_5, 2$)
isFree($P_1, 1$)	isFree($P_4, 1$)
	isFailedCaptured($P_4, 1$)
isFree($P_1, 2$)	isFree($P_4, 2$)
	isFailedCaptured($P_4, 2$)
isFree($P_1, 3$)	isFree($P_4, 3$)
	isFailedCaptured($P_4, 3$)
isFree($P_2, 1$)	isFree($P_5, 1$)
	isFailedCaptured($P_5, 1$)
isFree($P_2, 2$)	isFree($P_5, 2$)
	isFailedCaptured($P_5, 2$)
isCaptured($P_2, 3$)	isFree($P_5, 3$)
	isFailedCaptured($P_5, 3$)
snap($P_1, C5, 1$)	snap($P_4, C17, 1$)
snap($P_1, C10, 2$)	snap($P_4, C34, 2$)
snap($P_1, C10, 3$)	snap($P_4, C0, 3$)
snap($P_2, C9, 1$)	snap($P_5, C6, 1$)
snap($P_2, C10, 2$)	snap($P_5, C34, 2$)
snap($P_2, C10, 3$)	snap($P_5, C7, 3$)
samePlace($P_1, P_2, 2$)	samePlace($P_4, P_5, 2$)
samePlace($P_2, P_1, 2$)	samePlace($P_5, P_4, 2$)
samePlace($P_1, P_2, 3$)	
samePlace($P_2, P_1, 3$)	

our domain, we introduce new predicate variables *captureType* (whose domain is {capturing, failedCapturing}), *freeType* (over {freeing, failedFreeing}), and *stateType* over

$$\{\text{isCaptured, isFailedCaptured, isFree, isFailedFree}\}$$

For instance, variabilizing a first-order ML formula

$$\text{freeing}(a, b, t) \Rightarrow \neg\text{enemies}(a, b)$$

yields a second-order ML formula

$$freeType(a, b, t) \Rightarrow \neg enemies(a, b)$$

(note that *freeType* is now a variable). Instantiating back to first-order yields two formulas

$$freeing(a, b, t) \Rightarrow \neg enemies(a, b)$$

and

$$failedFreeing(a, b, t) \Rightarrow \neg enemies(a, b)$$

As far as agents' behavior is concerned, in the CTF domain, isCaptured is equivalent to isFailedFree, and isFree is equivalent to isFailedCaptured. As we will soon see, the theory augmentation process learns these equivalence classes and other relationships between states from training examples by expanding and subsequently refining formula H5 in Fig. 2.5. While we could work with only the isCaptured predicate and its negation to represent agents' states, we feel that having explicit failure states makes our discussion clearer. Furthermore, future work will need to address hierarchies of activities, including their failures. In that context, a representation of explicit failure states may not only be convenient, but may be necessary.

Next, we instantiate all predicate variables in $\mathcal{M}_S^2$ to produce a new first-order ML theory $\mathcal{M}_S'$ that contains the original theory $\mathcal{M}_S$ in its entirety plus new formulas that correspond to failed captures and frees (step 2). Since events that are, *e.g.*, nearly captures appear similar to actual successful captures, our hypothesis is that we do not need to drastically modify the original "successful" formulas in order to model the failed activities as well. In practice, the above process of lifting and instantiating indeed results in a good seed theory. While we could emulate the lifting and grounding steps with a scheme of copying formulas and renaming predicates in the duplicates appropriately, we cast our approach in principled second-order Markov logic, which ties our work more closely to previous research and results in a more extensible framework. Specifically, second-order Markov logic has been successfully used in deep transfer learning [17] and predicate invention [45]. Therefore, an interesting direction of future work is to combine our theory augmentation and refinement with transfer and inductive learning—operating in second-order ML—to jointly induce models of failed attempts of different activities in different domains, while starting with a single model of only successful activities in the source domain.

Typical structure learning and inductive logic programming techniques start with an initial (perhaps empty) theory and iteratively grow and refine it in order to find a form that fits the training data well. In order to avoid searching the generally huge space of hypotheses, a declarative bias is either specified by hand or mined from the data. The declarative bias then restricts the set of possible refinements of the formulas that the search algorithm can apply. Common restrictions include limiting the formula length, and adding a new predicate to a formula only when it shares at least one variable with some predicate already present in the formula. On the other hand, in our approach, we first generate our seed theory by instantiating all the activity-related predicate variables. To put it into context of structure learning, we expand the input model in order to generate a large seed theory, and then apply bottom-up (data-driven) learning to prune the seed theory, whereby the training data guides our search for formulas to remove as well as for an optimal set of weights on the remaining formulas. We conjecture that any failed attempt at an activity always violates at least one constraint that holds for successful executions of the activity. The experiments below support this conjecture.

The pruning is done in steps 3 and 4 of Algorithm 2.1. The function findIncompatibleFormulas($F, \mathcal{M}'_S$) returns a set of hard formulas in $\mathcal{M}'_S$ that are *incompatible* with the set of examples of failed interactions F. We say that a formula c is compatible with respect to a set of examples F if F logically entails c ($F \models c$). Conversely, if F does not entail c, we say that c is incompatible w.r.t. F.[6] We explain how to find incompatible formulas in the next section.

In step 4 of Algorithm 2.1, we simply remove all incompatible formulas ($\mathcal{I}$) from the theory. At this point, we have our $\mathcal{M}_{S+F}$ model, where hard formulas are guaranteed logically consistent with the examples of failed activities (because we removed the incompatible hard formulas), as well as with the successful activities (because they were logically consistent to start with). However, the soft formulas in $\mathcal{M}_{S+F}$ are missing properly updated weights (in Markov logic, the weight of each hard formula is simply set to $+\infty$). Therefore, we run Markov logic weight learning using theBeast package (step 5).

Recall that theBeast implements the cutting plane meta solving scheme for inference in Markov logic, where the ground ML network is reduced to an integer linear program that is subsequently solved by the LpSolve ILP solver. We chose this approach as opposed to, *e.g.*, MaxWalkSAT that may find a solution that is merely locally optimal, since the resulting run times are still relatively short (under an hour even for training and testing even the most complex model). Weights are learned discriminatively, where we directly model the posterior conditional probability of the hidden predicates given the observed predicates. We set theBeast to optimize the weights of the soft formulas via supervised on-line learning using margin infused relaxed algorithm (MIRA) for weight updates while the loss function is computed from the number of false positives and false negatives over the hidden atoms. Note that if any of the soft formulas are truly irrelevant with respect to the training examples, they are not picked out by the findIncompatibleFormulas() function, but their weights are set to zero (or very close to zero) in the weight learning step (line 5 in Algorithm 2.1). These zero-weighted formulas are subsequently removed in the following step. Note that the weight learning process does not need to experience a "cold" start, as an initial setting of weights can be inherited from the input theory $\mathcal{M}_S$.

Finally, we return the learned theory $\mathcal{M}_{S+F}$, whose formulas are optimally weighted with respect to *all* training examples. In the Experiments and Results section below, we will use $\mathcal{M}_{S+F}$ to recognize both successful and failed activities.

---

[6]Since in our domain, each example is a complete truth assignment, testing entailment is equivalent to checking if $F \cup c$ is logically consistent.

Algorithm 2.2 (findIncompatibleFormulas) Find formulas in a ML theory that are logically inconsistent with examples of execution of failed activities

---

Input: F: a set of examples of failed activities
$\quad\quad\mathcal{T}$: unrefined ML theory of successful and failed activities
Output: smallest set of formulas that appear in $\mathcal{T}$ and are unsatisfiable in the worlds in F

1: $O \Leftarrow$ extractObjects(F)
2: $\mathcal{T}_{\text{hard}} \Leftarrow \mathcal{T} \setminus \mathcal{T}_{\text{soft}}$
3: **integer** $n \Leftarrow 0$
4: **boolean** result $\Leftarrow$ **false**
5: **while** result == **false do**
6:      $\mathcal{T}^c \Leftarrow \mathcal{T}_{\text{hard}}$
7:      remove a new n-tuple of formulas from $\mathcal{T}^c$
8:      **if** for the current n, all n-tuples have been tested **then**
9:          $n \Leftarrow n + 1$
10:    **end if**
11:    result $\Leftarrow$ testSAT(F, $\mathcal{T}^c$, O)
12: **end while**
13: **return** $\mathcal{T}_{\text{hard}} \setminus \mathcal{T}^c$

Algorithm 2.1 also returns the incompatible hard formulas $\mathscr{I}$. We will see how $\mathscr{I}$ is used to extract the intended goal of the activities in the Sect. 2.5.3, but first, let us discuss step 3 of Algorithm 2.1 in more detail.

2.5.2.2 Consistency Check: Finding Incompatible Formulas

Now we turn to our method for finding incompatible formulas (summarized in Algorithm 2.2). Since our method leverages satisfiability testing to determine consistency between candidate theories and possible worlds (examples),[7] Algorithm 2.2 can be viewed as an instance of learning from interpretations—a learning setting in the inductive logic programming literature [18].

As input, we take a set of examples of failed activities F and a seed theory $\mathcal{T}$ (*e.g.*, produced in step 2 of Algorithm 2.1). The output is the smallest set of hard formulas that appear in $\mathcal{T}$ and are logically inconsistent with F. The algorithm first extracts the set of all objects O that appear in F (step 1 in Algorithm 2.2), while keeping track of the type of each object. For example, suppose there are only two example worlds in F shown in Table 2.3. Then *extractObjects*(F) returns $\{P_1, P_2, P_7, P_8, C_3, C_5, 1, 2\}$.

In step 2, we limit ourselves to only hard formulas when testing compatibility. We do so since we can *prove* incompatibility only for hard formulas. Soft constraints

---

[7]This is often referred to as the *covers* relation in inductive logic programming.

Table 2.3 Two simple examples of a logical representation a failed capture event	Example 1	Example 2
	$\mathrm{snap}(P_1, C_5, 1)$	$\mathrm{snap}(P_7, C_3, 2)$
	$\mathrm{snap}(P_2, C_5, 1)$	$\mathrm{snap}(P_8, C_3, 2)$
	$\mathrm{failedCapturing}(P_1, P_2, 1)$	$\mathrm{failedFreeing}(P_2, P_5, 2)$

can be violated many times in the data and yet we may not want to eliminate them. Instead, we want to merely adjust their weights, which is exactly what we do in our approach. Therefore, $\mathscr{T}_{\mathrm{hard}}$ contains only hard formulas that appear in $\mathscr{T}$. Next, on lines 5 through 12, we check if the entire unmodified $\mathscr{T}_{\mathrm{hard}}$ is compatible (since for $n = 0$, we do not remove any formulas). If it is compatible, we return an empty set indicating that all the hard formulas in the original seed theory $\mathscr{T}$ are compatible with the examples. If we detect incompatibility, we will need to remove some, and perhaps even all, hard formulas in order to arrive at a logically consistent theory. Therefore, we incrementally start removing n-tuples of formulas. That is, in the subsequent $|\mathscr{T}_{\mathrm{hard}}|$ iterations of the while loop, we determine if we can restore consistency by removing any one of the hard formulas in $\mathscr{T}_{\mathrm{hard}}$. If we can, we return the set $\mathscr{T}_{\mathrm{hard}} \setminus f_i$, where f_i is the identified and removed incompatible formula. If consistency cannot be restored by removing a single formula, we in turn begin considering pairs of formulas ($n = 2$), triples ($n = 3$), *etc.* until we find a pruned theory $\mathscr{T}^c$ that is consistent with *all* examples.

In general, we do need to consider n-tuples of formulas, rather than testing each formula in isolation. Consider formula H2 in Fig. 2.5, which can be split into seven conjoined implications, each having two predicates. Induced formulas pertaining to failed attempts at freeing will include ones that share a common antecedent that is sometimes true, but their respective consequents are at the same time both false. Here is a concrete instantiated example in propositional logic:

$$\cdots$$

$$\mathrm{failedFreeing}(P_1, P_2, 34) \Rightarrow \mathrm{isCaptured}(P_2, 34)$$

$$\mathrm{failedFreeing}(P_4, P_5, 45) \Rightarrow \mathrm{isFree}(P_5, 46)$$

$$\cdots$$

The training examples will include atoms such as

$$\cdots$$

$$\mathrm{failedFreeing}(P_1, P_2, 34)$$

$$\mathrm{failedFreeing}(P_4, P_5, 45)$$

$$\neg \mathrm{isFree}(P_5, 46)$$

$$\neg \mathrm{isCaptured}(P_2, 34)$$

$$\cdots$$

(Following the closed-world assumption, the two negated atoms would actually not appear in the training data, but we explicitly include them in this example for clarity.)

Now, removing either one of the formulas does not restore consistency of the theory and the examples. We need to remove *both* offending formulas to find a solution. Furthermore, attempting to find inconsistent formulas independently of each other in general results in pruning the theory too drastically and the result strongly depends on the order in which we choose to test formulas. This simple examples illustrates how hard formulas interact and that they do need to be considered jointly.

We also note that some hard formulas model physical constraints or inviolable rules of capture the flag, and therefore hold *universally*. Appropriately, these formulas are not eliminated by Algorithm 2.2. As an example, consider formula H1 in Fig. 2.5, which asserts that each player occupies exactly one cell at any given time. This formula is satisfied in games that include both successful and failed activities. On the other hand, consider formula H8 in the same figure. It contains a captured player to the cell he was captured in (following the "captured players cannot move" rule of CTF). While this holds for successful capturing events, it does not necessarily hold for failed attempts at capturing. Therefore, when rule H8 is expanded via second-order ML, only some of the derived formulas are going to be consistent with the observations.

Specifically, the candidate formula in Eq. (2.6) will be pruned away, as it is inconsistent with the training examples, *i.e.*, players that were only nearly captured continue to be free to move about. However, the remaining three variants of formula H8 will not be pruned away. Equation (2.7) will always evaluate to true, since if someone attempts to re-capture an already captured player a, a does indeed remain stationary. Similarly, Eq. (2.8) is also consistent with all the example CTF games because if there is a failed attempt at capture immediately followed by a successful capture, the captured player does remain in place from time t and beyond. Finally, Eq. (2.9) is compatible as well, since it is the original formula H8 that is consistent with the observations.

$$\forall a, t, c: \quad \big(\text{isFailedCaptured}(a, t) \land \text{isFailedCaptured}(a, t+1) \land \text{snap}(a, c, t)\big)$$
$$\Rightarrow \text{snap}(a, c, t+1) \tag{2.6}$$

$$\forall a, t, c: \quad \big(\text{isCaptured}(a, t) \land \text{isFailedCaptured}(a, t+1) \land \text{snap}(a, c, t)\big)$$
$$\Rightarrow \text{snap}(a, c, t+1) \tag{2.7}$$

$$\forall a, t, c: \quad \big(\text{isFailedCaptured}(a, t) \land \text{isCaptured}(a, t+1) \land \text{snap}(a, c, t)\big)$$
$$\Rightarrow \text{snap}(a, c, t+1) \tag{2.8}$$

$$\forall a, t, c: \quad \big(\text{isCaptured}(a, t) \land \text{isCaptured}(a, t+1) \land \text{snap}(a, c, t)\big)$$
$$\Rightarrow \text{snap}(a, c, t+1) \tag{2.9}$$

The function *testSAT*() (line 11 in Algorithm 2.2) checks whether a given candidate theory $\mathscr{T}^c$ is compatible with the examples F by the following process.

First, we ground $\mathcal{T}^c$ using the objects in O, thereby creating a ground theory $\mathcal{G}$. For example, if $\mathcal{T}^c = \{p(x) \Rightarrow q(x)\}$ and $O = \{B, W\}$, the grounding would be $\mathcal{G} = \{p(B) \Rightarrow q(B), p(W) \Rightarrow q(W)\}$. Then we check if $\mathcal{G} \cup F_{\text{hidden}}$ is satisfiable using the miniSAT solver, where F_{hidden} is simply the set of hidden atoms that appear in F. Intuitively, this corresponds to testing whether we can "plug in" the worlds in F into $\mathcal{T}^c$ while satisfying all the hard constraints. Though satisfiability is an NP-complete problem, in practice $testSAT()$ completes within tenths of a second even for the largest problems in our CTF domain.

For instance, suppose $F_{\text{hidden}} = \{p(B), \neg q(B)\}$. Then we test satisfiability of the formula

$$\big(p(B) \Rightarrow q(B)\big) \wedge \big(p(W) \Rightarrow q(W)\big) \wedge p(B) \wedge \neg q(B)$$

In this case we cannot satisfy it since we are forced to set $p(B)$ to *true* and $q(B)$ to *false*, which renders the first clause—and therefore the whole formula—*false*.

An alternative approach to pruning formulas via satisfiability testing, as we have just described, would be to treat both types of formulas (hard and soft) in the inflated theory $\mathcal{M}'_S$ as strictly soft formulas and learning a weight for each formula from examples of both successful and failed game events. However, this introduces several complications that negatively impact the system's performance as well as model clarity. First, the number of formulas in the inflated theory can be exponentially larger than in the seed theory. While the instantiation of the second-order ML representation can be quantified to limit this expansion, we still have worst-case exponential blow-up. By treating all formulas as soft ones, we now need to potentially learn many more weights. This is especially problematic for activities that occur rarely, as we may not have enough training data to properly learn those weights. Eliminating the hard candidate formulas by proving them inconsistent dramatically reduces the number of parameters we have to model. While satisfiability testing is NP-complete, weight learning in Markov logic entails running inference multiple times, which is itself a #P-complete problem.

The second reason for distinguishing between soft and hard formulas is the resulting clarity and elegance of the final learned model $\mathcal{M}_{S+F}$. Even in situations when we have enough training data to properly learn a large number of weights, we run into overfitting problems, where neither the structure nor the parameters of the model represent the domain in a natural way. Our experiments have shown that if we skip the pruning stage (steps 3 and 4 in Algorithm 2.1), the model's recognition performance does not differ from that of a pruned model in a significant way (p-value of 0.45). However, we end up with a large number of soft formulas with a mixture of positive and negative weights that the learning algorithm carefully tuned and balanced to fit the training data. They however bear little relationship to the concepts in the underlying domain. Not only does this make it very hard for a human expert to analyze the model, but it makes it even harder to modify the model.

For these reasons, softening all hard formulas is, in general, infeasible. An interesting direction of future work will be to identify a small amount of *key* inconsistent hard formulas to soften, while eliminating the rest of the inconsistent hard formulas. This however entails searching in a large space of candidate subsets of softened formulas, where each iteration requires expensive re-learning of all weights.

Note that Algorithm 2.2 terminates as soon as it finds a compatible theory that requires the smallest number of formula-removals. We also experimented with an active learning component to our system, where we modify Algorithms 2.1 and 2.2 such that they present *several* possible refinements of the theory to the user who then selects the one that looks best. The proposed modifications are shown both at the ML theory level with modified sections (formulas) highlighted as well as at the data level where the program shows the inferred consequences of those modifications. For each candidate modification, the corresponding consequences are displayed as a collection of animations where each animation shows what the results of activity recognition would be if we committed to that particular candidate theory. Note that even people who do not have background in ML can interact with such a system since the visualization is easy to understand. Interestingly, in the case of captures and frees, the least modified theory that the "off-line" version of the algorithm finds is also the best one and therefore there is no need to query the user. One can view this as a differential variant of Occam's razor. However, for different activities or other domains, the active learning approach may be worth revisiting and we leave its exploration for future work.

Finally, general structure learning techniques from statistical-relational AI and from inductive logic programming are not applicable as a substitute for our theory augmentation algorithm for several reasons. The main reason is that, for efficiency reasons, existing techniques in the literature typically operate over a very restricted set of formula templates. That is, they consider only Horn clauses, or only formulas without an existential quantifier, or only formulas with at most k literals or with at most l variables, and so on. This set of restrictions is part of the language bias of any given approach. While in principle, structure learning is possible without a language bias, one often has to carefully define one for the sake of tractability (see Sect. 2.7 for details). In our approach, the language bias is defined implicitly as discussed in Sect. 2.5.2.1.

2.5.3 Extracting the Goal from Success and Failure

Recall that applying the theory augmentation process (Algorithm 2.1) on the CTF seed theory of successful interactions (shown in Figs. 2.5 and 2.6) induces a new set of formulas that capture the structure of failed activities and ties them together with the existing formulas in the seed theory.

The logically inconsistent formulas $\mathscr{I}$ that Algorithm 2.2 returns are ones that are not satisfiable in the worlds with failed activities. At the same time, variants of those formulas were consistent with the examples of successful actions occurring in the games. Therefore, $\mathscr{I}$ represents the *difference* between a theory that models only successful activities and the augmented theory of both successful and failed actions, that has been derived from it. Intuitively, the difference between success and failure can be viewed as the intended purpose of any given activity a rational agent executes, and consequently as the goal the agent has in mind when he engages in that particular activity. In Sect. 2.6, we will explore the goals extracted from the CTF domain in this fashion.

2.5.4 Identifying Interesting Game Situations

Suppose we are interested in detecting segments of the games of capture the flag that are in some sense interesting. People's interests vary from person to person, and even within any one person over time. Therefore, we focus on identifying game segments that are novel, in the sense that the dynamics of the game suddenly change, and a sequence of events takes place, which is dissimilar to what happened prior as well as to what follows.

How can we automatically identify such moments from players' location? Moreover, how can we pinpoint which particular players are the main participants in such an interesting situation? Intuitively, we represent each second of a game in terms of the amount of agreement among players' velocity vectors. We then propose a novelty detection process based on convolution with a special kernel.

We define the similarity between the velocity of player i and player j as their dot product scaled by the current distance d between the two players:

$$\phi(\mathbf{v}_i, \mathbf{v}_j) = e^{-d(i,j)}(\mathbf{v}_i \cdot \mathbf{v}_j). \tag{2.10}$$

The dot product term takes into account the respective magnitudes of players' velocity vectors, as well as the angle between them. The larger the magnitudes, and the smaller the angle, the higher similarity score we assign. Since the players cannot see what is happening in the game at large distances, neither can they communicate, a correlation in motion of players far apart is almost certainly random. The exponential term in Eq. (2.10) imposes an exponential decay on the similarity score ϕ as we increase the distance between the players ($d(i, j)$), thereby forcing the similarity metric to focus on more localized correlation patterns. A high correlation in the velocities of two players i and j means that the players are following a very similar trajectory over the given period of time. In effect, our similarity measure ϕ tends to be maximal for pairs of players, who are nearby each other, and who are moving at a high-speed in the same direction.

We can now aggregate individual pair-wise similarities ϕ to represent the motion of an entire team of players, and to contrast the behavior of one team against that of the opposing team. As we outlined above, each second s_i of a game is represented by a three element vector, that captures the agreement of players' velocities within team 1, the agreement of players' velocities within team 2, and the agreement of velocities of players across teams:

$$\mathbf{g}_{s_i} = \left(\sum_{(i,j) \in \text{T1}} \phi(\mathbf{v}_i, \mathbf{v}_j), \sum_{(i,j) \in \text{T2}} \phi(\mathbf{v}_i, \mathbf{v}_j), \sum_{(i,j) \in \text{OP}} \phi(\mathbf{v}_i, \mathbf{v}_j) \right).$$

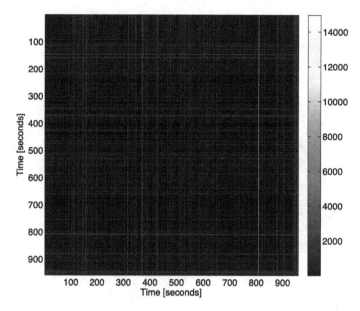

Fig. 2.7 Self-similarity matrix for an entire game of capture the flag. The hotter (more *white*) a given pixel with coordinates (i, j) is, the less are game seconds $\mathbf{g}_{s_i}$ and $\mathbf{g}_{s_j}$ similar to each other

In the first and second element of $\mathbf{g}_{s_i}$, we sum over all combinations of pairs of players (7 choose 2) within team 1 (T1) and team 2 (T2), respectively. In the third element, we sum over all combinations of opponent pairs (OP). This feature vector is tailored for detecting dynamic segments of a game with a lot of "action," however the proposed technique is general and can be applied to detect other types of player behavior as well, such as patrolling the home base, guarding a captured player *etc*.

Now we are ready to construct the self-similarity matrix S for game g, which contains the similarity between all pairs of game seconds $\mathbf{g}_{s_i}$. S is a square t by t matrix, where t is the number of seconds in game g. Each element of S is the L2 norm between the two corresponding game seconds:

$$S(i, j) = \|\mathbf{g}_{s_i} - \mathbf{g}_{s_j}\|_2.$$

An example self-similarity matrix is shown in Fig. 2.7. The hotter (more white) a given pixel with coordinates (i, j) is, the less are game seconds $\mathbf{g}_{s_i}$ and $\mathbf{g}_{s_j}$ similar to each other. Note that the diagonal elements $S(i, i)$ are all zero (black). We see short episodes of interesting activity (light colors) interleaved by monotonous segments (dark color), where not much dynamics occurs. Especially dominant are times around 150 seconds, then between 300 and 400 seconds, and finally near 800 seconds into the game. After that we observe moderately turbulent activity as the game climaxes.

We can automatically extract interesting game segments by convolving a self-similarity matrix with a "checkered" Gaussian kernel shown in Fig. 2.8. Mathemat-

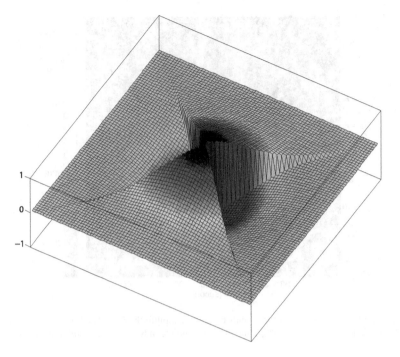

Fig. 2.8 Illustration of the "checkered" Gaussian kernel we use for convolution during detection of interesting game segments

ically, we can express the kernel as

$$f_c(i, j; \sigma) = \begin{cases} e^{-\frac{i^2+j^2}{2\sigma^2}} & \text{if } (i, j) \text{ lies in the first or third quadrant,} \\ -e^{-\frac{i^2+j^2}{2\sigma^2}} & \text{otherwise.} \end{cases} \quad (2.11)$$

To illustrate the convolution process, consider the two three-dimensional Figs. 2.8 and 2.9. Figure 2.9 visualizes the self-similarity matrix for the first 200 seconds of a game. The higher (and also the more red) a given point is in the surface plot, the more similar the corresponding seconds of the game are. Now imagine convolving this matrix with the checkered Gaussian kernel from Fig. 2.8 by sliding the kernel along the matrix's diagonal, while keeping the center of the kernel aligned with the diagonal elements of the matrix. Every time the kernel is convolved with a time window that contains an abrupt change from a high similarity to a low similarity, such as when the kernel is centered at element $(60, 60)$ in the self-similarity matrix, it produces a large negative correlation score. Plateau regions, such as the beginning of this particular game result in intermediate correlation, whereas regions containing a transition from a low similarity to a high similarity produce a large positive

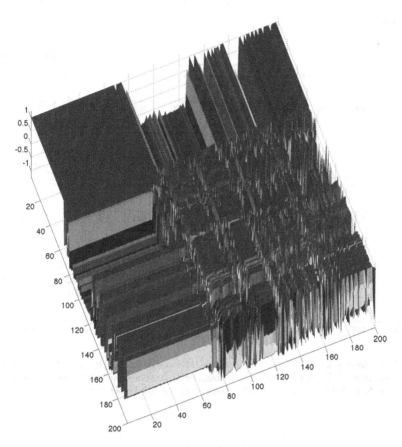

Fig. 2.9 A three dimensional visualization of the self-similarity matrix of the first 200 seconds of a game of capture the flag

score. Formally, the convolution process can be written as

$$N(t) = (f_c * S)(t) = \sum_{x=-\frac{L}{2}}^{\frac{L}{2}} \sum_{y=-\frac{L}{2}}^{\frac{L}{2}} f_c(x, y) S(t + x, t + y), \qquad (2.12)$$

where L is the width as well as the height of the kernel f_c, and the matrix S is appropriately padded around its "edges" to allow convolution along the entire diagonal. The resulting function $N(t)$ is often called the novelty function in the audio processing literature and has been successfully applied, perhaps most notably, in visualizing and classifying music [28, 66]. In our experiments, we set $\sigma = \frac{L}{2}$ when generating the checkered kernel (*cf.* Eq. (2.11)), but we found that the actual value of σ has a small effect on the quality of the results.

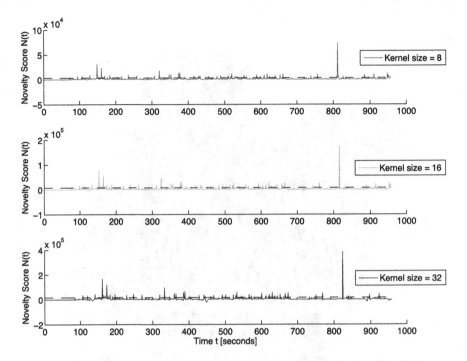

Fig. 2.10 Novelty scores obtained by convolving the game represented by the self-similarity matrix shown in Fig. 2.7 with kernels of various size. The *dashed line* in each plot depicts one standard deviation. Note that the score is very robust even as we vary the kernel size

Figure 2.10 shows the novelty scores obtained by convolving the game represented by the self-similarity matrix depicted in Fig. 2.7 with kernels of various size. The larger the area of the kernel, the more context it takes into account when calculating correlations. However, as we increase the size, we are more likely to overlook brief, but significant changes in game dynamics. Additionally, the exact time of occurrence of an interesting segment becomes harder to identify, as the larger kernel aggregates information from sizable areas of the self-similarity matrix. Nonetheless, as we see in Fig. 2.10, our technique is quite robust over a wide range of kernel sizes.

Now we can automatically identify interesting game situations by thresholding the novelty score. We can also accurately pinpoint which players are the dominant actors in each interesting game segment by examining their contributions to the corresponding feature vectors $\mathbf{g}_{s_i}$. In the experiments below, we will explore how well do the high-activity game segments detected by our system align with human judgement.

This concludes discussion of our models and methodology, and now we turn to experimental evaluation of the framework presented above.

2.6 Experiments and Results

We evaluate our approach along the three major directions outlined in Sect. 2.5 (Methodology), while focusing on answering the five research questions formulated *ibidem*. The structure of this section closely follows that of the Methodology section.

In a nutshell, we are first interested in how our Markov logic models perform on the standard multi-agent activity recognition task—labeling successful activities— and how their performance compares to the alternative models. Second, we examine the augmented model that captures both successful and failed attempts at activities. This is the model $\mathscr{M}_{S+F}$ induced by Algorithm 2.1, which also lets us extract the intended goal of the activities in question. Third, we compare the performance of $\mathscr{M}_{S+F}$ on the task of jointly recognizing *all four* activities with that of an alternative model. Finally, we investigate to what extent the reasoning about failed attempts does help in recognition of successfully executed activities, and how the interesting game segment detection approach compares to the judgement of human experts.

All experiments are performed on our capture the flag dataset consisting of four separate games. The dataset is summarized in Table 2.4, where for each game we list the number of raw GPS readings and the number of instances of each activity of interest. We evaluate the models via four-fold cross-validation, always training on three games (if training is required for a model) and testing against the fourth. For each experimental condition below, we report precision, recall, and F1 scores attained by each respective model over the four cross-validation runs. We have purposefully chosen to split the data so that each cross-validation fold directly corresponds to a separate game of CTF for conceptual convenience and clarity. As we discussed above, the events occurring in the games often have far-reaching consequences. For example, most captured players are never freed by their allies. Therefore, a capture at the beginning of a game typically profoundly influences the entire rest of the game. For this reason, splitting the games randomly or even manually would introduce unnecessary complications, as most of the segments would have dependencies on other segments. By enforcing that each fold exactly corresponds with a different game, we make each fold self-contained.

To quantify the statistical significance of the pair-wise differences between models, we use a generalized probabilistic interpretation of F1 score proposed by Goutte and Gaussier [30]. Namely, we express F1 scores in terms of gamma variates derived from models' true positives, false positives, and false negatives ($\lambda = 0.5$, $h = 1.0$, *cf.* Goutte and Gaussier [30]). This approach makes it possible to compare our results to future work that may apply alternative models on similar, but not identical, datasets. A future comparison may, for instance, include additional games or introduce random splits of the data. We note that standard statistical significance tests cannot be applied in those situations. All p-values reported are one sided, as we are interested if models' performance significantly *improves* as their level of sophistication increases.

Table 2.4 CTF dataset
overview: #GPS is the total
number of raw GPS readings,
#AC and #FC is the number
actual (successful) and failed
captures respectively, and
analogously for freeings (#AF
and #FF)

	#GPS	#AC	#FC	#AF	#FF
Game 1	13,412	2	15	2	1
Game 2	14,420	2	34	2	1
Game 3	3472	6	12	0	2
Game 4	10,850	3	4	1	0
Total	42,154	13	65	5	4

2.6.1 Recognition of Successful Activities

Recall that for both our two-step (2SML) and unified (UML) Markov logic models, we specify the Markov logic formulas by hand and optimize the weights of the soft formulas via supervised on-line learning. We run a modified version of the-Beast software package to perform weight learning and MAP inference. theBeast implements the cutting plane meta solving scheme for inference in Markov logic, where the ground ML network is reduced to an integer linear program that is subsequently solved by the LpSolve ILP solver. We chose this approach as opposed to, *e.g.*, MaxWalkSAT that can get "stuck" at a local optimum, since the resulting run times are still relatively short (under an hour even for training and testing even the most complex model).

At weight learning time, we use the margin infused relaxed algorithm (MIRA) for weight updates while the loss function is computed from the number of false positives and false negatives over the hidden atoms, as described in the Methodology section. The discretization step for the dynamic Bayesian network model (DBN) is implemented in Markov logic and is also executed in this fashion. The DBN model is trained via maximum likelihood as described in Sect. 2.4.2. The two deterministic baselines (B and B + S) do not require any training phase.

At inference time, we are interested in the most likely explanation of the data. In Markov logic, maximum *a posteriori* inference reduces to finding a complete truth assignment that satisfies all the hard constraints while maximizing the sum of the weights of the satisfied soft formulas. At testing time, theBeast Markov logic solver finds the most likely truth assignment to the hidden atoms as described above, and in this section we are specifically interested in the values of the capturing and freeing atoms.

In DBNs, the most likely explanation of the observations is equivalent to Viterbi decoding. The DBN model assigns either free or captured state to each player for every time step. We then label all transitions from free to captured state as capturing and all transitions from captured to free as freeing. Note that the DBN model is capable of determining which player is being freed or captured, but it does not model which player does the freeing or capturing. In our evaluation, we give it the benefit of the doubt and assume it always outputs the correct actor.

For all models, inference is done simultaneously over an entire game (on average, about 10 minutes worth of data). Note that we do not restrict inference to a (small)

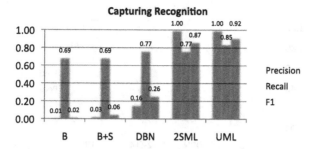

Fig. 2.11 Comparison of performance of the five models on capturing recognition while doing joint inference over both capturing and freeing events. See Table 2.5 for statistical significance analysis of the pairwise differences between models. (B = baseline model, B + S = baseline model with states, 2SML = two-step Markov logic model, UML = unified Markov logic model)

sliding time window. As the experiments described below show, many events in this domain can only be definitely recognized long after they occur. For example, GPS noise may make it impossible to determine whether a player has been captured at the moment of encounter with an enemy, but as the player thereafter remains in place for a long time, the possibility of his capture becomes certain.

Figures 2.11 and 2.12 summarize the performance of our models of successful capturing and freeing in terms of precision, recall, and F1 score calculated over the four cross-validation runs. For clarity, we present the results in two separate plots, but each model was jointly labeling both capturing and freeing activities. We do not consider the baseline model for freeing recognition as that activity makes little sense without having a notion of player state (captured or free).

We see that the unified approach yields the best results for both activities. Let us focus on capturing first (Fig. 2.11). Overall, the unified model labels 11 out of 13 captures correctly—there are only two false negatives. In fact, these two capture events are missed by *all* the models because they involve two enemies that appear unusually far apart (about 12 meters) in the raw data. Even the unified approach fails on this instance since the cost of adjusting the players' trajectories—thereby losing score due to violation of the geometry-based constraints—is not compensated for by the potential gain from labeling an additional capture.

Note that even the two-step approach recognizes 10 out of 13 captures. As compared to the unified model, it misses one additional instance in which the involved players, being moderately far apart, are snapped to mutually nonadjacent cells. On the other hand, the unified model does not fail in this situation because it is not limited by prior nonrelational snapping to a few nearby cells. However, the difference between their performance on our dataset is not statistically significant even at the 0.05 level (p-value of 0.32).

Both deterministic baseline models (B + S) perform very poorly. Although they yield a respectable recall, they produce an overwhelming amount of false positives. This shows that even relatively comprehensive pattern matching does not work at all in this domain. Interestingly, the performance of the DBN model leaves much to be desired as well, especially in terms of precision. While the DBN model is sig-

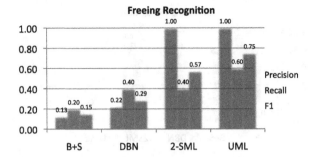

Fig. 2.12 Comparison of performance of our three models on freeing recognition while doing joint inference over both capturing and freeing events. See Table 2.6 for statistical significance analysis of the pairwise differences between models. (B + S = baseline model with states, 2SML = two-step Markov logic model, UML = unified Markov logic model)

Table 2.5 Summary of statistical significance (one sided p-values) of the pairwise differences between F1 scores for models of actual capturing. (B = baseline model, B + S = baseline model with states, DBN = dynamic Bayesian network model, 2SML = two-step Markov logic model, UML = unified Markov logic model)

	B + S	DBN	2SML	UML
B	0.0192	3.6×10^{-6}	5.1×10^{-7}	2.9×10^{-7}
B + S	–	5.9×10^{-5}	9.4×10^{-6}	1.4×10^{-6}
DBN	–	–	0.0002	8.0×10^{-5}
2SML	–	–	–	0.3230

nificantly better than both baselines (p-value less than 5.9×10^{-5}), it also achieves significantly worse performance than both the Markov logic models (p-value less than 0.0002; see Table 2.5).

Table 2.5 summarizes p-values of pairwise differences between models of actual (*i.e.*, successful) capturing. While the difference between the Markov logic-based models (2SML and UML) are not statistically significant (p-value of 0.32), pairwise differences in F1 scores between all other models are significant at the 0.02 level, and most often even at much lower p-values.

Though the unified model still outperforms its alternatives in the case of freeing recognition as well, its performance is further from ideal as compared to the capture recognition case (Fig. 2.12). It correctly identifies only 3 out of 5 freeing events in the games, but does not produce any false positives. This is partly due to the dependency of freeing on capturing. A failure of a model to recognize a capture precludes its recognition of a future freeing. Another reason is the extreme sparseness of the freeing events (there are only five of them in 40,000+ datapoints). Finally, in some instances players barely move after they had been freed. This may occur for a number of reasons ranging from already occupying a strategic spot to simply being tired. Such freeing instances are very challenging for any automated system, and even people familiar with the game to recognize (several situations would have

Table 2.6 Summary of statistical significance (one sided p-values) of the pairwise differences between F1 scores for models of actual freeing. (B + S = baseline model with states, DBN = dynamic Bayesian network model, 2SML = two-step Markov logic model, UML = unified Markov logic model)

	DBN	2SML	UML
B + S	0.2739	0.0733	0.0162
DBN	–	0.1672	0.0497
2SML	–	–	0.2743

been extremely hard to disambiguate if we didn't have access to our notes about data collection).

The two-step ML model does a slightly worse job than the unified model on freeing recognition. It correctly identifies only 2 out of 5 freeings for the same reasons as in the capturing recognition case. Similarly to models of actual captures, the difference between the unified and two-step freeing models is not statistically significant (p-value of 0.27).

Table 2.6 summarizes p-values of pairwise differences between models of actual (*i.e.*, successful) freeing. Here we see that only the difference between B + S and UML models is statistically significant (p-value of 0.01), whereas the differences between the rest of the model pairs are not statistically significant. Since there are only five instances of successful freeing, the 2SML model does not perform significantly better than the B + S model at the 0.05 significance level (p-value of 0.07). However, the UML model achieves better recognition results than even the DBN model with high confidence (p-value less than 0.05). Therefore, we see that although the 2SML model strictly dominates the non-Markov logic models when evaluated on capturing recognition, we need the full power of the unified ML model to strictly outperform the nonrelational alternatives for freeing. This suggests that as we move to more complex and more interdependent activities, relational and unified modeling approaches will be winning by larger and larger margins.

Even though the statistical significance tests suggest that 2SML is likely to give similar results to UML, it is important to note that 2SML, by design, *precludes* recognition of the activities in question in certain situations. Namely, as our experiments demonstrate, when the players are snapped to cells that are too far apart, the two-step model does not even consider those instances as candidates for labeling, and inevitably fails at recognizing them. Therefore, one needs to look beyond the p-values obtained when comparing the fully unified models to various alternatives.

As expected from the experiments with capturing recognition, both deterministic baseline models perform very poorly on freeing recognition as well. Not only do they produce an overwhelming amount of false positives, they also fail to recognize most of the freeing events.

Thus, we see that the models cast in Markov logic perform significantly better than both of the deterministic baseline models, and also better than the probabilistic, but nonrelational, DBN model. We note that the DBN model has the potential to be quite powerful and similar DBNs have been applied with great success in previous work on activity recognition from location data [24, 52]. It also has many similarities with the two-step ML model. They both share the same denoising and discretization step, and they both operate on the same observed data. The key difference is that the DBN model considers players individually, whereas the two-step ML model performs joint reasoning.

Looking at the actual CTF game data, we see several concrete examples of how this hurts DBN's labeling accuracy. For instance, consider a situation where two allies had been captured near each other. Performing inference about individual players in isolation allows the DBN model to infer that the two players effectively free each other, even though in reality they are both captured and cannot do so. This occurs because the DBN model is oblivious to the explicit states of one's teammates as well as opponents. Since capturing and freeing are interdependent, the obliviousness of the DBN model to the state of the actors negatively impacts its recognition performance for both activities. The example we just gave illustrates one type of freeing false positives. The hallucinated freeings create opportunities that often lead to false positives of captures, creating a vicious cycle. False negatives of freeing (capturing) events often occur for players who the model incorrectly believes have already been freed (captured) at a prior time.

Since the Markov logic based models are significantly better—with a high level of confidence—than the alternatives that are not fully relational, the experiments above validate our hypothesis that we need to exploit the rich relational and temporal structure of the domain in a probabilistic way and at the same time affirmatively answer research question Q1 (*Can we reliably recognize complex multi-agent activities in the CTF dataset even in the presence of severe noise?*). Namely, we show that although relatively powerful probabilistic models are not sufficient to achieve high labeling accuracy, we can gain significant improvements by formulating the recognition problem as learning and inference in Markov logic networks.

Now we turn to the evaluation of our method of learning models of both success and failure in people's activities.

2.6.2 Learned Formulas and Intentions

Applying the theory augmentation process (Algorithm 2.1) on the CTF seed theory (shown in Figs. 2.5 and 2.6) induces a new set of formulas that capture the structure of failed activities and ties them together with the existing formulas in the theory. We call this model $\mathcal{M}_{S+F}$. Figure 2.13 shows examples of new weighted formulas modeling failed freeing and capturing attempts that appear in $\mathcal{M}_{S+F}$.

First, note that our system correctly carries over the basic preconditions of each activity (contrast formulas S4 with S4′ and S5 with S5′ in Figs. 2.6 and 2.13 respectively). This allows it to *reliably* recognize both successful and failed actions instead of, *e.g.*, merely labeling all events that at some point in time appear to resemble a capture as near-capture. This re-use of preconditions directly follows from the language bias of the theory augmentation algorithm.

$$\forall a_1, a_2, t : \big[\big(\text{enemies}(a_1, a_2) \land \text{onHomeTer}(a_1, t)$$
$$\land\, \text{onEnemyTer}(a_2, t) \land \text{samePlace}(a_1, a_2, t) \land \text{isFree}(a_1, t)$$
$$\land\, \text{isFree}(a_2, t)\big) \Rightarrow \text{failedCapturing}(a_1, a_2, t)\big] \cdot 11.206 \qquad (\text{S4}')$$

$$\forall a_1, a_2, t : \big[\big(\lnot\text{enemies}(a_1, a_2) \land \text{onEnemyTer}(a_1, t)$$
$$\land\, \text{onEnemyTer}(a_2, t) \land \text{samePlace}(a_1, a_2, t) \land \text{isFree}(a_1, t)$$
$$\land\, \text{isCaptured}(a_2, t)\big) \Rightarrow \text{failedFreeing}(a_1, a_2, t)\big] \cdot 1.483 \qquad (\text{S5}')$$

$$\forall a_1, a_2, t : \big[\text{failedCapturing}(a_1, a_2, t)\big] \cdot (-0.0001) \qquad (\text{S6}')$$

$$\forall a_1, a_2, t : \big[\text{failedFreeing}(a_1, a_2, t)\big] \cdot (-0.002) \qquad (\text{S7}')$$

$$\lnot\forall a, t : \text{isFailedCaptured}(a, t) \oplus \text{isFree}(a, t) \qquad (\text{H5}')$$

$$\lnot\forall a, t : \text{isCaptured}(a, t) \oplus \text{isFailedFree}(a, t)$$

$$\lnot\forall a, t : \text{isFailedCaptured}(a, t) \oplus \text{isFailedFree}(a, t)$$

$$\forall a, t : \text{isFailedCaptured}(a, t) \Leftrightarrow \text{isFree}(a, t)$$

$$\forall a, t : \text{isCaptured}(a, t) \Leftrightarrow \text{isFailedFree}(a, t)$$

$$\forall a, t : \big(\text{isFree}(a, t) \land \text{isFailedCaptured}(a, t+1)\big)$$
$$\Rightarrow \big(\exists_{=1} a_1 : \text{failedCapturing}(a_1, a, t)\big) \qquad (\text{H6}')$$

$$\forall a, t : \big(\text{isCaptured}(a, t) \land \text{isFailedFree}(a, t+1)\big)$$
$$\Rightarrow \big(\exists_{=1} a_1 : \text{failedFreeing}(a_1, a, t)\big) \qquad (\text{H7}')$$

$$\boldsymbol{\lnot\forall a, t, c : \big(\text{isFailedCaptured}(a, t) \land \text{isFailedCaptured}(a, t+1) \land \text{snap}(a, c, t)\big)}$$
$$\boldsymbol{\Rightarrow \text{snap}(a, c, t+1)} \qquad \boldsymbol{(\text{H8}')}$$

Fig. 2.13 Example formulas, learned by Algorithm 2.1, that model unsuccessful capturing and freeing events. The crucial intent recognition formula (H8′) is highlighted in bold. Formulas eliminated by Algorithm 2.2 are preceded by the ¬ symbol, and are not included in the induced model $\mathcal{M}_{S+F}$. For concreteness sake, the values of the learned weights here come from one cross-validation run (and are similar in other runs)

Turning our attention to the learned hard formulas, we observe that the system correctly induced equivalence classes of the states, and also derived their mutual exclusion relationships (H5′). It furthermore tied the new failure states to their corresponding instantaneous interactions (H6′ and H7′).

Finally, the algorithm correctly discovers that the rule "*If a player is captured then he or she must remain in the same location*" (H8, Fig. 2.5) is the key distinction between a successful and failed capture (since players who were not actually captured can still move). Therefore, it introduces an appropriate rule for the failed captures (H8′, Fig. 2.13) explicitly stating that failed capturing does not confine the near-captured player to remain in stationary. An analogous process yields a fitting separation between failed and successful freeings. Namely, our model learns that an unsuccessfully freed player remains stationary. This learned difference between success and failure in players' actions directly corresponds to the goal of the activity and consequently the intent of rational actors. This difference is what our system outputs as the intended goal of capturing activity (and analogously for freeing).

These experimental results provide an evidence for a resounding "yes" to both Q2 (*Can models of attempted activities be automatically learned by leveraging existing models of successfully performed actions?*) and Q3 (*Does modeling both success and failure allow us to infer the respective goals of the activities?*) within the CTF domain.

We note that instead of applying our automated theory augmentation method, a person could, in principle, manually formulate a Markov logic theory of successful as well as failed activities by observing the games. After all, this is how we designed the initial seed model of successful events. However, this process is extremely time consuming, as one tends to omit encoding facts that to us, humans, seem self-evident but need to be explicitly articulated for the machine (*e.g.*, a single person cannot be at ten different places at once, or that a player is either free or captured but not both). It is also surprisingly easy to introduce errors in the theory, that are difficult to debug, mostly because of the complex weight learning techniques involved. Therefore, we believe that the theory augmentation method is a significant step forward in enhancing models' capabilities while requiring small amounts of human effort. As the complexity of domains and their models increases, this advantage will gain larger and larger importance.

2.6.3 Recognition of Both Successful and Failed Activities

We now compare the performance of our model $\mathcal{M}_{S+F}$ to an alternative (baseline) method that labels all four activities in the following way. Similarly to the baseline with states model for successful interactions defined in Sect. 2.5.1, there are two separate stages. First we snap each GPS reading to the nearest cell by applying only the geometric constraints (H1 and S1–S3) of our theory, and afterward we label the instances of our activities. The following labeling rule is applied. We loop over the whole discretized (via snapping) data set and look for instances where a pair of players a and b were snapped (in the first step) to either the same cell or to two adjacent cells at time t, they are enemies, b is not captured already, and a is on its home territory while b is not. If b moves (is snapped to a different cell at a later time) *without* having an ally nearby, we output $failedCapturing(a, b, t)$, otherwise we output $capturing(a, b, t)$. The labeling rule for freeing is defined analogously and all four events are tied together. We also tested a variant of the DBN model introduced in Sect. 2.5.1 that has two additional hidden state values for node S_t: isFailedFree and isFailedCaptured. However, the difference in the results obtained with this model was not statistically significant (p-value of 0.38), and therefore we focus on the conceptually more straightforward baseline model described above.

Model $\mathcal{M}_{S+F}$ is evaluated using four-fold cross-validation (always training on three games and testing against the fourth). Figure 2.14 compares both models in

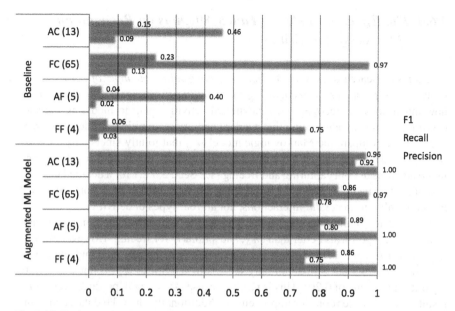

Fig. 2.14 Performance of the baseline and augmented ($\mathcal{M}_{S+F}$) models on joint recognition of successful and failed capturing and freeing. The F1 score of the augmented model is significantly better than that of the baseline for all four target activities (p-value less than 1.3×10^{-4}). AC = actual (successful) capturing, FC = failed capturing, AF = actual freeing, FF = failed freeing

terms of precision, recall, and F1 score. Note that all four activities are modeled *jointly* in both models. The F1 score of the augmented model is significantly better than that of the baseline for all four target activities (p-value less than 1.3×10^{-4}).

We see that the baseline model has, in general, a respectable recall but it produces a large number of false positives for all activities. The false positives stem from the fact that the algorithm is "greedy" in that it typically labels a situation where several players appear close to each other for certain period of time as a sequence of many captures and subsequent frees even though none of them actually occurred. Model $\mathcal{M}_{S+F}$ gives significantly better results because it takes full advantage of the structure of the game in a probabilistic fashion. It has a similar "over labeling" tendency only in the case of failed captures, where a single capture attempt is often labeled as several consecutive attempts. While this hurts the precision score, it is not a significant deficiency, as in practice, having a small number of short game segments labeled as possible near-captures is useful as well.

We also note that even though the original model (UML) did not contain any information on failed capturing nor failed freeing, the performance of $\mathcal{M}_{S+F}$ is respectable even for those two newly introduced activities. We only provided examples of game situations where those attempts occur and the system augmented itself and subsequently labeled all four activities. Thus, we see that we can indeed extend preexisting models in an automated fashion so that the unified model is capable of recognizing not only individual activities, but also both success and failure in people's behavior.

2.6.4 The Effect of Modeling Failed Attempts on Recognition of Successful Activities

To address research question Q4 (*Does modeling failed attempts of activities improve the performance on recognizing the activities themselves?*), we want to see how much does the recognition of attempted activities help in modeling the successful actions (the latter being the standard activity recognition problem). Toward that end, we compare the Markov logic model $\mathcal{M}_S$ that jointly labels only successful capturing and freeing with model $\mathcal{M}_{S+F}$ that jointly labels both successful and failed attempts at both capturing and freeing (see Sect. 2.5.2.1 for a detailed description of the two models). However, we evaluate them in terms of precision, recall, and F1 score only on *successful* interactions, not all four types of activities.

Figure 2.15 summarizes the results. We see that when evaluated on actual capturing, $\mathcal{M}_{S+F}$ performs better than $\mathcal{M}_S$, and similarly for freeing. However, the difference in F1 scores between a model that captures both attempted and successful activities ($\mathcal{M}_{S+F}$) and a model of only successful activities ($\mathcal{M}_S$) is not statistically significant (p-value of 0.20). This is partly because $\mathcal{M}_S$ already produces very solid results, leaving little room for improvement. Additionally, the CTF dataset contains relatively few events of interest. In terms of labeling performance at testing time, the difference between the two models is more than 11 % ($\mathcal{M}_S$ and $\mathcal{M}_{S+F}$ recognize, respectively, 14 and 16 out of 18 successful activities correctly). Thus, we believe the trends shown in Fig. 2.15 are promising and modeling attempted actions does improve recognition performance on both capturing and freeing, but evaluation on a dataset with a larger number of events is needed to show the difference to be statistically significant at a higher confidence level. However, this does not mean that recognizing attempts is unimportant. As we show above, our induced augmented model does recognize failed (as well as successful) activities in the complex CTF domain with high accuracy, and we argue this to be a significant contribution.

Finally, the comparison of $\mathcal{M}_S$ and $\mathcal{M}_{S+F}$ shows that applying our learning algorithm that augments a model with more recognition capabilities *does not hurt* model labeling performance. The fact that binary classification problems are typically easier to solve than their multi-class counterparts has been well reported on in machine learning literature [2]. Therefore, introducing new activities into a model, especially in an automated way, is likely to degrade its performance. Contrary to this intuition, our experiments show that $\mathcal{M}_{S+F}$ is no worse than $\mathcal{M}_S$ on successful activity recognition (*i.e.*, their intersection) with high confidence, even though $\mathcal{M}_{S+F}$ is clearly richer and more useful.

2.6.5 Identifying Interesting Game Situations

We now turn our attention to the evaluation of the automatic detection of interesting game segments, as stated in our research question Q5. Specifically, we explore how

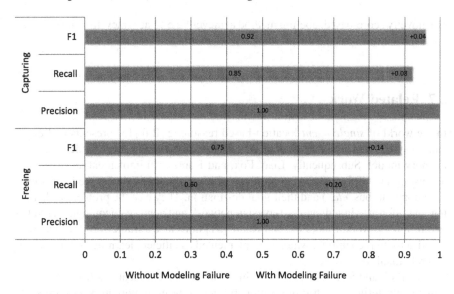

Fig. 2.15 Considering unsuccessfully attempted activities strictly improves performance on standard activity recognition. *Blue bars* show scores obtained with the unified Markov logic model that considers only *successful* activities ($\mathcal{M}_S$). The *red bars* indicate the additive improvement provided by the augmented model that considers both *successful and failed* activities ($\mathcal{M}_{S+F}$, the output of Algorithm 2.1). Each model labels its target activities jointly, we separate capturing and freeing in the plot for clarity. Precision has value of 1 for both models. F1 scores obtained when explicitly modeling failed attempts are not statistically different from F1 scores obtained without modeling attempts at a high confidence level (p-value of 0.20). However, these results still show the importance of reasoning about people's attempts when recognizing their activities; see text for details

do the high-activity game segments detected by our system align with human judgement. We divided each game into 20 second intervals and prepared a visualization of each segment over the map of the campus map using our Google maps web application (see Fig. 2.1). The 20 second segment length was chosen as the smallest time in which one can determine if a game situation is interesting or not with sufficient confidence. This produced a total of 151 different game segments.

We then show each segment individually to five subjects ($n = 5$) familiar with the capture the flag domain, and asked them to label each segment as either "interesting" or "uninteresting." At the same time, the novelty detection system described in Sect. 2.5.4 ($L = 32$) labeled each segment in the same manner. It selected the "interesting" label for game segments that contain at least one second with the absolute value of the novelty score larger than two standard deviations of all the novelty scores within that game.

We measure the inter-annotator agreement by Fleiss' kappa (κ) [27]. Over all four games, the five annotators show substantial agreement: $\kappa = 0.63$. Therefore, we take their majority vote as the ground truth against which we evaluate the automated system. It is interesting that even a relatively vague notion of an interesting versus uninteresting game situation results in a high agreement across annotators.

The novelty score-based labeling method achieves 92.5 % accuracy, thereby exhibiting a substantial agreement with human judgement.

2.7 Related Work

In the world of *single-agent* location-based reasoning, Bui [13] presents and evaluates a system for probabilistic plan recognition cast as an abstract hidden Markov memory model. Subsequently, Liao, Fox, and Kautz [50] implement a system for denoising raw GPS traces and simultaneously inferring individuals' mode of transportation (car, bus, *etc.*) and their goal destination. They cast the problem as learning and inference in a dynamic Bayesian network and achieve encouraging results. In a follow-up work, Liao, Fox, and Kautz [51] introduce a framework for location-based activity recognition, which is implemented as efficient learning and inference in a relational Markov network.

Ashbrook and Starner [3] focus on inferring significant locations from raw GPS logs via clustering. The transition probabilities between important places are subsequently used for a number of user modeling tasks, including location prediction. Eagle and Pentland [24] explore harnessing data collected on regular smart phones for modeling human behavior. Specifically, they infer individuals' general location from nearby cell towers and Bluetooth devices at various times of day. Applying a hidden Markov model (HMM), they show that predicting if a person is at home, at work, or someplace else can be achieved with more than 90 % accuracy. Similarly, Eagle and Pentland [25] extract significant patterns and signatures in people's movement by applying eigenanalysis to smart phone logs.

Hu, Pan, Zheng, Liu, and Yang [36] concentrate on recognition of interleaving and overlapping activities. They show that publicly available academic datasets contain a significant number of instances of such activities, and formulate a conditional random field (CRF) model that is capable of detecting them with high (more than 80 %) accuracy. However, they focus solely on single-agent household activities.

People's conversation has been the primary focus of *multi-agent* modeling effort [9]. In the fields of multi-agent activity recognition and studies of human behavior, researchers have either modeled conversation explicitly as, for example, Busetta, Serafini, Singh, and Zini [14], or have leveraged people's communication implicitly via call and location logs from mobile phones. This data has been successfully used to infer social networks, user mobility patterns, model socially significant locations and their dynamics, and others [24, 26]. This is arguably an excellent stepping stone for full-fledged multi-agent activity recognition since location is, at times, practically synonymous with one's activity (*e.g.*, being at a store often implies shopping) [81], and our social networks have tremendous influence on our behavior [67].

Additionally, a number of researchers in machine vision have worked on the problem of recognizing events in videos of sporting events, such as impressive recent work on learning models of baseball plays [31]. Most work in that area has focused on recognizing individual actions (*e.g.*, catching and throwing), and the state of the art is just beginning to consider relational actions (*e.g.*, the ball is thrown from player A to player B). The computational challenges of dealing with video data make it necessary to limit the time windows of a few seconds. By contrast, we demonstrate in this work that many events in the capture the flag data can only be disambiguated by considering arbitrarily long temporal sequences. In general, however, both our work and that in machine vision rely upon similar probabilistic models, and there is already some evidence that statistical-relational techniques similar to Markov logic can be used for activity recognition from video [12, 82].

Looking beyond activity recognition, recent work on relational spacial reasoning includes an attempt to locate—using spacial abduction—caches of weapons in Iraq based on information about attacks in that area [77]. Additionally, Abowd, Atkeson, Hong, Long, Kooper, and Pinkerton [1] present a location- and context-aware system, Cyberguide, that helps people explore and fully experience foreign locations. Horvitz, Apacible, Sarin, and Liao [35] explore an intelligent and nonintrusive navigation system that takes advantage of predictions of traffic conditions along with a model of user's knowledge and competence. Finally, Kamar and Horvitz [40] explore automatic generation of synergistic plans regarding sharing vehicles across multiple commuters.

An interesting line of work in cognitive science focuses on intent and goal recognition in a probabilistic framework [4, 5]. Specifically, they cast goal inference as inverse planning problem in Markov decision processes, where Bayesian inversion is used to estimate the posterior distribution over possible goals. Recent extensions of this work begin to consider simulated multi-agent domains [6, 7, 83]. Comparison of the computational models against human judgement in synthetic domains shows a strong correlation between people's predicted and actual behavior. However, the computational challenges involved in dealing with the underlying partially observable Markov decision processes are prohibitive in more complex domains with large state spaces, such as ours.

The focus of our work is on a different aspect of reasoning about people's goals. Rather than inferring a distribution over possible, *a priori* known goals, we automatically *induce* the goals of complex multi-agent activities themselves.

Other researchers have concentrated on modeling behavior of people and general agents as reinforcement learning problems in both single-agent and multi-agent settings. Ma [55] proposes a system for household activity recognition cast as a single-agent Markov decision process problem that is subsequently solved using a probabilistic model checker. Wilson and colleagues address the problem of learning agents' *roles* in a multi-agent domain derived from a real-time strategy computer game [88, 89]. Experiments in this synthetic domain show strongly encouraging results. While we do not perform role learning ourselves, we anticipate that the work of Wilson *et al.* is going to play an important role in learning hierarchies of people's activities. In our capture the flag domain, one can imagine automatically identifying a particular player as, for example, a defender and subsequently leveraging this information to model his or her behavior in a more "personalized" way.

Hong [34] concentrates on recognizing the goal of an agent in the course of her activities in a deterministic, but relational setting. Interesting work on goal recognition has been also applied to computer-aided monitoring of complex multi-agent systems, where relationships between agents are leveraged to compensate for noise and sparse data [41]. By contrast, in our work we focus on *learning* the respective goals of a given set of multi-agent activities in a probabilistic setting. The knowledge is in turn leveraged to achieve a stronger robustness of the other recognition tasks. Similarly to the approach of Hong [34], our system does not need a supplied plan library either.

Our work also touches on anomaly detection since our system reasons about the failed attempts of the players. Anomaly detection concerns itself with revealing segments of the data that in some way violate our expectations. For an excellent survey of the subject, we refer the reader to Chandola, Banerjee, and Kumar [15]. In the realm of anomaly detection within people's activities, Moore and Essa [60] address the problem of error detection and recovery card games that involve two players recorded on video. Their system models the domain with a stochastic context-free grammar and achieves excellent results.

We note that recognizing a failed attempt at an activity is more fine-grained a problem than anomaly detection. The failed event is not just anomalous in general.[8] Rather, it is the specific distinction between success and failure in human activities that we are interested in. And the distinction lies in the fact that an unsuccessful attempt does not yield a certain desired state whereas a successful action does. This desired state is exactly what our approach extracts for each activity in question. To our knowledge, there exists no prior work on explicit modeling and recognition of attempted activities or on learning the intended purpose of an activity in a multi-agent setting.

One of the components of our contribution focuses on *joint* learning and inference across multiple tasks (capturing, freeing, and their respective attempted counterparts). This is in contrast with the traditional "pipeline" learning architecture, where a system is decomposed into a series of modules and each module performs partial computation and passes the result on to the next stage. The main benefits of this set-up are reduced computational complexity and often higher modularity. However, since each stage is myopic, it may not take full advantage of dependencies and broader patterns within the data. Additionally, even though errors introduced by each module may be small, they can accumulate beyond tolerable levels as data passes through the pipeline.

An extensive body of work has shown that joint reasoning improves model performance in a number of natural language processing and data mining tasks including information extraction (*i.e.*, text segmentation coupled with entity resolution) [69], co-reference resolution [70], information extraction coupled with co-reference resolution [87], temporal relation identification [54, 92], and record de-duplication [16, 22]. Similarly to our work, some of the above models are cast in Markov logic. However, prior work uses sampling techniques to perform learning and inference, whereas we apply a reduction to integer linear programming. Interestingly, Denis

---

[8] A situation where a player in CTF moves through the campus at a speed of 100 mph and on her way passes an enemy player is certainly anomalous (and probably caused by GPS sensor noise), but we do not want to say that it is a failed attempt at capturing.

and Baldridge [21] jointly address the problems of anaphoricity and co-reference via a *manual* formulation of an integer linear program.

Joint activity modeling has also been shown to yield better recognition accuracy, as compared to "pipeline" baselines as well as baselines that make strong inter-activity independence assumptions. Wu, Lian, and Hsu [91] perform joint learning and inference over concurrent single-agent activities using a factorial conditional random field model. Similarly, Helaoui, Niepert, and Stuckenschmidt [33] model interleaved activities in Markov logic. They distinguish between foreground and background activities and infer a time window in which each activity takes place from RFID sensory data. By contrast, we focus on joint reasoning about multi-agent activities and attempts in a fully relational—and arguably significantly more noisy—setting.

Manfredotti, Hamilton, and Zilles [58] propose a hierarchical activity recognition system formulated as learning and inference in relational dynamic Bayesian networks. Their model jointly leverages observed interactions with individual objects in the domain and the relationships between objects. Since their method outperforms a hidden Markov model by a significant margin, it contributes additional experimental evidence that a relational decomposition of a domain improves model quality.

Landwehr, Gutmann, Thon, Philipose, and De Raedt [49] cast single-agent activity recognition as a relational transformation learning problem, building on transformation-based tagging from natural language processing. Their system induces a set of transformation rules that are then used to infer activities from sensory data. Since the transformation rules are applied adaptively, at each step, the system leverages not only observed data, but also currently assigned labels (inferred activities). However, the transformation rules are learned in a greedy fashion and experiments show that the model does not perform significantly better than a simple HMM. On the other hand, their representation is quite general, intuitive, and extensible. As we will see, our Markov logic model has a similar level of representational convenience while performing global—instead of greedy—optimization in a significantly more complex domain.

The denoising component of our model can be formulated as a tracking problem. Prior work proposed a relational dynamic Bayesian network model for multi-agent tracking [57]. Their evaluation shows that considering relationships between tracked entities significantly improves model performance, as compared to a nonrelational particle filter baseline. By contrast, our work explores *joint* tracking and activity recognition. However, each GPS reading is annotated with the identity of the corresponding agent. The work of Manfredotti and Messina [57] suggests that our model can be generalized, such that the associations between GPS and agent identities are *inferred* and need not be observed.

Our Markov logic theory can be viewed as a template for a conditional random field [48], an undirected graphical model that captures the *conditional* probability of hidden labels given observations, rather than the *joint* probability of both labels and observations, as one would typically do in a directed graphical model. Conditional random fields have been extensively applied to activity recognition, and their superior labeling performance over generative models has been demonstrated in a number of both single-agent and multi-agent domains [36, 51, 53, 84, 85]. This is the main reason we cast our models in Markov logic, rather than in directed models such as relational Bayesian networks [38] and their dynamic counterparts [56], probabilistic relational models [29, 47], Bayesian logic programs [42], and first-order conditional influence language [64].

Since Markov logic is based on, and in fact subsumes, finite first-order logic, we immediately gain access to a number of techniques developed in the rich field of traditional logic. Current Markov logic solvers take advantage of the underlying logical structure to perform more powerful optimizations, such as Alchemy's MC-SAT [68]. We also leverage this relationship between Markov and first-order logic when inducing an augmented model. Furthermore, presence of dependency cycles introduces additional problems in directed graphical (relational) models. Thus, the fact that, in Markov logic, knowledge can be expressed as weighted first-order formulas combined with the above factors make it a powerful framework best suited for the multi-agent reasoning tasks considered in this work.

Traditional hidden Markov models operate over an alphabet of unstructured (*i.e.*, "flat") symbols. This makes relational reasoning difficult, as one has to either propositionalize the domain, thereby incurring combinatorial increase in the number of symbols and model parameters, or ignore the relational structure and sacrifice information. Logical hidden Markov models (LHMMs) have been proposed to address this problem [43]. LHMMs are a generalization of standard HMMs that compactly represents probability distributions over sequences of logical atoms rather than flat symbols. LHMMs have been proven strictly more powerful than their propositional counterparts (HMMs). By applying techniques from logic-based reasoning, such as unification, while leveraging the logical structure component of the model, Kersting, De Raedt, and Raiko [43] show that LHMMs often require fewer parameters and achieve higher accuracy than HMMs.

LHMMs have been recently applied to activity recognition. In the context of intelligent user interfaces, Shen [78] designs and evaluates a LHMM model for recognition of people's activities and workflows carried out on a desktop computer. Natarajan, Bui, Tadepalli, Kersting, and Wong [65] propose a hierarchical extension of LHMMs along with an efficient particle filter-based inference technique, and apply it to activity recognition problems in synthetic domains. Both lines of work show that LHMMs can be learned and applied efficiently, and perform better than plain HMMs.

However, LHMMs are a generative model and therefore are not ideal for pure labeling and recognition tasks, where we typically do not want to make strong independence assumptions about the observations, nor do we want to explicitly model dependencies in the input space. TildeCRF—a relational extension of traditional conditional random fields—has been introduced to address this issue [32]. TildeCRF allows discriminative learning and inference in CRFs that encode sequences of logical atoms, as opposed to sequences of unstructured symbols. TildeCRF specifically focuses on efficient learning of models of sequential data via boosting, and is subsumed by Markov logic, which can produce both discriminative and generative models. We cast our model in the latter framework to make it more general, extensible, and interpretable.

PRISM, a probabilistic extension of Prolog, has been shown to subsume a wide variety of generative models, including Bayesian networks, probabilistic context-free grammars, HMMs (along with their logical extension) [75, 76]. However, since the focus of PRISM is on representational elegance and generality, rather than scalability, the sheer size of the state space and complexity of our CTF domain precludes its application here.

Finally, our Markov logic theory augmentation process is related to structure learning, transfer learning, and inductive logical programming. In fact, Algorithm 2.1 implements a special case of structure learning, where we search for a target theory that explains the training data well, while our declarative bias forces the target theory to differ from the source theory only as much as necessary. Again, with the intuition that failed attempts are similar to their failed counterparts. A number of researchers have focused on structure learning specifically in Markov logic networks. This includes early work on top-down structure learning, where clauses in the knowledge base are greedily modified by adding, flipping, and deleting logical literals [44]. This search is guided by the likelihood of the training data under the current model. Mihalkova and Mooney [59] exploit patterns in the ground Markov logic networks to introduce a bottom-up declarative bias that makes their algorithm less susceptible to finding only local optima, as compared to alternative greedy methods. Similarly, Kok and Domingos [46] introduce a bottom-up declarative bias based on lifted hypergraph representation of the relational database. This bias then guides search for clauses that fit the data. Since the hypergraph is lifted, relational path finding tractable. Interesting work on predicate invention applies relational clustering technique formulated in second-order Markov logic to discover new predicates from relational databases [45]. The above systems are capable of modeling relatively rich family of logical formulas. Other approaches perform discriminative structure learning and achieve excellent results, but focus on a restricted set of types of formulas (*e.g.*, Horn clauses) [11, 37]. Davis and Domingos [17] successfully use second-order Markov logic in deep transfer learning. They lift the model of the source domain to second-order ML and identify high-level structural patterns. These subsequently serve as declarative bias for structure learning in the target domain. By its very nature, the inductive logic programming discipline has extensively studied structure learning in deterministic, as well as probabilistic settings (*e.g.*, [18, 20, 61]). In fact, our theory augmentation algorithm can be viewed as an efficient Markov logic based version of theory refinement, a well-established ILP technique that aims to improve the quality of a theory in terms of simplicity, fit to newly acquired data, efficiency or other factors [90].

Our approach differs from all this work in three main points. First, our declarative bias is defined implicitly by the seed theory of successful activities. Therefore, our theory augmentation algorithm is not limited to any hard-wired set of formula types it can consider. Rather, the search space is defined at run time by extracting motifs from the seed theory. The second distinction lies in computational tractability and exactness of the results. By distinguishing between soft and hard formulas, we are able to search through candidate formulas in a systematic, rather than greedy manner. Consequently, our final learned model requires fewer parameters, which is especially important when the amount of training data is relatively small. Additionally, our weight learning does not experience cold starts, as we leverage the seed theory. The final difference is that, to our knowledge, we are the first to explore structure learning in the context of interplay of success and failure, and their relationship to the intended goals of people's actions.

2.8 Conclusions

This chapter took on the task of understanding the game of capture the flag from GPS data as an exemplar of the general problem of inferring human interactions and intentions from sensor data. We have presented a novel methodology—cast in Markov logic—for effectively combining data denoising with higher-level relational reasoning about a complex multi-agent domain. Specifically, we have demonstrated that given raw and noisy data, we can automatically and reliably detect and recognize both successful and failed interactions in adversarial as well as cooperative settings. Additionally, we have shown that success, failure, and the goal of an activity are intimately tied together and having a model for successful events allows us to naturally learn models of the other two important aspects of life in a supervised fashion. Specifically, we have demonstrated that the intentions of rational agents are automatically discovered in the process of resolving inconsistencies between a theory that models successful instances of a set of activities and examples of failed attempts at those activities. We have also explored to what extend can we identify interesting game situations and key players from raw location data. The results produced by our system show a high agreement with the judgement of human experts.

We have formulated five research questions and designed experiments within the CTF domain that empirically answer them. Compared to alternative approaches to solving the multi-agent activity recognition problem, our augmented Markov logic model, which takes into account not only relationships among individual players, but also relationships among activities over the entire length of a game, although computationally more costly, is significantly more accurate on real-world data. Furthermore, we have illustrated that explicitly modeling unsuccessful attempts boosts performance on other important recognition tasks.

2.9 Future Work

Multi-agent activity recognition is especially interesting in the context of current unprecedented growth of on-line social networks—in terms of their size, popularity, and their impact on our "off-line" lives. In this paper, we show that location information alone allows for rich models of people's interactions, but in the case of on-line social networks, we additionally have access to the content of users' posts and both the explicit and the implicit network interactions. For instance, our preliminary study shows that, interestingly, about 20 % of Twitter users reveal their location with each post. These data sources are now available to machines in massive volumes and at ever-increasing real-time streaming rate. We note that a substantial fraction of posts on services such as Facebook and Twitter talk about everyday activities of the users [63], and this information channel has become available to the research community only very recently. Thus, if we are able to reason about human behavior and interactions in an automated way, we can tap the colossal amounts of knowledge that is—at present—distributed across the whole population.

We are currently extending our model to handle not only explicit GPS traces, but also be able to *infer* the location of people who do not broadcast their GPS coordinates. The basic idea is, again, to leverage the structure of relationships among people. The vast majority of us participate in on-line social networks and typically some of our friends there do publish their location. We thus view the GPS-enabled people as noisy location sensors and use the network interactions and dynamics to estimate the location of the rest of the users. At present, we are testing this approach on public tweets.

Acknowledgements This chapter extends work published in Sadilek and Kautz [72–74]. We thank Sebastian Riedel for his help with theBeast, and to Radka Sadílková and Wendy Beatty for their helpful comments. This work was supported by ARO grant #W911NF-08-1-0242, DARPA SBIR Contract #W31P4Q-08-C-0170, and a gift from Kodak.

References

1. Abowd, G. D., Atkeson, C. G., Hong, J., Long, S., Kooper, R., & Pinkerton, M. (1997). Cyberguide: a mobile context-aware tour guide. *Wireless Networks, 3*(5), 421–433.
2. Allwein, E. L., Schapire, R. E., & Singer, Y. (2001). Reducing multiclass to binary: A unifying approach for margin classifiers. *Journal of Machine Learning Research, 1,* 113–141.
3. Ashbrook, D., & Starner, T. (2003). Using GPS to learn significant locations and predict movement across multiple users. *Personal and Ubiquitous Computing, 7,* 275–286.
4. Baker, C., Tenenbaum, J., & Saxe, R. (2006). Bayesian models of human action understanding. *Advances in Neural Information Processing Systems, 18,* 99.
5. Baker, C. L., Tenenbaum, J. B., & Saxe, R. R. (2007). Goal inference as inverse planning. In *Proceedings of the 29th annual meeting of the cognitive science society.*
6. Baker, C. L., Goodman, N. D., & Tenenbaum, J. B. (2008). Theory-based social goal inference. In *Proceedings of the thirtieth annual conference of the cognitive science society* (pp. 1447–1452).
7. Baker, C. L., Saxe, R. R., & Tenenbaum, J. B. (2011). Bayesian theory of mind: Modeling joint belief-desire attribution. In *Proceedings of the thirty-second annual conference of the cognitive science society.*
8. Baldwin, D. A., & Baird, J. A. (2001). Discerning intentions in dynamic human action. *Trends in Cognitive Sciences, 5*(4), 171–178.
9. Barbuceanu, M., & Fox, M. S. (1995). COOL: a language for describing coordination in multi agent systems. In *Proceedings of the first international conference on multi-agent systems (ICMAS-95)* (pp. 17–24).
10. Bell, R., Koren, Y., & Volinsky, C. (2007). Modeling relationships at multiple scales to improve accuracy of large recommender systems. In *KDD* (pp. 95–104). New York: ACM.

11. Biba, M., Ferilli, S., & Esposito, F. (2008). *Discriminative structure learning of Markov logic networks* (pp. 59–76). Berlin: Springer.
12. Biswas, R., Thrun, S., & Fujimura, K. (2007). Recognizing activities with multiple cues. In *Workshop on human motion* (pp. 255–270).
13. Bui, H. H. (2003). A general model for online probabilistic plan recognition. In *Eighteenth international joint conference on artificial intelligence (IJCAI-2003)*.
14. Busetta, P., Serafini, L., Singh, D., & Zini, F. (2001). Extending multi-agent cooperation by overhearing. In *Cooperative information systems* (pp. 40–52). Berlin: Springer.
15. Chandola, V., Banerjee, A., & Kumar, V. (2009). Anomaly detection: A survey. *ACM Computing Surveys, 41*, 15–11558.
16. Culotta, A., & McCallum, A. (2005). Joint deduplication of multiple record types in relational data. In *Proceedings of the 14th ACM international conference on information and knowledge management* (pp. 257–258). New York: ACM.
17. Davis, J., & Domingos, P. (2009). Deep transfer via second-order Markov logic. In *Proceedings of the 26th annual international conference on machine learning* (pp. 217–224). New York: ACM.
18. De Raedt, L. (2008). *Logical and relational learning*. New York: Springer.
19. De Raedt, L., & Kersting, K. (2008). Probabilistic inductive logic programming. In L. De Raedt, P. Frasconi, K. Kersting, & S. Muggleton (Eds.), *Lecture notes in computer science: Vol. 4911. Probabilistic inductive logic programming—theory and applications* (pp. 1–27). Berlin: Springer.
20. De Raedt, L., Frasconi, P., Kersting, K., & Muggleton, S. (Eds.) (2008). *Lecture notes in computer science: Vol. 4911. Probabilistic inductive logic programming—theory and applications*. Berlin: Springer.
21. Denis, P., & Baldridge, J. (2007). Joint determination of anaphoricity and coreference resolution using integer programming. In *Proceedings of NAACL HLT* (pp. 236–243).
22. Domingos, P. (2004). Multi-relational record linkage. In *Proceedings of the KDD-2004 workshop on multi-relational data mining*.
23. Domingos, P., Kok, S., Lowd, D., Poon, H., Richardson, M., & Singla, P. (2008). Markov logic. In L. De Raedt, P. Frasconi, K. Kersting, & S. Muggleton (Eds.), *Lecture notes in computer science: Vol. 4911. Probabilistic inductive logic programming—theory and applications* (pp. 92–117). Berlin: Springer.
24. Eagle, N., & Pentland, A. (2006). Reality mining: sensing complex social systems. *Personal and Ubiquitous Computing, 10*(4), 255–268.
25. Eagle, N., & Pentland, A. S. (2009). Eigenbehaviors: Identifying structure in routine. *Behavioral Ecology and Sociobiology, 63*(7), 1057–1066.
26. Eagle, N., Pentland, A., & Lazer, D. (2009). Inferring social network structure using mobile phone data. In *Proceedings of the National Academy of Sciences*.
27. Fleiss, J. L. (1971). Measuring nominal scale agreement among many raters. *Psychological Bulletin, 76*(5), 378.
28. Foote, J. (2000). Automatic audio segmentation using a measure of audio novelty. In *IEEE international conference on multimedia and expo. ICME 2000* (Vol. 1, pp. 452–455). New York: IEEE.
29. Friedman, N., Getoor, L., Koller, D., & Pfeffer, A. (1999). Learning probabilistic relational models. In *International joint conference on artificial intelligence* (Vol. 16, pp. 1300–1309).
30. Goutte, C., & Gaussier, E. (2005). *A probabilistic interpretation of precision, recall and f-score, with implication for evaluation* (pp. 345–359). Berlin: Springer.
31. Gupta, A., Srinivasan, P., Shi, J., & Davis, L. S. (2009). Understanding videos, constructing plots: Learning a visually grounded storyline model from annotated videos. In *CVPR*.
32. Gutmann, B., & Kersting, K. (2006). TildeCRF: conditional random fields for logical sequences. In *Machine learning: ECML 2006* (pp. 174–185). Berlin: Springer.
33. Helaoui, R., Niepert, M., & Stuckenschmidt, H. (2010). A statistical-relational activity recognition framework for ambient assisted living systems. In *Ambient intelligence and future*

trends—international symposium on ambient intelligence (ISAmI 2010) (pp. 247–254). Berlin: Springer.

34. Hong, J. (2001). Goal recognition through goal graph analysis. *The Journal of Artificial Intelligence Research, 15,* 1–30.
35. Horvitz, E., Apacible, J., Sarin, R., & Liao, L. (2005). Prediction, expectation, and surprise: Methods, designs, and study of a deployed traffic forecasting service. In *Twenty-first conference on uncertainty in artificial intelligence.*
36. Hu, D. H., Pan, S. J., Zheng, V. W., Liu, N. N., & Yang, Q. (2008). Real world activity recognition with multiple goals. In *UbiComp* (Vol. 8, pp. 30–39).
37. Huynh, T. N., & Mooney, R. J. (2008). Discriminative structure and parameter learning for Markov logic networks. In *Proceedings of the 25th international conference on machine learning* (pp. 416–423). New York: ACM.
38. Jaeger, M. (1997). Relational Bayesian networks. In *Proceedings of the 13th conference on uncertainty in artificial intelligence* (pp. 266–273).
39. Jordan, M. I. (1998). *Learning in graphical models.* Dordrecht: Kluwer Academic.
40. Kamar, E., & Horvitz, E. (2009). Collaboration and shared plans in the open world: Studies of ridesharing. In *IJCAI.*
41. Kaminka, G. A., Tambe, D. V. P. M., Pynadath, D. V., & Tambe, M. (2002). Monitoring teams by overhearing: A multi-agent plan-recognition approach. *Journal of Artificial Intelligence Research, 17.*
42. Kersting, K., & De Raedt, L. (2000). Bayesian logic programs. In *Proceedings of the work-in-progress track at the 10th international conference on inductive logic programming.*
43. Kersting, K., De Raedt, L., & Raiko, T. (2006). Logical hidden Markov models. *The Journal of Artificial Intelligence Research, 25*(1), 425–456.
44. Kok, S., & Domingos, P. (2005). Learning the structure of Markov logic networks. In *Proceedings of the 22nd international conference on machine learning* (pp. 441–448). New York: ACM.
45. Kok, S., & Domingos, P. (2007). Statistical predicate invention. In *Proceedings of the 24th international conference on machine learning* (pp. 433–440). New York: ACM.
46. Kok, S., & Domingos, P. (2009). Learning Markov logic network structure via hypergraph lifting. In *Proceedings of the 26th annual international conference on machine learning* (pp. 505–512). New York: ACM.
47. Koller, D. (1999). Probabilistic relational models. In *Inductive logic programming* (pp. 3–13). Berlin: Springer.
48. Lafferty, J. (2001). Conditional random fields: Probabilistic models for segmenting and labeling sequence data. In *International conference on machine learning (ICML)* (pp. 282–289). San Mateo: Morgan Kaufmann.
49. Landwehr, N., Gutmann, B., Thon, I., Philipose, M., & De Raedt, L. (2007). Relational transformation-based tagging for human activity recognition. In *Proceedings of the 6th international workshop on multi-relational data mining (MRDM07)* (pp. 81–92).
50. Liao, L., Fox, D., & Kautz, H. (2004). Learning and inferring transportation routines. In *Proceedings of the nineteenth national conference on artificial intelligence.*
51. Liao, L., Fox, D., & Kautz, H. (2005). Location-based activity recognition using relational Markov networks. In *IJCAI.*
52. Liao, L., Patterson, D. J., Fox, D., & Kautz, H. (2007). Learning and inferring transportation routines. *Artificial Intelligence, 171*(5–6), 311–331.
53. Limketkai, B., Fox, D., & Liao, L. (2007). CRF-filters: Discriminative particle filters for sequential state estimation. In *IEEE international conference on robotics and automation* (pp. 3142–3147).
54. Ling, X., & Weld, D. S. (2010). Temporal information extraction. In *Proceedings of the twenty fifth national conference on artificial intelligence.*
55. Ma, Z. (2008). *Modelling with PRISM of intelligent system.* MSc. Thesis, Linacre College, University of Oxford.

56. Manfredotti, C. (2009). Modeling and inference with relational dynamic Bayesian networks. In *Advances in artificial intelligence* (pp. 287–290). Berlin: Springer.
57. Manfredotti, C., & Messina, E. (2009). Relational dynamic Bayesian networks to improve multi-target tracking. In *Advanced concepts for intelligent vision systems* (pp. 528–539). Berlin: Springer.
58. Manfredotti, C., Hamilton, H., & Zilles, S. (2010). Learning RDBNs for activity recognition. In *Neural information processing systems*.
59. Mihalkova, L., & Mooney, R. J. (2007). Bottom-up learning of Markov logic network structure. In *Proceedings of the 24th international conference on machine learning* (pp. 625–632). New York: ACM.
60. Moore, D., & Essa, I. (2001). Recognizing multitasked activities using stochastic context-free grammar. In *Proceedings of AAAI conference*.
61. Muggleton, S. (2002). Learning structure and parameters of stochastic logic programs. In *Proceedings of the 12th international conference on inductive logic programming* (pp. 198–206). Berlin: Springer.
62. Murphy, K. P. (2002). *Dynamic Bayesian networks: representation, inference and learning*. Ph.D. thesis, University of California, Berkeley.
63. Naaman, M., Boase, J., & Lai, C.-H. (2010). Is it really about me?: message content in social awareness streams. In *CSCW'10: Proceedings of the 2010 ACM conference on computer supported cooperative work* (pp. 189–192). New York: ACM.
64. Natarajan, S., Tadepalli, P., Altendorf, E., Dietterich, T. G., Fern, A., & Restificar, A. (2005). Learning first-order probabilistic models with combining rules. In *Proceedings of the 22nd international conference on machine learning* (pp. 609–616). New York: ACM.
65. Natarajan, S., Bui, H. H., Tadepalli, P., Kersting, K., & Wong, W. (2008). Logical hierarchical hidden Markov models for modeling user activities. In *Proc. of ILP-08*.
66. Paulus, J., Müller, M., & Klapuri, A. (2010). Audio-based music structure analysis. In *Proceedings of the international symposium on music information retrieval* (pp. 625–636).
67. Pentland, A. S. (2008). *Honest signals: how they shape our world*. Cambridge: The MIT Press.
68. Poon, H., & Domingos, P. (2006). Sound and efficient inference with probabilistic and deterministic dependencies. In *Proceedings of the national conference on artificial intelligence* (Vol. 21, p. 458). Menlo Park: AAAI Press.
69. Poon, H., & Domingos, P. (2007). Joint inference in information extraction. In *Proceedings of the 22nd national conference on artificial intelligence* (Vol. 1, pp. 913–918). Menlo Park: AAAI Press.
70. Poon, H., & Domingos, P. (2008). Joint unsupervised coreference resolution with Markov logic. In *Proceedings of the conference on empirical methods in natural language processing* (pp. 650–659). Association for Computational Linguistics.
71. Riedel, S. (2008). Improving the accuracy and efficiency of map inference for Markov logic. In *Proceedings of the twenty-fourth conference annual conference on uncertainty in artificial intelligence (UAI-08)*, Corvallis, Oregon (pp. 468–475). New York: AUAI Press.
72. Sadilek, A., & Kautz, H. (2010). Modeling and reasoning about success, failure, and intent of multi-agent activities. In *Mobile context-awareness workshop, twelfth ACM international conference on ubiquitous computing*.
73. Sadilek, A., & Kautz, H. (2010). Recognizing multi-agent activities from GPS data. In *Twenty-fourth AAAI conference on artificial intelligence*.
74. Sadilek, A., & Kautz, H. (2011). Location-based reasoning about complex multi-agent behavior. *Journal of Artificial Intelligence Research*. AI Access Foundation.
75. Sato, T., & Kameya, Y. (2001). Parameter learning of logic programs for symbolic-statistical modeling. *Journal of Artificial Intelligence Research*.
76. Sato, T., & Kameya, Y. (2008). New advances in logic-based probabilistic modeling by PRISM. In *Probabilistic inductive logic programming* (pp. 118–155). Berlin: Springer.

77. Shakarian, P., Subrahmanian, V. S., & Spaino, M. L. (2009). SCARE: A Case Study with Baghdad. In *Proceedings of the third international conference on computational cultural dynamics*. Menlo Park: AAAI Press.
78. Shen, J. (2009). *Activity recognition in desktop environments*. Ph.D. Thesis, Oregon State University.
79. Shoenfield, J. R. (1967). *Mathematical logic*. Reading: Addison-Wesley.
80. Singla, P., & Domingos, P. (2005). Discriminative training of Markov logic networks. In *Proceedings of the national conference on artificial intelligence* (Vol. 20, p. 868). Menlo Park: AAAI Press.
81. Tang, K. P., Lin, J., Hong, J. I., Siewiorek, D. P., & Sadeh, N. (2010). Rethinking location sharing: exploring the implications of social-driven vs. purpose-driven location sharing. In *Proceedings of the 12th ACM international conference on ubiquitous computing* (pp. 85–94). New York: ACM.
82. Tran, S., & Davis, L. (2008). Visual event modeling and recognition using Markov logic networks. In *Proceedings of the 10th European conference on computer vision*.
83. Ullman, T. D., Baker, C., Macindoe, O., Evans, O., Goodman, N., & Tenenbaum, J. (2010). Help or hinder: Bayesian models of social goal inference. In *Advances in neural information processing systems (NIPS)* (Vol. 22).
84. Vail, D. L. (2008). *Conditional random fields for activity recognition*. Ph.D. Thesis, Carnegie Mellon University.
85. Vail, D. L., & Veloso, M. M. (2008). Feature selection for activity recognition in multi-robot domains. In *Proceedings of AAAI* (Vol. 2008).
86. Wang, J., & Domingos, P. (2008). Hybrid Markov logic networks. In *Proceedings of the 23rd national conference on artificial intelligence* (Vol. 2, pp. 1106–1111). Menlo Park: AAAI Press.
87. Wellner, B., McCallum, A., Peng, F., & Hay, M. (2004). An integrated, conditional model of information extraction and coreference with application to citation matching. In *Proceedings of the 20th conference on uncertainty in artificial intelligence* (pp. 593–601). Menlo Park: AAAI Press.
88. Wilson, A., Fern, A., Ray, S., & Tadepalli, P. (2008). Learning and transferring roles in multi-agent mdps. In *Proceedings of AAAI*.
89. Wilson, A., Fern, A., & Tadepalli, P. (2010). Bayesian role discovery for multi-agent reinforcement learning. In *Proceedings of the 9th international conference on autonomous agents and multiagent systems* (Vol. 1, pp. 1587–1588). International Foundation for Autonomous Agents and Multiagent Systems.
90. Wrobel, S. (1996). First order theory refinement. In *Advances in inductive logic programming* (pp. 14–33). Amsterdam: IOS Press.
91. Wu, T., Lian, C., & Hsu, J. Y. (2007). Joint recognition of multiple concurrent activities using factorial conditional random fields. In *Proc. 22nd conf. on artificial intelligence (AAAI-2007)*.
92. Yoshikawa, K., Riedel, S., Asahara, M., & Matsumoto, Y. (2009). Jointly identifying temporal relations with Markov logic. In *Proceedings of the joint conference of the 47th annual meeting of the ACL and the 4th international joint conference on natural language processing of the AFNLP* (Vol. 1, pp. 405–413). Association for Computational Linguistics.

Chapter 3
Energy-Accuracy Trade-offs of Sensor Sampling in Smart Phone Based Sensing Systems

Kiran K. Rachuri, Cecilia Mascolo, and Mirco Musolesi

Abstract A large number of context-inference applications run on off-the-shelf smart phones and infer context from the data acquired by sensing from the sensors embedded in these devices. The use of efficient and effective sampling techniques is of key importance for these applications. Aggressive sampling can ensure a more fine-grained and accurate reconstruction of context information but, at the same time, continuous querying of sensor data might lead to rapid battery depletion. In this chapter, we present a design methodology to evaluate energy-accuracy trade-offs for querying sensor data in continuous sensing mobile systems, and an adaptive sensor sampling methodology that relies on dynamic selection of sampling functions depending on history of context events. We also report on the experimental evaluation of a set of functions that control the rate at which the data are sensed from the accelerometer, Bluetooth, and microphone sensors, and we show that a dynamic adaptation mechanism provides a better energy-accuracy trade-offs compared to simpler function based rate control methods. Furthermore, we show that the suitability of these mechanisms varies for each of the sensors.

3.1 Introduction

Modern smart phones have many sensors embedded in them: accelerometers can be used to infer user activity, Bluetooth to detect colocation, GPS receivers to infer location, microphones to infer speech/noise, magnetometers to detect direction, cameras to capture images, and proximity sensors to detect the proximity of the phone (usually screen) with any object. However, the development of mobile context-

K.K. Rachuri (✉) · C. Mascolo
Computer Laboratory, University of Cambridge, Cambridge CB3 0FD, UK
e-mail: kkr27@cam.ac.uk

C. Mascolo
e-mail: cm542@cam.ac.uk

M. Musolesi
School of Computer Science, University of Birmingham, Birmingham B15 2TT, UK
e-mail: m.musolesi@cs.bham.ac.uk

T. Lovett, E. O'Neill (eds.), *Mobile Context Awareness*,
DOI 10.1007/978-0-85729-625-2_3, © Springer-Verlag London Limited 2012

aware applications has always been limited due to energy, processing, and memory constraints. With the advent of high-end phones like Samsung Galaxy S2 [19] (that is equipped with 1200 MHz dual-core processor and 1 GB RAM), the processing and memory limitations are overcome to a great extent. However, battery capacity has not seen similar level of growth and energy is still a scarce resource on mobile phones and should be expended judiciously by the applications. For example, it is reported in [21] that the battery charge of a Nokia N95 [12] smart phone lasts less than 5 hours when sensing data from accelerometer, GPS, microphone, and Wi-Fi sensors using a predefined static (and aggressive) sampling rate. It is also shown in [8] that the CenceMe application lasts around 6.22 hours with no other applications running on the phone. In other words, context-aware applications are by definition resource intensive, since they continuously query data from the sensors of the phone. There is a need for adaptive mechanisms for querying the sensor data in an energy efficient way by considering the application requirements in terms of energy and accuracy, and provide the sensor data to these applications.

As an initial step towards a larger framework, in this chapter, we present a design methodology to evaluate and study the energy-accuracy trade-offs of sampling rate control mechanisms for querying sensor data in continuous sensing mobile systems. These aspects are in some respects orthogonal to the problem of intelligent mechanisms for uploading data to a back-end [10], even if the sampling rate can also be tuned according to the corresponding transmission rate. However, some applications perform local computation on the phones and only then transmit the information to a remote server via GPRS or Wi-Fi.

We present some preliminary results by evaluating a set of functions that control the rate at which the data should be sensed from the accelerometer, Bluetooth, and microphone sensors for a predefined set of classifiers used in various mobile context-aware applications. In this work, we focus on context events that are represented by a stream of discrete states, such as streams of user activities, like walking, sitting, in conversation, and so on. We do not consider context information that is measured in a given continuous range, such as temperature. The contributions of this work can be summarized as follows:

- We propose a methodology for studying the energy-accuracy trade-offs for querying data in continuous sensing applications using a set of sampling functions selected dynamically according to the stream of context events. In particular, we discuss the choice of parameters of a dynamic adaptation algorithm that switches among a set of sampling functions based on the analysis of the stream of past events.
- We demonstrate that the dynamic adaptation mechanism is better in terms of accuracy compared to the other simple sampling rate control methods based on static functions.
- We show experimentally that a dynamic adaptation mechanism provides a better trade-off compared to simpler function based rate control methods. Furthermore, we show that the suitability of these mechanisms varies for each of the sensors.

The remainder of the chapter is organized as follows: in Sect. 3.2 we describe our design methodology and the dynamic adaptation scheme. In Sect. 3.3 we present the evaluation of the proposed dynamic scheme along with a set of static functions with respect to energy-accuracy trade-offs. We then present the related work in Sect. 3.4, and finally, we conclude the chapter in Sect. 3.5.

3.2 Adaptive Sampling Based on Dynamic Selection of Functions

Context-aware applications require data from the sensors in mobile phones to be queried on a continuous basis. Even though this helps in delivering services to the user, it consumes a considerable amount of energy and thereby decreases their battery life. Most importantly, these applications may not be of high importance to the user compared to making and receiving calls. Therefore, the sensor sampling rate has to be optimized in order for the user to turn on and use/run these applications. In order to address the energy-accuracy trade-offs of context-aware applications, we propose a methodology that exploits a set of functions to adjust the sampling rate of sensors based on the current observed data. The sensor data are either queried periodically or aperiodically according to the sampling function used. We define two parameters *viz.*, *minSamplingInterval* and *maxSamplingInterval*. The former is the minimum sleep interval between two successive sensor readings and the later is the maximum sleep interval. If the sensor sampling interval for a sensor is always set to *minSamplingInterval*, then the accuracy of classifiers will be high (due to aggressive data sampling). However, the energy expended will also be considerable. On the other hand, if the sampling interval is always set to *maxSamplingInterval*, then the energy consumption is minimized but the accuracy decreases. To achieve a balance between energy and accuracy and to satisfy application requirements, we advocate the use of function based sampling, where the sampling interval varies between *minSamplingInterval* and *maxSamplingInterval* values.

We classify context events into two classes *viz.*, *missable* and *unmissable*. A *missable* event indicates that no interesting external phenomenon has happened and the corresponding sensor can sleep during this time. An *unmissable* event is an event of interest observed in the environment that should not be missed by the sensor. If there are no "interesting" events observed (*i.e.*, missable events), then the sampling interval increases (*i.e.*, sampling rate decreases) from its current value to *maxSamplingInterval* based on a *back-off function*. Similarly, if the event is classified as unmissable, then the sampling interval decreases (*i.e.*, sampling rate increases) from its current value to *minSamplingInterval* based on an *advance function*. The classification of an event as missable or unmissable is application dependent. For example, let us assume that the current sampling sleep interval of microphone is s. If no interesting events are observed (classifier detects that none of the users are speaking), then the rate of sampling has to be decreased to save battery life. One way to do it is by increasing the sleep interval to e^s. If there are no events in the next iteration as well, then we further increase the interval and so on until it reaches a maximum value (*maxSamplingInterval*). Even though this might save energy (as exponential function increases the sleep interval aggressively), there might be a case that we

Table 3.1 Back-off and Advance functions

Type	Back-off function	Advance function
Linear	$k \times x$	x/k
Quadratic	x^2	$\sqrt{x}$
Exponential	e^x	$\log_e x$
Minimum	N/A	$minSamplingInterval$
Maximum	$maxSamplingInterval$	N/A

might miss some interesting events during the sleep time. The choice of the advance and back-off functions and of the *minSamplingInterval* and *maxSamplingInterval* parameters play a crucial rule in the energy-accuracy trade-offs for the various context inference components. Examples of back-off and the advance functions (also used in the evaluation section) are given in Table 3.1. The back-off function is invoked when there are no interesting events observed and advance function is invoked otherwise.

The functions take into consideration the previous state and not the full or partial history of the context events. Moreover, they can be considered static (no dynamic adaptation). One further step is to dynamically switch these functions based on past observations of sensor data. For our evaluation, we adopt the adaptive technique showed in Algorithm 3.1. The idea is to use the functions according to the consistency of the observed sensor data, *i.e.*, the function changes from least to most "aggressive" based on the number of consecutive sampling of the same state. By adopting this mechanism, small state changes do not have a large effect on the sampling interval. More refined techniques can be implemented, however, since the goal of this work is primarily to present a methodology for tuning the parameters of adaptive sampling functions by analyzing energy-accuracy trade-offs, we limit our discussion, methodological analysis, and performance evaluation to this simple mechanism.

3.3 Evaluation

In this section we describe the dataset used for the evaluation and then present the results of the performance evaluation of the proposed techniques considering accelerometer, Bluetooth, and microphone sensors. The main goals of our evaluation are to find the optimal sensor sampling combinations of advance and back-off functions for each of the sensors and classifiers.

3.3.1 Dataset

Trace files with ground-truth information for accelerometer, Bluetooth, and microphone sensors were collected from 10 users for 24 hours using the EmotionSense

Algorithm 3.1 Dynamic adaptation algorithm

```
sleep(sleepInterval)
interestingEvent = senseAndClassify(sensorId)
if (interestingEvent == TRUE) then
    uninterestingSequence = 0
    interestingSequence + = 1
    sequence = interestingSequence
else
    interestingSequence = 0
    uninterestingSequence + = 1
    sequence = uninterestingSequence
end if
if (sequence < linearThreshold) then
    function = linear
else if (sequence < quadraticThreshold) then
    function = quadratic
else
    function = exponential
end if
sleepInterval = update(function, sleepInterval, interestingEvent)
if (sleepInterval ≥ maxSamplingInterval) then
    sleepInterval = maxSamplingInterval
else if (sleepInterval ≤ minSamplingInterval) then
    sleepInterval = minSamplingInterval
end if
```

platform [15] running on Nokia 6210 Navigator [13] phones. In order to extract the microphone sensor traces, audio samples of 5 seconds length were recorded continuously with a sleep period of 1 second between consecutive recordings. Colocation data for the Bluetooth sensor traces were queried continuously with a sleep duration of 3 seconds between successive queries. The accelerometer sensor is sampled continuously for movement information with an interval of 1 second.

As discussed above, the events generated from the data of each sensor can be of two types, *viz.*, "unmissable" and "missable" events. In the case of the microphone sensor, an unmissable event corresponds to some audible voice data being heard in the environment and a missable event corresponds to silence. These events are generated based on a GMM classifier [1] capable of classifying whether an audio trace contains any conversation. For the Bluetooth sensor traces, an unmissable event corresponds to a change in the number of colocated users, whereas a missable event indicates that there is no change. The change in colocated users is measured based on the variation of number of Bluetooth devices detected in the proximity of a user. We assume reliable Bluetooth readings, however, techniques to identify outliers can also be applied. In the case of the accelerometer sensor, the unmissable event corresponds to movement of a user and a missable event indicates that the

Fig. 3.1 Percentage of missed events vs linear threshold for Bluetooth sensor

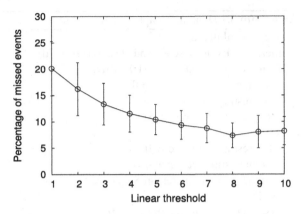

Fig. 3.2 Energy consumption vs linear threshold for Bluetooth sensor

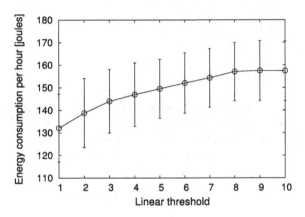

user is stationary. Although both of these events are unmissable, it is sufficient to detect just one of them since we have just two possible events, so we choose "user moving event" as unmissable. The accuracy is measured in terms of the percentage of missed events. An event is said to be missed when there is an unmissable event recorded in the trace file while the sensor is not actively queried. The energy consumption is measured using the Nokia Energy Profiler [11].

3.3.2 Results

In order to find optimal values of thresholds used in the dynamic adaptation algorithm for the Bluetooth sensor, we varied one of them by fixing the other. Figures 3.1 and 3.2 show the accuracy and energy consumption by varying the *linearThreshold* value. From these results, we selected a value of 3 for *linearThreshold* as the benefits in terms of accuracy after that are negligible.

Figures 3.3 and 3.4 show the effect of increasing the value of *minSampling-Interval* on the percentage of missed events and energy consumption for the

Fig. 3.3 Percentage of
missed events vs minimum
sampling interval for
Bluetooth sensor

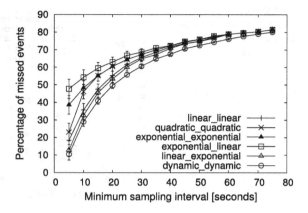

Fig. 3.4 Energy
consumption vs minimum
sampling interval for
Bluetooth sensor

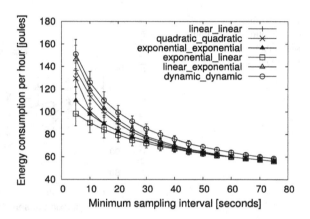

Bluetooth sensor. Figures 3.5 and 3.6 show the effect of increasing the value of
maxSamplingInterval on the percentage of missed events and energy consumption for the Bluetooth sensor. Note that the format of the legend in all the plots
is ⟨*backoff function*⟩_⟨*advance function*⟩. We can observe that all these curves stabilize at certain values. Therefore, high values of these intervals do not necessarily
imply low accuracy and high savings in energy. It should suffice to use the values after which there are no considerable improvements in terms of performance.
The dynamic adaptation function is best in terms of accuracy compared to the other
functions for most of the cases; however, it is not always the worst in terms of energy consumption. With respect to the Bluetooth sensor (Figs. 3.3 and 3.4), for a
minSamplingInterval value of 5, the best performing function (dynamic adaptation)
is more accurate than the worst (exponential_linear) by a factor of 5, whereas, in
terms of energy consumption the gain ratio is 1.5. So, in this case, the gain in accuracy is much higher than the compromise in terms of energy consumption using
the dynamic adaptation method. Figures 3.5 and 3.6 show the *maxSamplingInterval* variation for Bluetooth sensor. We observe a similar behavior with respect to
variation of *maxSamplingInterval* too.

Fig. 3.5 Percentage of missed events vs maximum sampling interval for Bluetooth sensor

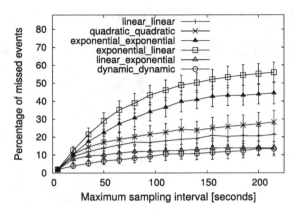

Fig. 3.6 Energy consumption vs maximum sampling interval for Bluetooth sensor

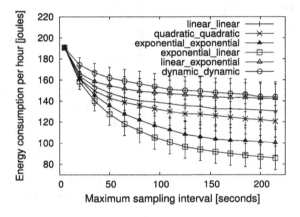

Figures 3.7 and 3.8 show the effect of increasing the value of *minSamplingInterval* on the percentage of missed events and energy consumption for the accelerometer sensor. With respect to the accelerometer sensor, the difference among the combinations in terms of energy consumption is negligible, whereas the difference with respect to accuracy is not. For a *minSamplingInterval* value of 3, the best performing function is 20 % more accurate than the worst, whereas the difference in terms of energy consumption is only 1 %. Thus, the dynamic adaption method can be used to sample the accelerometer sensor without worrying about energy consumption as it provides better accuracy. Figures 3.9 and 3.10 show the effect of increasing the value of *minSamplingInterval* on the percentage of missed events and energy consumption for the microphone sensor. With respect to the microphone sensor, we can observe that for a *minSamplingInterval* value of 25, the accuracy of *linear_exponential* is only 3 % less than that of dynamic adaption method, however, the energy saving of the former is 11 % better than the latter. This is due to high energy consumption for processing audio data locally on the phone. Therefore, *linear_exponential* is a better option for this sensor.

Fig. 3.7 Percentage of missed events vs minimum sampling interval for accelerometer

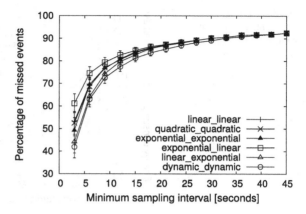

Fig. 3.8 Energy consumption vs minimum sampling interval for accelerometer

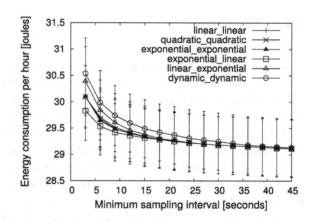

Fig. 3.9 Percentage of missed events vs minimum sampling interval for microphone sensor

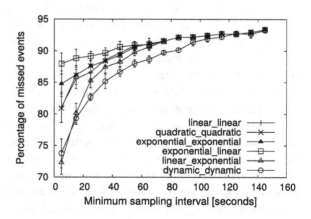

Fig. 3.10 Energy consumption vs minimum sampling interval for microphone sensor

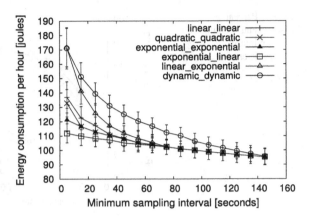

3.4 Related Work

There are many works that deal with inferring various kinds of contextual information based on smart phones [4, 5, 7, 17]. These works infer contextual information such as speaker identification [9, 15], activity recognition [8, 18, 21]. Some systems that used purpose-built devices for measuring the contextual information include the Sociometer [3] and the Mobile Sensing Platform [2]. In EmotionSense [15], we used a linear back-off function to adjust the sampling rate of the sensors. More recently, in SociableSense [16], we used a learning technique to control the sampling rate of the sensors and we also compared the performance of the dynamic adaptation scheme with the learning mechanism.

Energy efficiency is a key issue in mobile sensing system design, and for this reason, it has been investigated in many recent works. In this section, we present a brief selection of relevant projects. The *EEMSS system* [21] is probably the most relevant work: this platform uses a hierarchical sensor management strategy to recognize user states as well as to detect state transitions. *SeeMon* [6] is a context monitoring service for mobile devices based on several sensors, and it achieves energy efficiency by performing context recognition only when the there is a change in the context. In [10] the authors show that continuous sensing is a viable option for mobile phones by adopting efficient data uploading (to a remote server) strategies. *SALSA* [14] addresses the problem of energy-delay trade-offs in smart phone applications, in particular for delay-tolerant settings. The authors present an algorithm based on Lyapunov optimization, which achieves energy efficiency by adapting to channel conditions and deferring data transmissions according to them. In [9], the authors present a framework for mobile smart phones which can perform collaborative inference and is self-extending (based on self-evolving classifiers) and utilizes colocated mobile phones to achieve better accuracy and scalability. Finally, several energy saving schemes for mobile devices are discussed and compared in [20].

3.5 Conclusions

In this chapter, we discussed a design methodology to evaluate energy-accuracy trade-offs for querying sensor data in smart phone based mobile systems, and also presented its evaluation with respect to a set of functions that control the rate at which the data should be sensed from the accelerometer, Bluetooth, and microphone sensors. We also discussed a dynamic algorithm that switches among these functions based on the context history. The results show that the dynamic adaptation scheme is better in terms of accuracy, however, the suitability of these functions varies for each of the sensors.

We plan to explore the function based sampling rate control further by considering additional functions, and also evaluate their suitability to different types of classifiers. Our future research agenda includes the design of techniques for combining intelligent sampling *and* uploading to back-end servers for further processing, *i.e.*, mechanisms that are able to optimize the sampling and uploading processes at the same time.

Acknowledgements This work was supported through the Gates Cambridge Trust at the University of Cambridge, and the EPSRC grants EP/C544773, EP/F033176, and EP/D077273.

References

1. Bishop, C. M. (2007). *Pattern recognition and machine learning*. Berlin: Springer.
2. Choudhury, T., Borriello, G., Consolvo, S., Haehnel, D., Harrison, B., Hemingway, B., Hightower, J., Klasnja, P. P., Koscher, K., LaMarca, A., Landay, J. A., LeGrand, L., Lester, J., Rahimi, A., Rea, A., & Wyatt, D. (2008). The mobile sensing platform: an embedded activity recognition system. *IEEE Pervasive Computing, 7*(2), 32–41.
3. Choudhury, T., & Pentland, A. (2003). Sensing and modeling human networks using the sociometer. In *Proceedings of the IEEE international symposium on wearable computers (ISWC '03)*.
4. Gaonkar, S., Li, J., Choudhury, R. R., Cox, L., & Schmidt, A. (2008). Micro-blog: sharing and querying content through mobile phones and social participation. In *Proceedings of the ACM international conference on mobile systems, applications and services (MobiSys '08)*. New York: ACM.
5. Hong, L., Jun, Y., Zhigang, L., Nicholas, L., Tanzeem, C., & Andrew, C. (2010). The Jigsaw continuous sensing engine for mobile phone applications. In *Proceedings of the ACM conference on embedded network sensor systems (Sensys '08)*. New York: ACM.
6. Kang, S., Lee, J., Jang, H., Lee, H., Lee, Y., Park, S., Park, T., & Song, J. (2008). SeeMon: scalable and energy-efficient context monitoring framework for sensor-rich mobile environments. In *Proceedings of the ACM international conference on mobile systems, applications and services (MobiSys '08)*. New York: ACM.
7. Kukkonen, J., Lagerspetz, E., Nurmi, P., & Andersson, M. (2009). BeTelGeuse: a platform for gathering and processing situational data. *IEEE Pervasive Computing, 8*(2), 49–56.
8. Miluzzo, E., Lane, N. D., Fodor, K., Peterson, R., Lu, H., Musolesi, M., Eisenman, S. B., Zheng, X., & Campbell, A. T. (2008). Sensing meets mobile social networks: the design, implementation and evaluation of the CenceMe application. In *Proceedings of the ACM conference on embedded network sensor systems (SenSys '08)*. New York: ACM.

9. Miluzzo, E., Cornelius, C. T., Ramaswamy, A., Choudhury, T., Liu, Z., & Campbell, A. T. (2010). Darwin phones: the evolution of sensing and inference on mobile phones. In *Proceedings of the ACM international conference on mobile systems, applications and services (MobiSys '10)*. New York: ACM.

10. Musolesi, M., Piraccini, M., Fodor, K., Corradi, A., & Campbell, A. T. (2010). Supporting energy-efficient uploading strategies for continuous sensing applications on mobile phones. In *Proceedings of the international conference on pervasive computing (Pervasive '10)*. Berlin: Springer.

11. Nokia Energy Profiler. http://store.ovi.com/content/17374.

12. Nokia N95. http://www.forum.nokia.com/devices/N95.

13. Nokia 6210 Navigator. http://europe.nokia.com/find-products/devices/nokia-6210-navigator.

14. Ra, M. R., Paek, J., Sharma, A. B., Govindan, R., Krieger, M. H., & Neely, M. J. (2010). Energy-delay tradeoffs in smartphone applications. In *Proceedings of the ACM international conference on mobile systems, applications and services (MobiSys '10)*. New York: ACM.

15. Rachuri, K. K., Musolesi, M., Mascolo, C., Rentfrow, P. J., Longworth, C., & Aucinas, A. (2010). EmotionSense: a mobile phones based adaptive platform for experimental social psychology research. In *Proceedings of the ACM international conference on ubiquitous computing (UbiComp '11)*. New York: ACM.

16. Rachuri, K. K., Mascolo, C., Musolesi, M., & Rentfrow, P. J. (2011). SociableSense: exploring the trade-offs of adaptive sampling and computation offloading for social sensing. In *Proceedings of the ACM international conference on mobile computing and networking (MobiCom '11)*. New York: ACM.

17. Raento, M., Oulasvirta, A., Petit, R., & Toivonen, H. (2005). ContextPhone: a prototyping platform for context-aware mobile applications. *IEEE Pervasive Computing, 4*(2), 51–59.

18. Reddy, S., Mun, M., Burke, J., Estrin, D., Hansen, M., & Srivastava, M. (2010). Using mobile phones to determine transportation modes. *ACM Transactions on Sensor Networks, 6*(2), 1–27.

19. Samsung Galaxy S2. http://www.samsung.com/global/microsite/galaxys2.html.

20. Viredaz, M. A., Brakmo, L. S., & Hamburgen, W. R. (2003). Energy management on Handheld devices. *ACM Queue, 1*(7), 44–52.

21. Wang, Y., Lin, J., Annavaram, M., Jacobson, Q. A., Hong, J., Krishnamachari, B., & Sadeh, N. (2009). A framework of energy efficient mobile sensing for automatic user state recognition. In *Proceedings of the ACM international conference on mobile systems, applications and services (MobiSys '09)*. New York: ACM.

Chapter 4
Acceleration Noise Correction for Transfer Inference Using Accelerometers on Mobile Devices

Hisao Setoguchi, Yuzo Okamoto, Naoki Iketani, Kenta Cho, Masanori Hattori, and Takahiro Kawamura

Abstract The acceleration noise generated in the ordinary usage of mobile devices (e.g. when "taking out" the devices or operating them) interferes with estimation of the means of migration using accelerometers on the devices. We developed a correction method for the noise generated when users take out devices, change their posture, and operate the devices. The method uses the changes of acceleration and the operation events acquired from the operating systems of the mobile devices to detect the period of noises. The result of evaluation shows that the method using the acceleration changes improves the precision of the context inference approximately 5 %, and the method using the operation events corrects the inference mistaking resting for boarding.

4.1 Introduction

We developed a context-aware engine that infers a user's location and means of migration with multiple sensors [1]. This engine uses the data from accelerometer and GPS. It uses the accelerometer to classify the means of migration into 4 classes: resting, boarding, walking, and running. And it uses the GPS to identify a user's current location and destination as Points of Interest. Using this information, the engine determines the life scene (e.g. he/she is taking a train to work, he/she is walking home), and information or services matching the user's context can be offered by changing the behavior of the system according to the life scene. However, when a user takes out a device, changes posture, and operates the device, the acceleration generated in the motions causes the context-aware engine to make mistakes in the transfer inference. We call the acceleration that causes such problems the acceleration noise. In order to deal with the acceleration noise, we implemented correction methods that detect the noise segments and eliminate them. The methods are based on (1) the changes of acceleration and (2) the event published by the operation system of the mobile devices. In addition, we evaluated the correction methods using real mobile devices in our daily life. Using these acceleration correction methods,

H. Setoguchi (✉) · Y. Okamoto · N. Iketani · K. Cho · M. Hattori · T. Kawamura
Corporate Research & Development Center, Toshiba Corporation, Tokyo, Japan

T. Lovett, E. O'Neill (eds.), *Mobile Context Awareness*,
DOI 10.1007/978-0-85729-625-2_4, © Springer-Verlag London Limited 2012

we are able to realize high-precision transfer inference. This high precision of the inference of the life scene is a prerequisite for the provision of high-quality services to users.

4.2 Acceleration Noises

4.2.1 Definition of Acceleration Noises

In this paper, the acceleration noises are the acceleration generated in the motion irrelevant to the migration. The acceleration noises improperly magnify the statistics used in the context inference (e.g. the maximum, mean and variance of acceleration), and the statistics of the noises are similar to those of walking and boarding. Therefore, the inference mistaking the noises for walking and boarding occurs.

4.2.2 Classification of Acceleration Noises

We observe the acceleration noises and classify them into three classes. The patterns of acceleration of noises are shown in Figs. 4.1, 4.2 and 4.3. In each figure, the horizontal axis is time axis, and the vertical axis is acceleration axis. Each figure covers the range of around 1.7 minutes. The unit of acceleration is the Newtonian constant of gravitation ([G]).

4.2.2.1 Taking-out Noise

Taking-out noises are generated when a user takes out a device or puts a device in a bag. The pattern of the acceleration is shown in Fig. 4.1.

In the case of Taking-out noises, large changes of acceleration and changes of direction of devices are observed. These changes in acceleration are similar to those in walking and boarding. Therefore, the context-aware engine will mistake Taking-out noises for walking and boarding.

4.2.2.2 Waggling Noise

Waggling noises are generated when a user changes posture (e.g. standing/sitting up straight, changing the direction of the body). The pattern of the acceleration is shown in Fig. 4.2.

Waggling noises are generated frequently when a user keeps a device close to his/her body (e.g. in a pocket). The impacts generated by unexpected touching of the devices are also included in Waggling noises. Waggling noises are associated with large changes of acceleration, which are similar to those of walking and boarding. Therefore, the context-aware engine will mistake Waggling noises for walking and boarding.

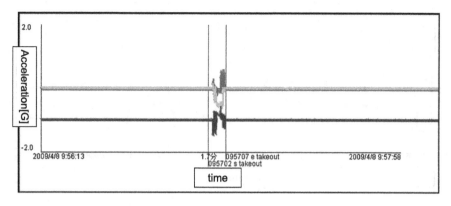

Fig. 4.1   Sample of Taking-out noise

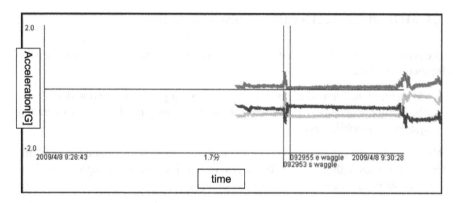

Fig. 4.2   Sample of Waggling noise

4.2.2.3 In-Operation Noise

In-Operation noises are generated when a user touches the buttons or screen of a device (e.g. writing e-mails, starting applications). The pattern of the acceleration is shown in Fig. 4.3.

In-Operation noises are not associated with large changes of acceleration, but the noises may last for a long period. The period of the noise ranges from a moment to several minutes according to the sequence of operations. In-Operation noises are similar to the acceleration observed in the case of trains or buses, and therefore the context-aware engine will mistake In-Operation noises for boarding.

Noises other than those of the three classes may occur. For example, the acceleration observed when a user dances while a device is in his/her pocket will interfere with the context inference. However, dealing with these three classes of noises covers most of the scenes where noises occur in the course of ordinary usage of mobile devices. Therefore, in this paper, we focus on these three classes of noises.

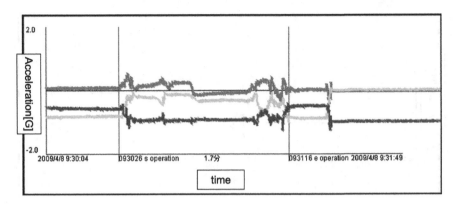

Fig. 4.3 Sample of In-Operation noise

4.3 Methods of Acceleration Noise Correction

The noise correction module judges if the acceleration data segment is noise by the following methods:

1. The method that detects the noises by preprocessing the acceleration data.
2. The method that detects the noises based on the event published by the operating system on a mobile device.

We deal with Taking-out noises and Waggling noises with method 1, and In-Operation noises with method 2. We refrain from using data in the segments judged to be noises to avoid mistakes in context inference.

4.3.1 Noise Correction Based on Acceleration Changes

The sequence of the correction method based on the changes of acceleration is shown in Fig. 4.4.

In this sequence, first, the data is put into a buffer. This method weakens the response of context inference, but the effect of the delay is minimized by using the latest result of context inference.

4.3.2 Feature Values Used in Noise Correction

In the noise correction, three feature values are calculated. These feature values involve low calculation cost in order to drive the noise correction on mobile devices at a practical speed.

Fig. 4.4 Sequence of noise
correction based on the
acceleration changes

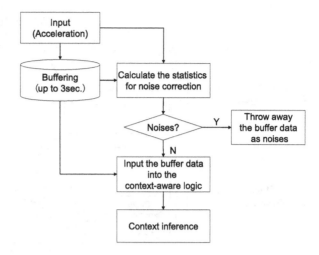

4.3.2.1 Degree of Direction Change

This feature value is used to detect Taking-out noises and Waggling noises. The
unit is the radian. This feature value is a large value when there is a rotation or
a direction change of the devices observed in the Taking-out noises and Waggling
noises segments.

4.3.2.2 Degree of Impact Change

This feature value is used to detect Taking-out noises and Waggling noises. The unit
is [G]. This feature value is a large value when a device receives an impact. The
value is small when the user is walking. Hence, using this feature value keeps the
context-aware engine from mistaking walking and boarding for noises. A side effect
is that when the user starts or stops walking, this feature value may be large and the
context-aware engine may mistake walking for noises. This causes the delay of context inference. However, the noise correction method should eliminate the mistakes
of context inference though it causes the delay of context inference. Therefore, we
judged this delay to be tolerable.

4.3.2.3 Walking Pace

This feature value is used to avoid mistaking walking and running for noises. The
unit is [counts/(5 s)]. The noises are detected with Degree of Direction Change and
Degree of Impact Change when the user is walking or running, Degree of Direction Change and Degree of Impact Change may be unexpectedly large values. This
causes the inference mistaking walking and running for noises. To avoid this, we use
Walking Pace. Since the value of Walking Pace is similar to the number of steps, the

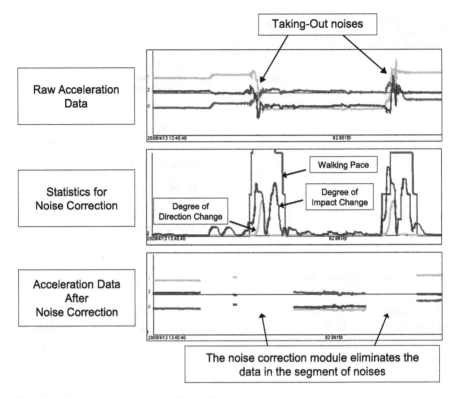

Fig. 4.5 Noise correction based on the acceleration changes

walking and running segments are distinguishable from that of noises if Walking Pace is a large value. The result of the noise correction using these three feature values is shown in Fig. 4.5.

As shown in the middle of Fig. 4.5, the value of the Degree of Direction Change and Degree of Impact Change is large in the Taking-out noises segment. However, the value of Walking Pace is below the threshold according to which the noise correction judges the acceleration to be that of walking and running. Using these feature values, the noise correction can detect the Taking-out noises segment and eliminate the acceleration data in the segment properly, as shown at the bottom of Fig. 4.5.

4.3.3 Noise Correction Based on the OS Events

The noise correction method based on OS events is a measure for In-Operation noises. Smartphones are the main target of our noise correction. The operating systems running on these devices publish the events when users operate the devices (e.g. press a button, touch the screen), and, in almost all cases, In-Operation noise occurs at the same time. Therefore, we eliminate these noises with the following methods:

1. If the engine receives OS events, it discards the acceleration data in the buffer, and records the time when the event occurred.
2. The engine will not use the acceleration data for context inference from the time of the last event to 5 seconds later.

As well as the acceleration-based methods, the noise correction based on OS events also uses the buffer and uses only the data confirmed not to be noises. Since users do not always operate devices continuously; the engine does not use the data for 5 seconds after an operation event occurs. We decided this length of time based on the result of a preliminary experiment, but the optimal length varies according to the patterns of device usage. The data of many users should be examined and this is a subject for future work.

4.4 Evaluation

4.4.1 Evaluation on the Effect of Noise Correction Based on the Acceleration Changes

We evaluated the effect of noise correction by comparing the precision. The evaluation setting was as follows:

- **Devices Used:** T-Mobile G1 (HTC Dream)
- **Number of Participants:** Three persons
- **Entire Length of Data:** 22 hours and 54 minutes

We collected the data using the devices in our daily life. The data covers the scenes where participants are resting, walking, running, or boarding vehicles, and the noises showed in the data.

The results of the evaluation are shown in Tables 4.1 and 4.2. The overall precision of the context inference is improved from 86.3 % to 91.1 %. The recall of

Table 4.1 Precision of context inference before adapting noise correction based on the acceleration changes

Precision of context inference *before* adapting noise correction

	Precision	Recall	F-measure
Resting	0.831	0.866	0.848
Walking	0.846	0.996	0.915
Running	1.000	0.838	0.912
Boarding	0.968	0.758	0.850
Total	0.863	0.863	0.863

Table 4.2 Precision of context inference after adapting noise correction based on the acceleration changes

Precision of context inference *after* adapting noise correction			
	Precision	Recall	F-measure
Resting	0.831	0.931	0.879
Walking	*0.981*	0.993	0.987
Running	0.992	0.849	0.915
Boarding	0.968	*0.830*	0.887
Total	0.911	0.911	*0.911*

resting and boarding is improved substantially, and the improvement in precision of walking is outstanding. This result shows that the noise correction reduces the inference that mistakes resting and boarding for walking. In addition, we examined the tolerance of Taking-out noise. The examination involves Taking-out a device 10 times from bags, and 10 times from pockets. The result shows that the noise correction eliminates the segment with acceleration noise properly. The pattern of acceleration noise is shown in Fig. 4.5. Moreover, the method of reducing the Waggling noises is effective in noise segments other than Taking-out, Waggling, and In-Operation noises; when we start and stop walking alternately (e.g. when shopping), the noise correction detects the noises on the border between resting and walking segments, and the context-aware engine detects each resting and walking segment properly.

4.4.2 Review on the Effects of Noise Correction Based on the OS Events

The noise correction based on the OS events is effective for In-Operation noises. We confirm its effectiveness through an examination in which the devices are operated for 5 minutes while placed on a table, and then operated for 5 minutes while held in the hand. The operation of the devices consisted of playing a game, writing an e-mail, and browsing the Web. The result of noise correction is shown in Fig. 4.6.

The real context is resting. The context-aware engine without the noise correction makes the inference mistaking resting for boarding. In contrast, the context-aware engine with the noise correction infers properly in the resting segment. This result suggests that the noise correction based on the OS events works.

4.5 Related Work

Much work has focused upon accelerometer noise. In [2], a Kalman filter is used to reduce the random noise from an accelerometer. Although this approach is effective

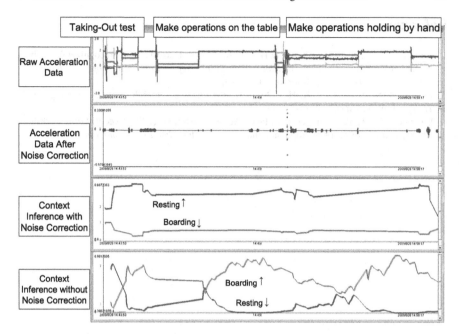

Fig. 4.6 Effect of the noise correction based on the OS events

for random noise, our goal is to deal with the noises generated in the course of ordinary usage of mobile devices, and therefore the approach for random noises may be unsuitable for our purpose. In [3], Hidden Markov Models (HMM) and Linear Discriminant Analysis (LDA) are used for context inference in workshop activities. They define actions irrelevant to the workshop activities as noises in order to avoid mistakes in the context inference and with this approach they detect the noises. However, using both HMM and LDA may result in higher computation costs than in the case of our approach, and moreover, the use of many sensors mounted on various parts of the body, which is necessary in their work, would be unsuitable for users of mobile devices.

4.6 Conclusion

We have shown that the acceleration noises in the ordinary usage of mobile devices can cause mistakes in context inference. We implemented a correction method for acceleration noises; the method based on the acceleration changes improves the precision of the context inference from 86.3 % to 91.1 %, and the method based on the OS events deals with the noises arising in the course of device operation. Subjects for future work are a measure for users' unexpected motions, examination of the correction methods involving many users, and classification of the state of holding devices to improve the precision of context inference.

References

1. Cho, K., Iketani, N., Setoguchi, H., & Hattori, M. (2009). Human activity recognizer for mobile devices with multiple sensors. In *Proc. of the 2009 symposia and workshops on ubiquitous, autonomic and trusted computing* (pp. 114–119).
2. Liu, H. H. S., & Pang, G. K. H. (2001). Accelerometer for mobile robot positioning. *IEEE Transactions on Industry Applications, 37*(3), 812–819.
3. Lukowicz, P., Ward, J., Junker, H., Stäger, M., & Tröster, G. (2004). Recognizing workshop activity using body worn microphones and accelerometers. *Pervasive Computing*, 18–32.

Chapter 5
Mobile Sensing of User's Motion and Position Context for Automatic Check-in Suggestion and Validation

Cristina Frà, Massimo Valla, Alessio Agneessens, Igor Bisio, and Fabio Lavagetto

Abstract Users are increasingly interested in mobile social applications that allow them to share opinions, comments and votes about places (restaurants, shops, etc.). Among these, check-in applications are spreading rapidly. In this paper we illustrate a system able to automatically validate users' check-in in a place exploiting device's sensors and inferred knowledge of context (motion activity, nearby friends). Additionally, the system allows check-in suggestion to users staying in a place for a required amount of time. A description of the service scenario, of the architecture and its technical components is given, focusing on how raw context data from accelerometer onboard the device is used to recognize users' motion situation and how it is combined with GPS position to validate check-ins.

5.1 Introduction and Motivation

Users are increasingly interacting with advanced and innovative services that allow them to stay in touch with their social network, to connect with other users and to exchange contents or suggestions often linked to their everyday life. A lot of interest is emerging on mobile social applications like Foursquare [3] that allow a user to check-in in a place and share this information with other users, providing comments and votes about venues (restaurants, events, etc.). Check-in applications are spreading rapidly for several reasons: users like to share with their social network what they are doing, where they are, their opinions about a place, etc. Such applications are also very attractive for place owners that are interested in advertising their business, making their commercial activities (like restaurants, bars, shops, etc.) more visible and offering for example special discounts to customers that collect a minimum number of check-ins. Another use is to collect statistics about profiles of people checking-in the place, information that may be very important for the owner to better direct his business.

C. Frà (✉) · M. Valla
Telecom Italia S.p.A., Turin, Italy

A. Agneessens · I. Bisio · F. Lavagetto ·
University of Genova, Genova, Italy

T. Lovett, E. O'Neill (eds.), *Mobile Context Awareness*,
DOI 10.1007/978-0-85729-625-2_5, © Springer-Verlag London Limited 2012

A weak point of these mobile services is that is difficult to validate a check-in to guarantee the owner of a place that the customer has actually stayed in the place for required amount of time after checking-in. To take commercial advantages, users could in fact check-in while not being physically there or just pass-by a place and sign-in without really staying.

In this paper we describe a solution that allows commercial operators to deal only with actual check-ins without having to worry about complex and custom validation processes. The check-in validation is done in a completely automatic and context-based way, making the access to these services easier, more convenient and more secure for both users and place owners.

This method exploits the improvements in mobile devices hardware (i.e. embedded sensors) and their increasing processing power. The basic idea is to combine context data coming from different sources (the GPS receiver and the accelerometer onboard the device) to automatically infer that a user has been in a place for the minimum amount of time requested by the place owner to validate the check-in. The user's position allows a first level of validation based on the comparison with the geographical positions of the place. To exploit the embedded accelerometer we propose a method that using raw data coming from it is able to infer four different user's motions situations (idle, still, walking and running). The knowledge of the user's motion situation enables a second validation phase that is performed after the user enters the place, where typically the GPS doesn't fix. While inside, the GPS is automatically switched off in order to save battery, while the accelerometer is turned on and data coming from it is periodically evaluated. If using the motion situation provided by the device the application recognized that the user has been in that place for the requested time (for example because in the evaluated period his motion has been mostly idle or still) the check-in is considered valid and "certified".

This approach fits in a more general client-server context framework and is implemented on the device. Raw sensor and inferred information is sent to a server that makes it available to context-based applications through a web API.

The proposed solution has been implemented on Android OS smartphones taking into account limitations of mobile devices while performing motion sensing. Even if computation power and battery capacity are less critical aspects, they still remain important mostly if they are used for added-value services and not for basic and higher priority activities like voice calls. For this reason we paid much attention to energy saving aspects: for example the GPS is switched off for a while when the user is indoors. Furthermore the accelerometer is involved and invoked only after the user enters in a place and the rate of its reading is in the range of minutes. A more frequent knowledge of the user's physical activity is uselessly energy consuming since the target application doesn't need this accuracy.

5.2 System Architecture

In Fig. 5.1 is represented the overall architecture of the system. The Check-in application we described is enabled by a general client-server Context Framework [5].

Fig. 5.1 System architecture

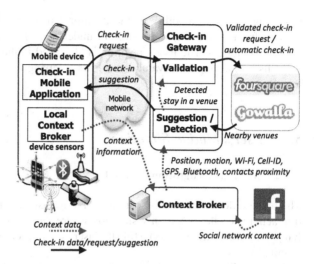

On the client side is implemented a Local Context Broker (LCB) that collects data from different sources (in this example the GPS receiver and the accelerometer) and infers higher level context information (the user's motion situation). The LCB implements the energy saving policies described previously, enabling and disabling the hardware sensors according to the device environment: the accelerometer is not used if the GPS receiver has a valid fix since the target application needs to know the user's motion only if he is indoor. Similarly the LCB switches off the GPS receiver for a while when it doesn't provide a valid position and starts to read data from the accelerometer. Both raw and inferred context data are sent to the server side of the framework, where a Context Broker makes this information available to all applications through a web API.

5.3 Context Collection and Classification

5.3.1 User's Position

Modern smartphones are equipped with an embedded GPS receiver; applications can obtain a position from the operating system. The LCB application interacts with the device's GPS APIs and sends, if available, the position to the Context Broker.

The LCB sends additional information to the platform to infer user's position: the identifier of the current mobile cell and the lists of Bluetooth and Wi-Fi nearby access points. Information about cell, Bluetooth and Wi-Fi will be used to infer or verify the user's position if not directly available on the device (for example if the GPS receiver cannot return a position based on satellites).

Knowledge of the user's position enables the first phase of the check-in validation process: evaluating the distance between the user and the position of the venue. By reasoning on the availability of the position (for example evaluating if it comes directly from a GPS fix) is possible to understand if the user is actually inside a venue or outdoors. The user's position is also used in the Place Detection process since its monitoring and evaluation allows inferring user's stay nearby a specific location.

5.3.2 User's Motion Situation

5.3.2.1 Motion Recognition Method

The method described in this section is able to distinguish four different user motion activities: idle (is the only situation where the phone is not on the user but is lying somewhere motionless), still (the user is sitting or still standing), walking or running.

The algorithm assumes that each data sample produced by the accelerometer onboard the device represented the acceleration in m/s^2 measured on three orthogonal axes. A data frame consists of F seconds of samples and is acquired every T seconds; this allows to switch off the accelerometer for $T - F$ seconds after every frame acquisition avoiding to waste battery. Each frame is associated to a feature vector in order to be classified. Once the vector has been calculated it is used by a classifier to associate the frame to one of the activity class described previously. For this task we used a decision tree [7], a common classifier used also in similar activity recognition works [6].

A single-frame classifications may not be sufficiently reliable to directly infer the user's activity; therefore, a way to sum up a certain number of time-distributed frame-based classifications over a broader time span is needed. Groups of W consecutive frames are organized in windows. The number of frames in each window has to be set carefully since it affects the computation result making the algorithm more reactive to motion changes or conversely more vulnerable to occasionally misclassified frames. Consecutive windows are overlapped by O frames. Figure 5.2 represents the data acquisition process; the involved parameters, that have been fine tuned in the proposed method, are the following:

- Δ: minimum time that must elapse between consecutive windowed decisions;
- W: number of frames in each window;
- O: number of frames shared by consecutive windows;
- N: time between consecutive frames, expressed in number of frames. It is equivalent to considering a frame-acquisition period $T = (N + 1) \times F$, where F is the frame duration expressed in seconds.

Such parameters are tied by the following expression:

$$(W - O) \times T \geq \Delta, \quad \text{or equivalently } (W - O) \geq \lceil \Delta / T \rceil$$

Each windowed decision assigns the current window to one of the four considered classes, based on a given decision policies.

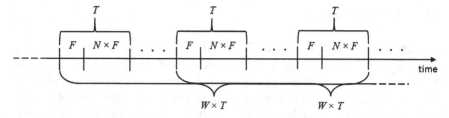

Fig. 5.2 Datagram representing raw accelerometer data acquisition

Four different decision policies were evaluated and compared, as detailed in the following:

Majority Decision   The simplest windowed decision policy is a majority-rule decision: the window is associated to the class with the most frames in the window. While it is clearly simple to implement and computationally inexpensive, the majority-rule windowed decision treats all frames within a window in the same way, without considering when the frames occurred or the single frame classifications' reliability.

Time-Weighted Decision   This method gives different a weight to every window's frame according to its position in the window and assigns a window to the class with the highest total weight. A frame will have a greater weight the closer it is to the end of the window, under the assumption that more recent classifications should be more useful to determine the current user motion status. In order to determine what weight to give to frames, two weighting functions were designed and compared: a Gaussian function and a negative exponential function.

Score-Weighted Decision   This method assigns to each frame a score representing how reliable its classification is. As in the case of the time-weighted decision, a window is associated to the class with the highest total weight. The scoring method used in our implementation [9] takes advantage of the fact that each leaf of a decision tree represents a region in the feature space defined by a set of inequalities determined by the path from the tree root to the leaf. It is based on the idea that the closer a frame's feature vector is to the decision boundary, the more unreliable the frame's classification will be, under the hypothesis that the majority of badly classified samples lie near the decision boundary. The basic idea is that the closer a frame's feature vector is to the decision boundary, the more unreliable the frame's classification will be, under the hypothesis that the majority of badly classified samples lie near the decision boundary.

Joint Score/Time-Weighted Decision   Another windowed decision policy is given by combining the temporal weights and the classification scores into a single, joint time-and-score weight. Fusion is obtained simply by multiplying the corresponding time weight and classification score, since both are between 0 and 1.

5.3.2.2 Method Training

Dataset Acquisition   The dataset employed in the experiments was acquired by four volunteers; each one acquired about one hour of data for each motion class described previously. During data acquisition the device was kept in four different positions in the user's front or rear pants pocket. For every combination of two and three users, the dataset was then divided into a training set for classifier training and a distinct test set for performance evaluation purposes.

Parameters Setting   The algorithm depends on some parameters (i.e. the number of frames in every window, the number of frames shared by consecutive windows, the time between consecutive frames, etc.) that have to be carefully tuned in order to achieve the best trade-off between results accuracy and a good usage of the device resources.

An additional ad hoc sequence of data not included in the dataset described before was acquired; the motion activities performed in random order during it was labelled and these labels was used as ground truth. At first, a single-frame classification is performed on the sequence, producing recognized-class labels and classification scores: incorrectly classified frames are associated with low recognition scores. After single-frame classification is performed, windowed decision accuracy is evaluated for all admissible combinations of the parameters to be tuned.

5.3.2.3 Classification Results

In evaluating the performance of the proposed method, one must distinguish single-frame classification accuracy from windowed-decision accuracy: the former depends solely on the decision tree classifier and was evaluated on a test set, while the latter depends on what decision policy was used and was evaluated using the ad hoc sequence described in previous section.

Frame Classification Results   Of all evaluated classifiers, the one with the best single-frame accuracy produced a 98 % correct test set classification average. More in detail, the class with the best recognition accuracy is sitting (over 99 % of test set frames correctly recognized), while running is the activity with the lowest test set accuracy (95.2 %), with most of the incorrectly classified frames (approximately 4.6 % of the total) being misclassified as walking.

Windowed Decision Results   The results can be summed up in Fig. 5.3. Each column represents the percentage of evaluated parameter configurations in which each decision policy led to the best windowed decision accuracy.

Using only the time-based frame classification weighting doesn't seem to improve performance compared to the majority decision, while employing classifica-

Fig. 5.3 Windowed decision results. (M: majority decision, Te: exponential time weighting, Tg: Gaussian time weighting, S: classification score weighting, S + Te: joint classification score/exponential time weighting, S + Tg: joint classification score/Gaussian time weighting)

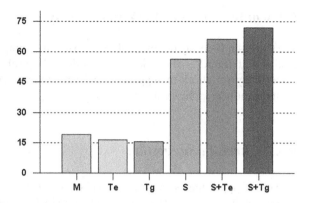

tion-score weighting, by itself or combined with time-weighting, led to significant improvements in windowed decision accuracy.

Overall, the best parameter configuration led to an 85.2 % windowed decision accuracy: it was obtained using 8-frame windows ($W = 8$), single-frame window overlap ($O = 1$), 16 second pauses between consecutive frames ($N = 4$), joint score/time frame weighting using a Gaussian function. Such decision policy led to an 11.1 % increase in windowed decision accuracy compared to the majority-rule decision.

Furthermore, using 16 second pauses between consecutive frames allows reducing the computational load by 80 % with respect to the case of constant accelerometer data acquisition (no pause between consecutive frames), thus reducing energy consumption while maintaining a satisfying recognition accuracy.

5.3.3 User's Contacts' Proximity

Our system is connected with external Social Networks, for example Facebook via Facebook Graph APIs [2], to retrieve information about user's friends and therefore his "social" context. The user can create ad hoc lists on the social network (if allowed) or directly on the context framework in order to assign specific meaning to groups of contacts: family, friends, colleagues etc. By combining information about contacts with the knowledge of the Bluetooth address of the device associated to a specific user, the Context Platform is able to infer information about user's contacts *proximity*. Proximity estimation is done using several technologies and combining different approaches like: comparison of users' geographical positions, evaluation of common Wi-Fi fingerprints and signal strengths, etc. More details are given in [1] about the implemented algorithm to compute proximity.

Knowledge of the user social situation (e.g. "he is with friends") enables check-in validation for groups of users, as explained later.

5.4 Context-Based Check-in Gateway

The Check-in Gateway represented in Fig. 5.1 is the component responsible for integration with the APIs of check-in web services. Two sub-components are in charge respectively for check-in suggestion and validation of check-in requests received from the mobile application.

5.4.1 Check-in Suggestion

One of the appealing aspects of check-in applications is the possibility for the user to become the "mayor" or the "boss" of a place by checking-in most times, to obtain social recognition or commercial benefits. An important issue is that manual check-ins are tedious and usually forgotten, especially when related to places the user visits routinely.

The Check-in gateway sub-module in charge of Place Detection is used to retrieve user's nearby venues and to detect stays. Information about nearby places is obtained from the APIs offered by Foursquare [3] and Gowalla [4] to search for points of interest close to a specified geographical location. The sub-module monitors the stay of the user device in a place using a combination of raw context data retrieved from the Context Platform. Our initial implementation exploits user's GPS position updates from the device, or uses position estimates calculated from other context data, e.g. Bluetooth, cell-ID and Wi-Fi, which is also updated to the Context Broker. Another approach, still under development, combines position with user's motion context, computed from filtered accelerometer sensing, to improve stay detection. The detection time depends on the place/venue type, since each type (e.g. restaurant, pub, etc.) is associated to a minimum time required to detect the stay.

When the component recognizes the user is staying in a place for the required time, the Check-in Gateway sends a check-in suggestion to the Mobile Check-in application. This message is shown to the user as an alert suggesting him to check-in in the venue. The user can ignore the suggestion (the place will not be suggested again), or he can accept and do the check-in, specifying that in the future he wants to be automatically checked-in every time the system recognizes he's staying at the venue.

5.4.2 Check-in Validation

As explained, one of the weak points in check-in applications is check-ins verification. To obtain commercial advantages, users could in fact check-in in a venue while not being physically there or just pass-by a place and sign-in without really staying. The Check-in Gateway acts as a validator for check-in requests coming from mobile applications and is in charge to forward the verified request to Foursquare and Gowalla using their check-in web APIs.

A first example of validation is instantaneous location-based certification. Every time the gateway receives a check-in request it invokes the Context Broker to retrieve user's location context. By comparing information like cell-ID position and device's declared GPS position with venue's coordinates, the check-in request can be considered valid and forwarded to external check-in web services.

However in many situations an instantaneous evaluation of the user's position is not enough to validate a check-in. For example, a restaurant owner can offer some promotional coupons to customers that actually dine there and not simply stay nearby for a while. In this case the validation module uses the place detection described in the previous section: user's context is used to perform user's stay detection in a place. A check-in for restaurant, for example, can be considered valid if Place Detector recognizes that 'user's position is in the venue range with an allowed accuracy of 50 meters and his motion is still or idle at least for 1 hour'.

A second example can be a check-in application related to jogging routes; runners can check-in in their favourite running routes sharing with their social network their performance results. By exploiting the knowledge of user's motion situation this action can be validated in two steps: first, checking the geographic user's closeness to the route and, second, evaluating his motion (that should be walking or running) during the required period of time.

Since the Context Platform is able to infer the social proximity situation of a user, applications can combine it with other context data to validate group check-ins or to validate a check-in only in a particular social context, e.g. the user is "with colleagues". We consider for example a pub owner that offers free drinks to customers who check-in in his venue together with at least three friends; or a restaurant owner that offers discounts to customers that check-in during a business lunch with colleagues.

5.5 Related Work

In recent years a significant amount of work has been done concerning context-aware services relying on data coming from GPS or accelerometers. Recently, thanks to the increasing native support of sensors onboard mobile devices, new applications for health-care, personal training, activity recognition, social networking, etc. that exploit the accelerometer are being proposed. For example CenceMe [6] uses the embedded accelerometer to continuously recognize the user's motion situation and allows him to share it with the social community. Some other applications instead need ad hoc sensors to work, for example [8] uses a recognition system that includes five tri-axial wireless wearable accelerometers.

The system described in this paper is based solely on the sensors embedded on mobile device, and combines raw data (GPS and accelerometer) to compute overall user's motion and position context which is used to validate the check-in. In addition, continuous sensor use is avoided to save battery power in two ways: first by using frame and windowed classification to avoid continuous accelerometer readings to compute the motion status; secondly by deactivating the GPS and accelerometer according to the inferred user situation.

5.6 Conclusions and Future Work

In this paper we described an energy-efficient context framework able to combine and to elaborate raw data from the user device to perform an automatic context-based validation of user's check-ins based on motion and position.

We paid special attention to the user's motion recognition sensor and its frame-based algorithm that reduces the activation of the accelerometer saving device battery. This sensor is suitable for future improvements relying on fusion and computation of available context data. For example the algorithm can be extended to take into account also the user's speed (obtained by GPS positions) to infer more complex motion situations like travelling or biking that can be offered as context information to additional applications.

References

1. Carlotto, A., Parodi, M., Bonamico, C., Lavagetto, F., & Valla, M. (2008). Proximity classification for mobile devices using wi-fi environment similarity. In *Proc. First ACM international workshop on mobile entity localization and tracking in GPS-less environments (MELT 08)*, September 2008, San Francisco, California, USA. doi:10.1145/1410012.1410023.
2. Facebook and Facebook Developer's API. http://www.facebook.com/. http://developers.facebook.com/. Last visit 1.10.2011.
3. Foursquare and Foursquare Developer's API. http://foursquare.com/. http://foursquare.com/apps/. Accessed 1.10.2011.
4. Gowalla and Gowalla Developer's API. http://gowalla.com. http://gowalla.com/api/docs. Accessed 1.10.2011.
5. Lamorte, L., Licciardi, C. A., Marengo, M., Salmeri, A., Mohr, P., Raffa, G., Roffia, L., Pettinari, M., & Cinotti, T. S. (2007). A platform for enabling context aware telecommunication services. In *Third workshop on context awareness for proactive systems*, Guildford, UK.
6. Miluzzo, E., et al. (2008). Sensing meets mobile social networks: the design, implementation and evaluation of the CenceMe application. In *SenSys '08: Proc. of the 6th ACM conference on embedded network sensor systems* (pp. 337–350). New York: ACM.
7. Quinlan, J. R. (1992). *C4.5: programs for machine learning*. San Mateo: Morgan Kaufmann.
8. Tapia, E. M., et al. (2007). Real-time recognition of physical activities and their intensities using wireless accelerometers and a heart rate monitor. In *Proc. of international symposium on wearable computers*. New York: IEEE Press.
9. Tóth, N., & Pataki, B. (2008). Classification confidence weighted majority voting using decision tree classifiers. *International Journal of Intelligent Computing and Cybernetics, 1*(2), 169–192.

Chapter 6
The Case for Context-Aware Resources Management in Mobile Operating Systems

Narseo Vallina-Rodriguez and Jon Crowcroft

Abstract Efficient management of mobile resources from an energy perspective in modern smart-phones is paramount nowadays. Today's mobile phones are equipped with a wide range of sensing, computational, storage and communication resources. The diverse range of sensors such as microphones, cameras, accelerometers, gyroscopes, GPS, digital compass and proximity sensors allow mobile apps to be context-aware whereas the ability to have connectivity almost everywhere has bootstrapped the birth of rich and interactive mobile applications and the integration of cloud services. However, the intense use of those resources can easily be translated into power-hungry applications. The way users interact with their mobile handsets and the availability of mobile resources is context dependent. Consequently, understanding how users interact with their applications and integrating context-aware resources management techniques in the core features of a mobile operating system can provide benefits such as energy savings and usability. This chapter describes how context drives the way users interact with their handsets and how it determines the availability and state of hardware resources in order to explain different context-aware resources management systems and the different attempts to incorporate this feature in mobile operating systems.

6.1 Introduction

Lithium-ion battery technologies have not experienced the same evolution as the rest of hardware components in mobile handsets. The battery capacity is limited by design factors such as size and weight, thus the only alternative left at the moment to extend their battery life is reducing the power consumption at the hardware level and designing more energy efficient applications and operating systems. However, despite the recent achievements in improving the energy efficiency by both

N. Vallina-Rodriguez (✉) · J. Crowcroft
Computer Lab, University of Cambridge, William Gates Building, 15 JJ Thomson Avenue,
Cambridge CB3 0FD, UK
e-mail: Narseo.Vallina-Rodriguez@cl.cam.ac.uk

J. Crowcroft
e-mail: Jon.Crowcroft@cl.cam.ac.uk

T. Lovett, E. O'Neill (eds.), *Mobile Context Awareness*,
DOI 10.1007/978-0-85729-625-2_6, © Springer-Verlag London Limited 2012

hardware and software vendors, mobile handsets still suffer from severe energy limitations. As the consumption of energy can be attributed to the use of particular hardware components (mainly sensors, displays and wireless interfaces), there is a clear need to discover new ways of reducing the use of such components without compromising the user experience and services delivered by mobile applications.

Generally, there is a energy-usability trade-off when managing networking and sensing resources in mobile systems. Typical software energy saving techniques aim at keeping hardware resources in low power mode for as long as possible. However, transitions between power modes can imply an energy cost depending on the power features of the resource. As an example, cellular interfaces present three power modes: DCH (Dedicated Channel) FACH (Forward Access Channel, an intermediate power mode popularly known as "*tail-energy*") and IDLE. In the case of WCDMA technologies, a large fraction of energy is wasted in these intermediate but still high-power states after the completion of a typical transfer in case there is going to be an immediate transmission once the current one is finished in order to improve the user experience in cellular networks. In GSM technologies, the time spent in the FACH state is much smaller compared to 3G (6 vs. 12 s) [1]. In fact, these transitions are typically related to applications running on the device and the interaction patterns of the user [2, 3].

On the other hand, the quality of resources such as cellular networks can vary depending on the location, time of the day and even season of the year [4]. Users tend to run a specific set of application (and consequently, they access an specific set of hardware resources) depending on the social or personal activity they are performing. Consequently, this dependency has implications in the energy consumption of the handset since both the state of resources and the way users interact with their handsets and applications are social and context-dependent. As an example, a mobile user can experience frequent periods of network blackouts in certain locations (specially when moving) so launching a network-intense video streaming application in these situations might not be the best idea.

Incorporating contextual information and energy-awareness as a key feature of mobile operating systems has been barely explored despite its enormous potential. In this chapter, we will show how mobile operating systems can exploit contextual information to adapt the system to the environment and the users' needs in order to extend the battery life of the handset without compromising the users' experience. In other words, the operating system can learn from user's interaction and mobility patterns to know what kind of resource is likely to be demanded by the user at a specific context and the state of these resources. In Sect. 6.2 we will show how users interaction is driven by context while Sect. 6.3.1 describes the dependency of resources availability (e.g. wireless interfaces and location sensors) with context. Finally, Sect. 6.4 describes two ongoing projects that are trying to incorporate context-aware features at the operating system level to manage resources: CondOS [5] and ErdOS [6].

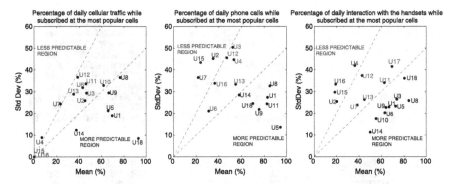

Fig. 6.1 User classification by their percentage of the usage/interaction with the 3G interface, telephony service and screen while subscribed at the most common cells (likely to be users' workplace and home). The x axis represents the daily average usage and the y axis the standard deviation. This information can be used to identify the places where the energy consumption will be higher and also to infer the predictability of the user interaction and the state of a resource

6.2 Are Users' Interaction with Their Handsets Driven by Context?

Several studies have tried to explore the impact of contextual information on mobile systems. As an example, *LiveLab* is an event-based resources logger for jail broken iPhone devices used to measure real-world smartphone usage and wireless networks [7]. Despite the fact that the results obtained are not statistically representative, they indicate that both users' interaction with the device and the state of the resources depend on contextual factors such as time and space [8].

Vallina-Rodriguez et al. performed a study using a background application to collect traces directly from 18 mature Android users during 2 weeks [2]. The dataset contains contextual information and more than 25 state and usage statistics from multiple resources and applications, sampled every 10 seconds. This analysis uses machine learning techniques to understand the dependencies between resources caused by users interaction and both spatial and temporal context. The paper demonstrates that energy demand and resource availability depend enormously on each participant's pattern of usage both in terms of which applications they ran and when and where they were doing so. This interaction can be very variable and dynamic both in time and space.

Spatial context affects how users interact with their handsets. Figure 6.1 shows three scatterplots of the average percentage of daily usage of the 3G interface, telephony and the screen versus its standard deviation while the users are subscribed to their three most popular cells. Users *U1*, *U5*, *U8*, *U9*, *U14* and *U18* have a strong routine due to their low variance and are quite likely to interact with certain resources in those locations. These users present a more predictable interaction pattern than other users who are likely to interact with their resources in non-frequent location and in transitions between them (e.g. while commuting).

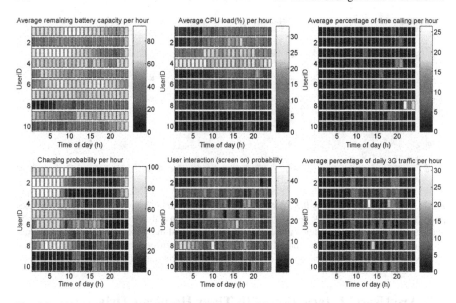

Fig. 6.2 Average usage and availability of different mobile resources for users *U1* to *U10* per hour of day. As in Fig. 6.1, this information can be used to identify peaks of usage and temporal patterns on those resources

However, temporal context also provides useful hints about how resources are used. Figure 6.2 plots the average usage and availability of different mobile resources such as battery, telephony, network, screen and CPU for ten users per hour of day. Each one of the x-axis bins represent an hour of the day and the colour indicates their averaged value during duration of the experiment. These results reveal that battery usage, charging opportunities and power limitations are well defined for some individuals in the temporal domain while others are more random. For instance, users such as *U2* and *U5*) and yet others present a much burstier pattern for specific resources.

While most resources available in mobile handsets can be recovered and reallocated once used by a process, energy can be only recovered when the user manually charges the handset. As a consequence, an energy-aware operating system must be able to estimate when energy will be consumed, how much energy will be available and when it will be recovered by predicting future charging opportunities and their uncertainty. Charging actions are in fact context-dependent and relatively predictable. Oliver [9] used classification methods to identify three distinct types of charging patterns among a large dataset of 17,300 Blackberry users. Those clusters are defined as "*opportunistic chargers*", "*light-consumers*" and "*night time chargers*". In their results, they evaluated that it is possible to predict the energy level on a mobile handset within 7 % error within an hour and within 28 % error within 24 hours.

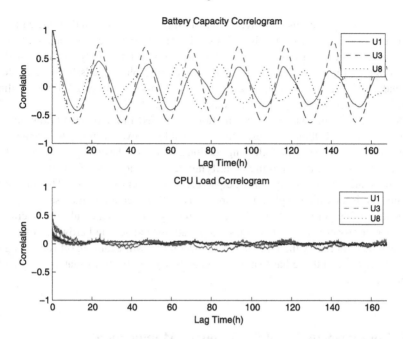

Fig. 6.3 Correlogram for the CPU load and the battery capacity for users *U1*, *U3* and *U8* during a period of 7 days. The battery capacity correlogram shows a clear pattern and a periodicity on the energy consumption and recharging cycle every 24 hours approximately while the CPU load is highly random

Figure 6.3 shows the *correlograms* or *autocorrelation plots* of the battery capacity and the CPU load for three users for a 7 day lag. Note that a correlogram is a plot of the sample autocorrelations versus the time lags. This kind of analysis helps to identify randomness and periodicities in a dataset. The correlogram clearly reveals that *U3* presents a clear charging periodicity of 24 hours approximately while *U8* does not have such a marked routine. However, those results highly depend on the resource analysed. As we can observe, the CPU load is not periodic at all indicating that CPU load might be more difficult to predict than battery capacity. This confirms that an efficient resources management technique must be user-centric and must try to identify the randomness, patterns and predictability of each individual user and device.

Nevertheless, Banerjee et al. in [10] claim that, despite the fact that there is a great variation among users, most of recharges happen when the battery has substantial energy left and a considerable portion of the recharges are driven by context (e.g. location and time). In a similar way, Ravi et al. proposed a system for context-aware battery management that warns the mobile user when it detects a power limitation before the next charging opportunity is going to happen [11]. This stops the system from compromising the execution and performance of crucial applications and services such as telephony and messaging by non-crucial ones. This system uses the current set of applications running, the battery discharging rate[1] and phone call logs as inputs of their forecasting algorithms. The results indicate that their algorithm can predict battery consumption and charging opportunities only for users with a low usage entropy. The main difficulty is predicting phone calls because of their dependency of the almost unpredictable social factors and the variability of calling patterns between weekends and weekdays.

As a conclusion, contextual information can be used to understand how mobile users interact with their devices. This can enable innovative ways to manage resources as we will see in the following sections. However, the entropy of users' interaction patterns and habits require identifying new techniques to efficiently leverage this information without impacting negatively on the user experience. The operating system can infer which applications are likely to be executed by the user at a given context and which resources might be required by them. As a result, the operating system can proactively pre-load these applications and set the hardware resources that will be required by them in the right power mode while turning off (or setting in low-power modes) those hardware components and applications that are not likely to be accessed.

6.3 Context-Aided Mobile Resource Management

In addition to users' interaction patterns with mobile handsets, the state and availability of mobile resources depend on contextual aspects. Two clear examples are:

- *GPS*. The number of visible satellites by the receiver affects the time to fix their location from the *cold-start*[2] phase and its accuracy. However, satellites are constantly moving in their orbits, the number of satellites visible for the receiver depends on time of day and the day [13]. Other aspects such as reflections and radio obstacles also affect the time required by the receivers (thus the energy required) to fix their location. Nevertheless, in the case of assisted-GPS, chips can vary depending on the availability of a cellular network to quickly access the ephemeris of the satellites [14] thus reducing considerably the time to fix the location.
- *Cellular interfaces*. The energy consumption of cellular interfaces and their quality of service depend on the receiving signal strength of the radio link [15]. As the *signal-to-noise ratio* (SNR) increases, more retransmissions at the link layer are required and therefore, more energy is consumed. As we can see in Fig. 6.4,

---

[1]Battery discharging rate might arguably not be the best indicator to measure energy consumption in mobile handsets. This signal is very noisy since it depends on hardware and users' habits and requires complex methods to be properly calibrated [12].

[2]If the GPS chip has not been used in a long time, then the *Time To First Fix* (TTFF) can be longer because it needs to download the satellites ephemeris and almanac before it can make the calculations. Usually, the GPS-receiver also needs 4 satellites to accurately fix its location. This is usually referred to as *cold start*. In cases when the chip was recently used (in the order of minutes or even few hours), the time to fix would be even faster (i.e. *warm start* and *hot start* phases).

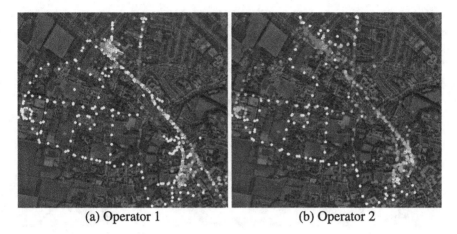

(a) Operator 1   (b) Operator 2

Fig. 6.4 Signal strength perceived by two identical co-located handsets in several locations in west and centre of Cambridge (UK) with different network operators. *Lighter points* indicate better signal strength

co-located nodes present different network coverage and quality depending on the location and the mobile operator. The signal strength is in fact, context-dependent. As any radio technology, the quality of the link can be affected by other aspects such as provider's network deployment, whether the node is indoors or outdoors, node's mobility, radio obstacles and radio interferences [16].

6.3.1 Wireless Interfaces

Mobile handsets present different wireless interfaces that range from cellular networks such as GPRS to LTE and IEEE 802.11 (i.e. WiFi) technologies. The key differentiators between these interfaces are their availability and their power states. The operating system could switch the type of network depending on which service is being requested by the user and the applications. The OS can select the optimal link for a wireless communication taking into account the energy-delay trade-off and applications requirements [1, 17, 18]. As a result, the system can adapt to channel conditions by leveraging contextual [19], local and historic information to decide whether and when it must defer a transmission in order to save energy.

As we can see in network coverage maps collected by crowd-sourcing means such as *OpenSignalMap* [20], the network availability and quality depend on location. *3GTest* [21] is a cross-platform application that checks the state of cellular networks and the performance of network-based applications. The traces from 30,000 mobile users all over the world confirm the impact of contextual aspects on the performance of cellular networks. Network properties can vary depending on the time-of-day and location for a specific operator, as Tan et al. [22] had also previously demonstrated for a more geographically limited environment such as Hong

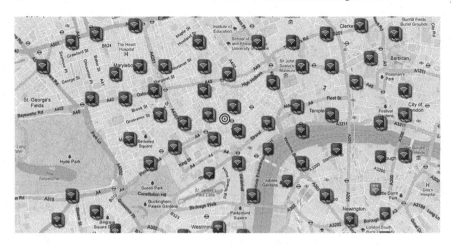

Fig. 6.5 Open IEEE 802.11g Access Points in London city center (UK). Snapshot obtained from WiFi Map UK [23]

Kong. A detailed knowledge of the network properties can help to identify bottle-necks in wireless network and also performance limitations and bugs in hardware, operating system and popular network-centric applications. In fact, the latency of the radio link depends on the current power state of the wireless machine. Based on historic data, the operating system can seamlessly enable caching mechanisms to applications accessing wireless interfaces and also supporting traffic shaping techniques to adapt the applications' traffic to the conditions of the wireless interface at a given location.

On the other hand, the availability of WiFi access points is reduced to specific locations as we can see for London city center (UK) in Fig. 6.5. IEEE 802.11 networks usually present a lower latency than cellular networks for transmitting data but they present a higher cost when the device is associating to the access point. As a consequence, reducing the energy cost of scanning and associating to the access point is essential. Because of this reason, most of the works described in this section try to leverage contextual information to smartly wake up the WiFi interface from sleep mode when it is likely to have an access point.

The operating system can adapt the AP's discovery enquiries to minimise the energy consumption while maximising the chances of having connectivity. The works by Agarwa et al. [24] and *Blue-Fi* [25] are two good examples to illustrate this claim. These papers describe how to save energy by exploiting other resources such as Bluetooth radios and contextual information to serve as a paging channel for IEEE 802.11 technologies. The results show that it is possible to save between 23 % to 48 % of energy compared to the present IEEE 802.11 standard operating modes with negligible impact on performance. The system can predict when there will be WiFi connectivity by combining contextual information obtained from Bluetooth scans contact-patterns and cell-tower information.

Likewise, *Context-for-wireless* is a context-aware intelligent switching algorithm between WiFi and cellular networks to reduce the energy consumption substantially [26]. *Context-for-wireless* leverages contextual information such as time, historic data, cellular network conditions and mobility to formulate the selection of wireless interfaces as a statistical decision problem and to predict future network conditions.

6.3.2 Location Sensors

Mobile applications tend to become context-aware. By simply looking at the applications market of mobile platforms such as *Android* and *iPhone*, it is possible to find a large number of context-aware applications and location-aware online services such as *Google Maps* and *Foursquare* [27]. Applications often need location data to update locally relevant information, to provide a service requested by the user and also to find nearby friends and places of interest.

Modern smartphones include different types of location sensors with different resolution and energy demands such as cellular network-based location providers, WiFi-based, A-GPS (Assisted-GPS), gyroscopes and compass. New location techniques are being investigated such as audio fingerprints [28], signal-strength fingerprints [29]. and geo-magnetism fingerprints [30]. Other solutions leverage phone sensors, audio beaconing infrastructures and opportunistic user-intersection (in space-time) to develop an electronic escort service formulated like routing packets in Delay-Tolerant Networks (DTNs) [31]. All these technologies are mainly focused on providing more efficient indoor localisation. However, most context-aware applications are based on standard sensors. They usually prefer A-GPS over its alternatives (e.g. network-based location providers such as *Skyhook* [32] and *Location-api* [19]) because of its accuracy despite its higher energy cost. Cellular network based location services present a mean error in the order of 300 m (can be in the order of several km) and, given a location they can report different locations because of radio link changes. As a consequence, the research community tried to find solutions to save energy when accessing location information without sacrificing accuracy [33] describes four alternative techniques to GPS sensing to reduce the energy consumption:

- **Substitution and Suppression** makes use of alternative location-sensing mechanisms (e.g. network-based location sensing or combined use of accelerometers and compass) that consumes less power than GPS. Substitution decides when to use more energy-efficient sensors instead of more energy-costly ones such as GPS. As a consequence, the system can automatically decrease the energy consumption of mobile sensing applications. On the other hand, suppression utilises less power-intensive sensors. As an example, it is possible to use accelerometers to suppress unnecessary GPS sensing if the user is static.

Table 6.1 Location sensing optimisations. Most of the works aimed to tackle the continuous location sensing challenge by combining different techniques. This table highlights the different methodologies used by each one of the solutions and the sensors they are using

Sensor-based optimisations						
Name	Sensors Used			Piggybacking	Probabilistic models	Adaptation
	GPS	Accel.	GSM			
EnLoc	✓	✓	✓		✓	
A-Loc	✓	✓	✓		✓	
EnTracked					✓	✓
RAPS	✓	✓	✓		✓	✓
Zhuang	✓	✓	✓	✓		✓
Caps	✓		✓		✓	

- **Piggybacking** synchronises the location sensing requests from multiple running location-based applications.[3]
- **Adaption** adjusts sensing parameters such as time and distance depending on the remaining battery capacity. This technique tries to find heuristics to adapt the sampling rate without sacrificing accuracy.
- **Probabilistic Models**. Some methodologies rely on probabilistic models of users' location to infer future locations to reduce the number of sensing reads.

Continuous location-sensing can be very costly in terms of energy. Several research projects tried to combine in a different way those techniques, mainly looking at the energy-accuracy tradeoff as it is summarised in Table 6.1.

EnLoc [35] provides a location sensing adaptive framework that exploits mobility patterns of the user and decides which sensor to use taking into account the accuracy-energy trade-off of the different location sensors available in mobile phones. The authors take advantage of users' *Logical Mobility Tree* (LMT). This model allows sampling at a few uncertainty points which may be sufficient for predicting future locations. EnLoc utilises dynamic programming to find the optimal localisation accuracy for a given energy budget: it decides which localisation sensor will be the best one for a given scenario and energy budget.

Similarly, *EnTracked* [36] estimates and predicts the system state and mobility of the user[4] to schedule position updates in order to minimise the power consumption while optimising robustness. *EnTracked* uses the GPS-estimated uncertainty to quickly schedule a new measurement if a potential bad measurement is performed.

---

[3]The energy consumption becomes even more significant if multiple applications are requesting location reads independently. Zhuang et al. [33] are the only ones who applie this technique. Android OS *Location Providers* follow a similar philosophy [34].

[4]The system only supports pedestrians as possible movement model and uses accelerometer to infer users' mobility.

Other solutions exploit Hidden Markov Models to predict the mobility of the users and they also take advantage of Bluetooth scans to identify static scenarios based on devices in the same location [37]. A more sophisticated version of the system was recently proposed in [38]. In this case, they use sensors such as radio fingerprints, accelerometer and compass with the collaboration of a server to estimate the time to sleep of the GPS receiver before the next positioning sensing.

A-Loc [39] incorporates probabilistic models of user location and sensor errors. It was implemented as a middleware solution for Android devices which requires applications' collaboration. A-Loc selects the most energy-efficient sensor to meet applications accuracy requirements which must be either specified explicitly by applications or automatically by the system. The system uses the probabilistic models to choose among different localisation methods and tunes the energy expenditure to dynamically meet the error requirements.

Other systems such as *RAPS* (Rate adaptive GPS-based positioning for smart-phones) [40] take inspiration from the observation that GPS accuracy in urban areas can be poor due to moving objects, trees' shade and building reflections. To solve this issue, RAPS uses location-time history of the user to estimate user velocity and adaptively turn on GPS in case the estimated uncertainty in the prediction exceeds the accuracy threshold. RAPS presents three different approaches: it allows synchronising GPS readings between neighbouring mobile devices to reduce power consumption, it blocks GPS reads when the user is subscribed to cellular base stations where it is unlikely to get a GPS read (e.g. an area where the user is usually indoors) and it exploits accelerometer data to estimate user velocity. It also proposes sharing position readings among nearby devices using Bluetooth in order to further reduce GPS activation. However, RAPS is mainly designed for pedestrian use, and a significant portion of the energy savings come from avoiding GPS activation when it is likely to be unavailable. The authors recently proposed newer approaches such as [41]. In this case, they try to combine the accuracy and energy complementary features of GPS and network-based solution. This paper is based on the observation that users exhibit consistency in their everyday routes, having a sequence of Cell-IDs. The system can provide an accurate estimation of user's position by monitoring the cell-ID transitions and using a history of GPS readings obtained within a cell. They use the Smith-Waterman algorithm for sequence matching between similar historic data. They look for a sub-sequence in the database that matches and they pick up the sequence that matches the best and they turn ON GPS when there is no good matching. However, such system has the limitation of not being able to detect small detours in common routes.

6.4   Context-Aware Mobile Operating Systems

In previous sections we have seen that the most commonly used hardware components by applications in mobile phones are context-dependent in terms of availability, energy cost as also users' interaction patterns. Current mobile operating systems are also multitasking. By executing **ps** in the terminal of an Android handset we can identify more than 60 processes running simultaneously. Many of these processes are context-aware and they are accessing shared resources such as sensors and wireless interfaces. However, battery capacity is still the main limitation in mobile systems and, as a consequence, mobile devices are likely to experience power limitations at any time depending on how intensely the users interact with them. Two mobile operating systems already aim to leverage contextual information to prolong the battery life on mobile handsets: CondOS [5] and ErdOS [6].

CondOS has been conceived after observing that context-awareness is already a reality in modern mobile platforms and applications. Mobile handsets support a diverse range of sensing hardware and they are capable of executing the algorithms required to process raw sensed data. However, the way contextual information is generated and provided to applications can be more efficient by integrating context-aware resources management techniques in the operating systems. If applications manage and generate their own context independently, the power consumption can increase. It is necessary to provide a central content provider that coordinates all the context requests and the operating system is the right place for that. They consider that raw-sensed data must be converted into *"contextual data units"* (CDUs) by the operating system. A CDU is defined as a higher level data abstraction compared to the current contextual data provided by modern mobile platforms. Those objects contain a unit of meaningful context data to applications such as *walking* or *commuting*). The authors also list the potential benefits that can be achieved with a context-aware OS:

- *Memory Management.* Actions such as *"running"* and *"walking"* may suggest the user to load a music player or a workout app. On the other hand, actions such as *"driving"* may suggest loading a navigator. The operating system can see how users' interacted previously with applications in order to pro-load them and set the hardware resources in the right power mode to improve the user experience.
- *Scheduling.* Context information can help to schedule processes while limiting the impact on battery life and user experience. CondOS suggests that context can directly influence process priorities based on the users' preferences and the applications that are likely to be executed at a given location.
- *I/O.* Contextual data can help to adapt notifications such as the ringing mechanism or the appropriate input method to the situation (e.g. voice search features might be useful while the user is walking but they might not be the best choice in a noisy environments or in the opera). The operating system can also adapt manage wireless interfaces aided with contextual information as we have already seen in Sect. 6.3.1.
- *Security.* Security can be adapted to the location. For example, security requirements can be relaxed at home, enabling interaction and sharing data with other devices in the home network. On the other hand, in public places the security policies can be more rigid in order to reduce the potential security and privacy risks.
- *Energy savings.* As we have seen in the previous sections, mobile operating systems can predict future charging opportunities from contextual information. The

operating system can manage applications and resources in order to meet the energy goals that users' interaction might impose. Moreover, having a central source of contextual information can potentially save energy by reducing the number of requests to the hardware resource. Applications can collaborate and share interests on resources in a similar fashion as Android OS does with its "*location providers*" [34].

Mobile operating systems need to make efficient and autonomous allocation decisions whilst maximising the users experience. Software should guarantee energy efficiency in addition to the traditional OS perspective of maximising performance [42]. Recently, energy-aware operating systems attracted the attention of the research community again with mobile operating systems such as Cinder [43] and ErdOS [6]. However, those two projects follow different philosophies about how energy management should be performed, and by whom.

Cinder follows the philosophy of ECOSystem [44] and Odyssey [45]. They try to leverage the interaction between applications and operating system without necessarily being context-aware. In the case of Odyssey, applications adapt to the available energy and resources to provide different quality of service to the users in runtime while ECOSystem fairly allocates energy shares to multiple hardware components and applications. *Cinder* [43] allocates energy to applications using two abstractions called *reserve* and *taps* to form a graph of resource consumption. When an application consumes a resource, the Cinder kernel reduces the right values in the corresponding reserve and its scheduler only allows threads to run if they have enough reserves to run. The rate at which the reserves are being consumed is controlled by the *taps* (a special-purpose thread whose only job is to transfer energy between reserves at proportional or constant rates). Once an application has consumed all its reserves, the kernel prevents its threads to perform more actions. Nevertheless, Cinder allows *reserve debits* between tasks for performing additional actions. Note that most of the modern mobile OSs usually give priority to foreground processes over the rest of the apps and non-system background processes in order to improve the user experience and also to prolong the battery life.

A different approach is followed by *ErdOS* [6]. This operating system[5] does not require interaction and communication means between applications and OS. It is completely seamless to applications. ErdOS also leverages contextual information to manage resources efficiently customised for each user. ErdOS was motivated by the observation that resources' state (e.g. GPS and cellular networks) and the usage patterns and habits of mobile users are diverse and highly context-dependent. As mobile systems present energy peaks caused by periods of high interaction from the users, managing and allocating computing resources to applications proactively based on predictions of the resources state and the users' demands is more flexible and efficient than algorithmic resources management. In order to support this feature, ErdOS monitors resources state, applications resource demands and users'

---

[5]ErdOS is conceived as an Android OS extension.

interaction patterns with applications. It learns from users' behaviour and habits (defined as the *users' activity* abstraction) to predict the future resources demands and the resources availability in an event-based fashion. In fact, users generally remain subscribed to a small set of base stations and the majority of interaction with their resources or applications takes place there. ErdOS builds a location-based model of resources usage and resources demands per location in order to predict power limitations and peaks of energy consumption. Such a model might help to detect malware and buggy applications by identifying situations where resources demand are out of the norm.

Additionally, the authors consider that computation should not be exclusively limited to local resources. Accessing resources in neighbouring handsets opportunistically can be beneficial both in terms of energy and usability by enabling access to resources that have the right power mode [46]. By considering the social activity of mobile phone users, we can see that large portions of a user's daily life are spent in close proximity of other mobile phone users with devices that incorporate similar hardware resources. Indeed, if we consider a commuter travelling by bus and using a location-based service on her mobile phone, there is a high probability that a significant number of co-commuters are also using their phone's GPS and cellular networks to interact with similar services. Additionally, in social events such as music concerts or sport events, large numbers of co-located users may use their phone to access the Internet simultaneously. This enables more opportunities for sharing resources opportunistically and, as a consequence, more opportunities to reduce the energy consumption. As a consequence, ErdOS tries to exploit this opportunity for improving the energy efficiency of mobile phone usage while making acceptable compromises in the QoS, by trying to aggregate, share and coordinate resources of multiple users at close proximity. Nevertheless, contextual information can play an important role in making ErdOS even more energy efficient by allowing the system to adapt the resources discovery enquiries and the privacy and security policies to the probability of discovering devices at a given location.

6.5 Summary

Mobile handsets are power-hungry devices because of the integration of power-hungry hardware resources such as touchscreen displays and location sensors. Moreover, they support Internet data services anytime (almost) anywhere so they are always connected to the network. All those resources bootstrap a rich ecosystem of mobile applications but their design is clearly driven by usability factors rather than energy efficiency. However, managing mobile resources from an energy-efficient perspective without diminishing the user experience is clearly one of the most challenging problems in mobile computing nowadays. Power management considerations often require certain actions to be deferred, avoided or slowed down to prolong battery life. In this chapter, we have seen that contextual information can be a useful source of data to manage hardware resources more efficiently in mobile systems. It can allow the operating system to dynamically predict the power states of the hardware components and applications behaviour at a given location. However, those techniques can impact on the user experience with the handsets and there is still an important work to be done in this space.

References

1. Balasubramanian, N., Balasubramanian, A., & Venkataramani, A. (2009). Energy consumption in mobile phones: a measurement study and implications for network applications. In *Proceedings of the 9th ACM SIGCOMM conference on Internet measurement conference, IMC '09*, New York, NY, USA (pp. 280–293). New York: ACM.
2. Vallina-Rodriguez, N., Hui, P., Crowcroft, J., & Rice, A. (2010). Exhausting battery statistics: understanding the energy demands on mobile handsets. In *Proceedings of the second ACM SIGCOMM workshop on networking, systems, and applications on mobile handhelds, MobiHeld '10*, New York, NY, USA (pp. 9–14). New York: ACM.
3. Trestian, I., Ranjan, S., Kuzmanovic, A., & Nucci, A. (2009). Measuring serendipity: connecting people, locations and interests in a mobile 3G network. In *Proceedings of the 9th ACM SIGCOMM conference on Internet measurement conference, IMC '09*, New York, NY, USA (pp. 267–279). New York: ACM.
4. Xu, Q., Gerber, A., Mao, Z. M., & Pang, J. (2011). AccuLoc: practical localization of performance measurements in 3G networks. In *Proceedings of the 9th international conference on mobile systems, applications, and services, MobiSys '11*, New York, NY, USA (pp. 183–196). New York: ACM.
5. Chu, D., Kansal, A., Liu, J., & Zhao, F. (2011). Mobile apps: It's time to move up to CondOS. In *USENIX HotOS*.
6. Vallina-Rodriguez, N., & Crowcroft, J. (2011). Erdos: achieving energy savings in mobile OS. In *Proceedings of the 6th ACM international workshop on mobility in the evolving Internet architectures, MobiArch'11*.
7. Shepard, C., Rahmati, A., Tossell, C., Zhong, L., & Kortum, P. (2011). LiveLab: measuring wireless networks and smartphone users in the field. *ACM SIGMETRICS Performance Evaluation Review, 38*, 15–20.
8. Falaki, H., Mahajan, R., Kandula, S., Lymberopoulos, D., Govindan, R., & Estrin, D. (2010). Diversity in smartphone usage. In *Proceedings of the 8th international conference on mobile systems, applications, and services, MobiSys '10*, New York, NY, USA (pp. 179–194). New York: ACM.
9. Oliver, E. (2010). Diversity in smartphone energy consumption. In *ACM workshop on wireless of the students, by the students, for the students*.
10. Banerjee, N., Rahmati, A., Corner, M. D., Rollins, S., & Zhong, L. (2007). Users and batteries: interactions and adaptive energy management in mobile systems. In *Proceedings of the 9th international conference on ubiquitous computing, UbiComp '07* (pp. 217–234). Berlin: Springer.
11. Ravi, N., Scott, J., Han, L., & Iftode, L. (2008). Context-aware battery management for mobile phones. In *PERCOM '08: Proceedings of the 2008 sixth annual IEEE international conference on pervasive computing and communications*, Washington, DC, USA (pp. 224–233). Washington: IEEE Computer Society.
12. Dong, M., & Zhong, L. (2011). Self-constructive high-rate system energy modeling for battery-powered mobile systems. In *Proceedings of the 9th international conference on mobile systems, applications, and services, MobiSys '11*, New York, NY, USA (pp. 335–348). New York: ACM.
13. Wing, M., Eklund, A., & Kellogs, L. (2005). Consumer-grade global positioning system (GPS) accuracy and reliability. *Journal of Forestry, 103*, 169–173.

14. Djuknic, G. M., & Richton, R. E. (2001). Geolocation and assisted GPS. *Computer*, *34*, 123–125.
15. Chakravorty, R., Katti, S., Crowcroft, J., & Pratt, I. (2003). Flow aggregation for enhanced TCP over wide-area wireless. In *Proc. IEEE INFOCOM* (pp. 1754–1764).
16. Chen, X., Zhai, H., Wang, J., & Fang, Y. (2005). A survey on improving TCP performance over wireless networks. In M. Cardei, I. Cardei, & D.-Z. Du (Eds.), *Resource management in wireless networking* (pp. 657–695). Dordrecht: Kluwer Academic.
17. Ra, M.-R., Paek, J., Sharma, A. B., Govindan, R., Krieger, M. H., & Neely, M. J. (2010). Energy-delay tradeoffs in smartphone applications. In *Proceedings of the 8th international conference on mobile systems, applications, and services, MobiSys '10*, New York, NY, USA (pp. 255–270). New York: ACM.
18. Pluntke, C., Eggert, L., & Kiukkonen, N. (2011). Saving mobile device energy with multipath TCP. In *Proceedings of the sixth international workshop on MobiArch '11*, New York, NY, USA (pp. 1–6). New York: ACM.
19. Location-Api. http://location-api.com/.
20. OpenSignalMap. http://opensignalmap.com/.
21. Huang, J., Xu, Q., Tiwana, B., Mao, Z. M., Zhang, M., & Bahl, P. (2010). Anatomizing application performance differences on smartphones. In *Proceedings of the 8th international conference on mobile systems, applications, and services, MobiSys '10*, New York, NY, USA (pp. 165–178). New York: ACM.
22. Tan, W. L., Lam, F., & Lau, W. C. (2008). An empirical study on the capacity and performance of 3G networks. *IEEE Transactions on Mobile Computing*, *7*, 737–750.
23. Wifi Map UK. http://www.wifimapuk.com/home/.
24. Agarwal, Y., Schurgers, C., & Gupta, R. (2005). Dynamic power management using on-demand paging for networked embedded systems. In *Proceedings of the 2005 Asia and South Pacific design automation conference, ASP-DAC '05*, New York, NY, USA (pp. 755–759). New York: ACM.
25. Ananthanarayanan, G., & Stoica, I. (2009). Blue-Fi: enhancing Wi-Fi performance using bluetooth signals. In *Proceedings of the 7th international conference on mobile systems, applications, and services, MobiSys '09*, New York, NY, USA (pp. 249–262). New York: ACM.
26. Rahmati, A., & Zhong, L. (2007). Context-for-wireless: context-sensitive energy-efficient wireless data transfer. In *Proceedings of the 5th international conference on mobile systems, applications and services, MobiSys '07*, New York, NY, USA (pp. 165–178). New York: ACM.
27. FourSquare. https://foursquare.com/.
28. Tarzia, S. P., Dinda, P. A., Dick, R. P., & Memik, G. (2011). Indoor localization without infrastructure using the acoustic background spectrum. In *Proceedings of the 9th international conference on mobile systems, applications, and services, MobiSys '11*, New York, NY, USA, (pp. 155–168). New York: ACM.
29. You, C.-W., Huang, P., Chu, H.-h., Chen, Y.-C., Chiang, J.-R., & Lau, S.-Y. (2008). Impact of sensor-enhanced mobility prediction on the design of energy-efficient localization. *Ad Hoc Networks*, *6*, 1221–1237.
30. Chung, J., Donahoe, M., Schmandt, C., Kim, I.-J., Razavai, P., & Wiseman, M. (2011). Indoor location sensing using geo-magnetism. In *Proceedings of the 9th international conference on mobile systems, applications, and services, MobiSys '11*, New York, NY, USA (pp. 141–154). New York: ACM.
31. Constandache, I., Bao, X., Azizyan, M., & Choudhury, R. R. (2010). Did you see Bob?: human localization using mobile phones. In *Proceedings of the sixteenth annual international conference on mobile computing and networking, MobiCom '10*, New York, NY, USA (pp. 149–160). New York: ACM.
32. SkyHook Wireless. http://www.skyhookwireless.com/.
33. Zhuang, Z., Kim, K.-H., & Singh, J. P. (2010). Improving energy efficiency of location sensing on smartphones. In *Proceedings of the 8th international conference on mobile systems, applications, and services, MobiSys '10*, New York, NY, USA (pp. 315–330). New York: ACM.

34. Android Developers. http://developer.android.com/reference/android/location/ LocationManager.html.
35. Constandache, I., Gaonkar, S., Sayler, M., Choudhury, R. R., & Cox, L. (2009). EnLoc: energy-efficient localization for mobile phones. In *IEEE INFOCOM 2009—The 28th conference on computer communications* (Vol. 4, pp. 2716–2720). New York: IEEE.
36. Kjaergaard, M. B., Langdal, J., Godsk, T., & Toftkjaer, T. (2009). Entracked: energy-efficient robust position tracking for mobile devices. In *Proceedings of the 7th international conference on mobile systems, applications, and services, MobiSys '09*, New York, NY, USA (pp. 221–234). New York: ACM.
37. Farrell, T., Cheng, R., & Rothermel, K. (2007). Energy-efficient monitoring of mobile objects with uncertainty-aware tolerances. In *Proceedings of the 11th international database engineering and applications symposium*, Washington, DC, USA (pp. 129–140). Washington: IEEE Computer Society.
38. Kjaergaard, M. B., Bhattacharya, S., Blunck, H., & Nurmi, P. (2011). Energy-efficient trajectory tracking for mobile devices. In *Proceedings of the 9th international conference on mobile systems, applications, and services, MobiSys '11*, New York, NY, USA (pp. 307–320). New York: ACM.
39. Lin, K., Kansal, A., Lymberopoulos, D., & Zhao, F. (2010). Energy-accuracy trade-off for continuous mobile device location. In *Proceedings of the 8th international conference on mobile systems, applications, and services, MobiSys '10*, New York, NY, USA (pp. 285–298). New York: ACM.
40. Paek, J., Kim, J., & Govindan, R. (2010). Energy-efficient rate-adaptive GPS-based positioning for smartphones. In *Proceedings of the 8th international conference on mobile systems, applications, and services, MobiSys '10*, New York, NY, USA (pp. 299–314). New York: ACM.
41. Paek, J., Kim, K.-H., Singh, J. P., & Govindan, R. (2011). Energy-efficient positioning for smartphones using Cell-ID sequence matching. In *Proceedings of the 9th international conference on mobile systems, applications, and services, MobiSys '11*, New York, NY, USA (pp. 293–306). New York: ACM.
42. Ellis, C. S., & Watt, M. (2000). Every joule is precious energy in computing. In *ACM SIGOPS*.
43. Roy, A., Rumble, S. M., Stutsman, R., Levis, P., Mazières, D., & Zeldovich, N. (2011). Energy management in mobile devices with the cinder operating system. In *Proceedings of the sixth conference on computer systems, EuroSys '11*, New York, NY, USA (pp. 139–152). New York: ACM.
44. Ellis, C. S. (1999). The case for higher-level power management. In *Proceedings of the seventh workshop on hot topics in operating systems, HOTOS '99*, Washington, DC, USA (p.162). New York: IEEE Computer Society.
45. Noble, B., Price, M., & Satyanarayanan, M. (1995). A programming interface for application-aware adaptation in mobile computing. In *2nd USENIX symposium on mobile and location-independent computing* (Vol. 8, No. 4, pp. 345–363).
46. Vallina-Rodriguez, N., Efstratiou, C., Xie, G., & Crowcroft, J. (2011). Enabling opportunistic resources sharing on mobile operating systems: Benefits and challenges. In *ACM S3 workshop*.

Chapter 7
A Scalable Sensor Middleware for Social End-User Programming

Salvador Faria and Vassilis Kostakos

Abstract A substantial amount of research has focused on developing sensor middleware targeted at various research communities such as networking and context awareness. This chapter presents SAWA, a sensor middleware based on Sensor Andrew aimed at social end-user programming. SAWA is designed to collect, present, share, and act on sensor data. First, it allows novice users to deploy a multitude of both physical and virtual sensors and actuators (e.g. temperature, light, unread email count, friend's status on Facebook, SMS, Tweet) and to aggregate this data in a central server. Users are able to access an online portal to visualize and explore their recorded data. In addition, they can request and share access to other users' sensor streams. Finally, they can create actions that are driven by sensor data—both physical and virtual, and both their own or any of their friends'. In addition to describing SAWA's architecture, this chapter presents case studies where this middleware was used. It is shown that in addition to being robust and scalable, SAWA opens up a series of new applications by allowing users to program sensors and actuators in a shared social environment.

7.1 Introduction

Sensors, or transducers, are devices that measure a physical quantity and convert it into a signal that can be read by an observer or by an instrument [8]. With big advances in processor technologies and wireless communications, sensor networks and home automation systems have been growing in recent years [5]. In these systems, many sensors distributed in an area collect various physical data such as temperature, humidity, motion, and light [4].

S. Faria (✉)
Madeira Interactive Technologies Institute, University of Madeira, Madeira, Portugal
e-mail: salvador.faria@m-iti.org

V. Kostakos
Department of Computer Science and Engineering, University of Oulu, Oulu, Finland
e-mail: vassilis@ee.oulu.fi

T. Lovett, E. O'Neill (eds.), *Mobile Context Awareness*,
DOI 10.1007/978-0-85729-625-2_7, © Springer-Verlag London Limited 2012

Researchers have previously developed many sensor-networking applications and middleware, but they are typically isolated, small-scale and short-lived experiments [10]. This highlights the necessity for interconnecting various sensors, both physical and virtual, in a scalable manner and using open protocols and technology.

This need is further exaggerated because with digital technology information available anywhere and anytime about the physical world has a potential value, and with sensor networks deployed across the globe by various organization, governments, scientist and general public, it becomes clear that data sharing is an important step to get more value [2]. With increasing penetration of embedded sensors in networked devices, such as GPS sensor in mobile phones, it is now possible to create applications that take into account the current state of the real world [3]. This kind of information may be useful to be shared in community places, such as social networks, where users may share their personal state with their friends.

Furthermore, collected data from sensors is normally difficulty to interpret, and combined with the fact that the specialists who interpret the data are usually not experts in computers, they need an easy tool to use to manage the collection of data [2]. Therefore, the sensing platform should help scientists to leverage computational power to simulate, visualize, manipulate, predict and gain intuition about monitored phenomenon [6]. Visual representation of data can be done in many ways, the most common are evolution charts. Evolution charts are charts that represent one measure over an evolving dimension, time for instance. These types of charts are useful to compare new data with previous data, as well with different periods of time.

Our intention is to build a system to facilitate the use and sharing of sensor data by providing a set of functionalities and a uniform access to these devices. The system allows users to network any sensing device by "registering" sensors and actuators, enables users to monitor their devices and define who has access to the recorded information; present data to users in form of charts thus giving a better interpretation and meaning to data; longitudinally record sensor data enabling monitoring; and allow for user policies to define sensor conditions and respective actions.

7.2 Related Work

There are different methods for retrieving data from sensors, continuous, event-oriented, query-oriented and hybrid. The method to use depends on network design and resources constraints, like power and limited communication. In continuous methods, the sensor data is sent continuously at predefined rate (e.g. temperature every hour). In event-oriented mode, the sensor data is sent when an event of interest occurs (e.g. presence in room). In query-oriented model, applications are responsible for defining witch events are of interest and then querying sensors (e.g "SELECT sensors WHERE temperature > 40 AND C02 > 15"). Finally the hybrid method is when more than one of the other three methods are used [9].

Online sensor-sharing services like Pachube and SensorPedia have the objective of applying the social networking principles to sensor data. Pachube is an innovative web service, which enables users to share and discover real time sensor data from objects, devices and spaces around the world. A user can easily register a sensor feed and start uploading sensor data. Recently Patchube started to offer triggers, allowing users to have URL event notification and experimental SMS notifications. The Pachube web service has the major advantages of an easy to use interface, a big community and a set of third party applications. A drawback is that Pachube relies on Representational State Transfer (REST) paradigm and not on a real-time transfer paradigm, limited support for actuators and basic triggers.

Our system is similar to Pachube, in the way it has similar objectives, allowing users to easily share sensor data and visualize them. Besides the these objectives, our system allows a high scalability, extensibility, security and privacy in the middleware. Our system allows multiple entities to subscribe to sensor data in a push method, define user access type and groups, encryption and other relevant XMPP Pub-Sub features. It also provides a web interface, where it is possible to manage sensors networks and devices, allowing users to add any sensor and actuator device with images and related information. From the web interface of our application it is possible to directly call commands in the actuators and create advanced policies, which can use different types of rules and actions.

7.2.1 Sensor Andrew

Sensor Andrew is a scalable campus-wide sensor middleware, developed with the objectives of supporting ubiquitous large-scale monitoring and infrastructure control [10]. It was developed by Carnegie Mellon University in order to integrate multiple systems, and designed to be extensible, easy to use, and secure while maintaining privacy. Its reliance on XMPP allows application developers to be able to transmit sensor data with no need to re-invent lower-level interfaces.

Sensor Andrew's objectives made it ideal for our needs:

- Ubiquitous large-scale monitoring and control: support for sensing and actuation.
- Ease of management, configuration and use: easy to use, manage and develop applications.
- Scalability and extensibility: support for any device, and support extensions
- Built-In security and privacy: support for security and privacy, encryption, key management, access control and user management.
- Infrastructure sharing: allow application to reuse of infrastructure devices.
- Evolvability: support for different computational paradigms and support changes.
- Robustness: built-in robustness and able to reconfigure itself.

A drawback of Sensor Andrew, however, is that it remains an expert tool, with no visual interface and all configurations taking place via scripts and options files in the command prompt. Therefore, a substantial amount of our work focused on adding an interface and visualization component to Sensor Andrew.

7.2.2 XMPP

The Extensible Messaging and Presence Protocol is an open protocol based on Extensible Markup Language (XML), designed for real time communications, being the XML the base format for exchanging information. With XMPP protocol it is possible to support a vast quantity of services, such as, channel encryption, authentication, presence, contact lists, one-to-one messaging, multi-party messaging, service discovery, notifications, structured data forms, workflow management and peer-to-peer media sessions [1].

XMPP is used by many types of applications, instant messaging, multi-party chat, voice and video calls, collaborations, lightweight middleware and content dissemination [7], also expanded to the domain of message-oriented middleware. Built to be extendible, the protocol has been extended with many features, including the Publisher-Subscriber paradigm. According to [11], by 2003 it was estimated that software using XMPP was installed in hundreds of server across the Internet and was used by ten millions of people. Most notably, services like Google chat and Facebook chat rely on this technology.

XMPP has more than 150 published extensions, including the publisher subscriber extension (XEP-060). The Pub-Sub extension defines a generic protocol, enabling any application to implement the most basic Pub-Sub features.

7.3 System Overview

Our system makes it possible for users to network physical and virtual sensors, and create policies to act upon the values of the sensors. For instance, it is possible to create a policy to alert a person via SMS when a particular value, e.g. of gas concentration, is detected. The system has potential for real-time uses, for non realtime, and it can be used also as data recording tool. A good example is monitoring energy consumption. It is possible to monitor many situations, like average time and frequency of use of television, computers, and lights turned on without any person present in the home.

Furthermore, using GPS technology it is possible to create policies to detect when a device enters or exits a geographical area. Considering a bus updating its GPS position every minute, a policy can be created to trigger a notification when a bus is detected in special area such as a bus stop. Given the built-in sharing capabilities of the system, the owner of the "bus sensor" (conceivably the bus operator) could choose to share the sensor readings with any member of the public. Subsequently, interested users could construct their own notification based on the bus position, as they see fit.

Finally, the system can be used to optimize energy consumption and to execute common human actions. It is possible to detect a person in a room and the system can turn automatically the lights on if the luminosity is sufficient (e.g. during day). And turn off the same lights when presence is not detected. Thus avoiding users to repeat continuously the same everyday actions as well can reduce energy consumptions.

7.3.1 User Interface

Our system provides user with instructions on how to network and connect their sensors to our infrastructure. This is possible in a number of ways, both using XMPP and HTTP GET. Here we do not describe this part of the process, but rather focus on the web front of our application.

The main interface (Fig. 7.1) consists of a menu, similar to a tree, starting from generic root options, and then subdividing into multiple sections. This menu allows us to expand the platform features without having to substantially change the menu or interface layout. From the first page the user is able to graphically browse her sensor networks and sensor networks that she has been granted access to. Sensor networks are groups of sensors, usually functioning as a group. Sensor networks are presented in the form of a mashup using Google maps. It is worth noting that sensor networks contain multiple sensors, and an individual sensor may contain multiple "variables" as in the case of an accelerometer that contains 3 variables for X, Y and Z.

The user is also able to create a list of sensor networks they have access to, as shown in Fig. 7.2. Here, each sensor network has an ID, a name and address, a number of associated sensors, a control model (open allow access to anyone, whitelist gives access to authorized users), and an owner.

Each sensor network can be probed for further information. In this case, a variety of details are shown about the network, including possible screenshots uploaded by other users (see Fig. 7.3), a detailed list of the sensors in this network, as well as the type of each sensor and its current recording state.

More information for each sensor can be shown on a separate page (see Fig. 7.4). This detailed contains the basic sensor information, an image gallery and the sensor variables list. Certain sensors, such as an accelerometer, may have multiple "variables": in the case of the accelerometer these are X, Y, and Z. In other cases, such as in the figure below, it is convenient to create aggregations of sensors, such as a "refrigerator sensor". In this case, we show a "sensor" that has a series of value relating to temperature, door status, gas levels, and whether any human is nearby.

In addition to sensors, sensor networks may also contain actuators. These are treated in a very similar way as sensors, except from the fact that they cannot record information and they have functions that can be called. Each actuator has a detailed page where all its attributes and functions are shown (see Fig. 7.5). In addition, the functions can be directly called for purposes of testing and daily usage. New functions can be added to actuators, but these functions are symbolic and must by interpreted appropriately by the actuator hardware. This most likely requires consultation of the hardware instructions and the device's specifications.

Given a set of sensors and actuators, a user can specify a policy (see Fig. 7.6). Policies consist of sensor values (it is noted that these sensors may not be owned by the owner herself but may be shared or public), actions, and a notification interval. The notification interval is the least amount of between subsequent executions of the actions. This feature avoids the continuous notifications when a policy is constantly matched, i.e. we do not want to receive an SMS notification every second. A policy

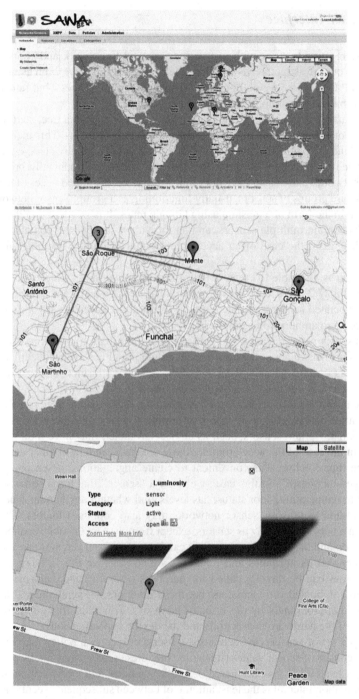

Fig. 7.1 Main Interface, showing an overview of available sensor networks (*top*), a summary of a particular network's structure (*middle*), and details about particular sensors (*bottom*)

Community Sensor Networks

ID	NAME	ADDRESS	SENSORS	ACCESS	OWNER	Info
6	sal_home	Estreito De Câmara, Portugal	6	open	salvador	
7	cqm_wine_lab	University of Madeira, CQM	1	whitelist	jcm	
8	Testiverkko	Gaula, Portugal	4	open	demo	
9	Oulu	Kuivasjärvi, Oulu, Finland	2	whitelist	uolevi	
10	co2_madeira	São Roque, Funchal, Portugal	3	whitelist	salvador	

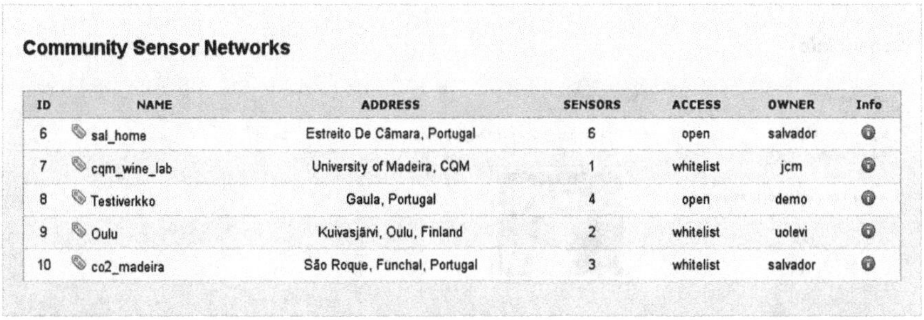

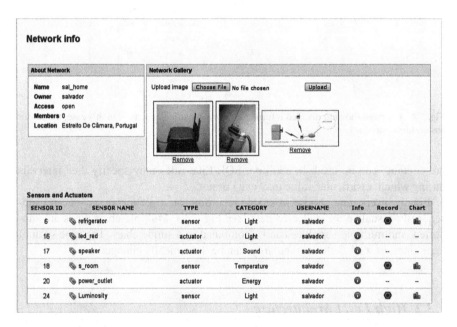

Fig. 7.2 Detail view of sensor networks

Network Info

About Network

Name sal_home
Owner salvador
Access open
Members 0
Location Estreito De Câmara, Portugal

Network Gallery

Upload image Choose File No file chosen Upload

Remove Remove Remove

Sensors and Actuators

SENSOR ID	SENSOR NAME	TYPE	CATEGORY	USERNAME	Info	Record	Chart
6	refrigerator	sensor	Light	salvador			
16	led_red	actuator	Light	salvador		--	--
17	speaker	actuator	Sound	salvador		--	--
18	s_room	sensor	Temperature	salvador			
20	power_outlet	actuator	Energy	salvador		--	--
24	Luminosity	sensor	Light	salvador			

Fig. 7.3 Detailed view of a particular sensor network. This includes a list of all the sensors in the network along with their current state

can have multiple rules which describe conditions under which policies should be fired. When a policy is fired, the actions are executed.

In Fig. 7.6 we created a policy named "gas_alert", the selected notification type is SMS, in the message field, and we use tags ({value}), to be replaced in the actual SMS. This policy contains only one rule, the defined rule uses gas_value variable, the operator '>' and the match value 100. The effect of this policy is to alert via SMS when there is a gas leak (gas_value > 100).

It is noted that rules may also use dates and times, while for variables of type string the operators "is", "is not", "starts with", "ends with", "contains" and "does

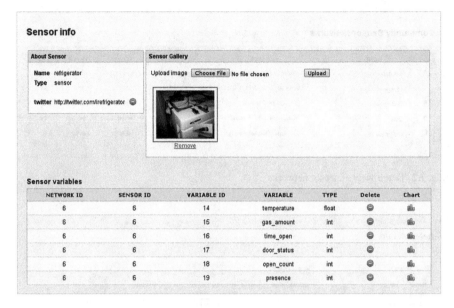

Fig. 7.4 The page showing detailed information about a particular sensor. In this case, the sensor has multiple variables

not contain" can be used. In addition, SQL-Like rules may specify date intervals during which a particular value may exist or not.

Finally, users may choose to enable recording on a particular sensor, and subsequently visualize the collected data (see Fig. 7.7). Multiple chart types are supported, and multiple variables can be combined in a single chart. The time span of their chart, as well as their granularity, can be dynamically changed.

7.3.2 High Level Architecture

The system consists of a number of components (see Fig. 7.8):

- *Web application*—The component responsible for presenting all information to users, and enabling users to manage their devices, associated options, and sharing preferences.
- *Datarecorder*—The service responsible for storing sensor data.
- *Actionchecker*—The service responsible for matching sensor input to existing policies, and trigger actions when a policy matches.
- *Scheduler*—The service responsible for handling new recording requests and new policies, and coordinating the datarecorder and actionchecker services.

Our system can be divided in two parts: (i) the middleware, composed by the XMPP server with publisher-subscriber support, which is responsible for transport-

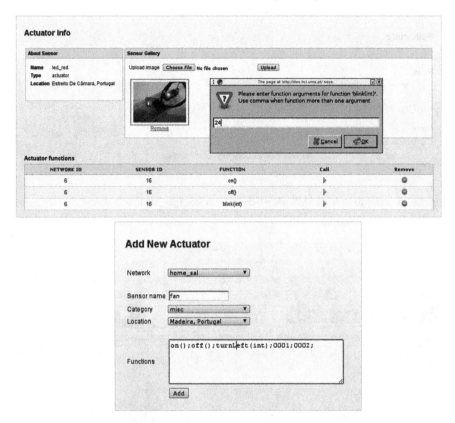

Fig. 7.5 *Top*: Detailed information for a particular actuator. In this case the actuator is an LED. In addition to details about the actuator, its functions are also shown and they can be called. Furthermore, new functions can be added. *Bottom*: adding a new actuator allows for the definition of functions. These functions are symbolic, and must be interpreted appropriately by the actuator hardware

ing and handling all sensor data, and (ii) the other part which consists of the web application and services.

The architecture style of our system is a passive shared repository, allowing for a loose coupling between system components. All interactions are made through the database, allowing a greater facility in modifying system components without affecting other components. The web application interacts with the middleware using a dedicated XMPP client, but most of the work done by the web application is stored in repository. As the figure shows, the services also use the repository to modify, read and create new entries. The datarecorder and actionchecker services connect to the XMPP server and the repository; these services listen for published data in Pub-Sub nodes and then process the sensor data according to user definitions in repository.

Finally, the system allows HTTP POST requests to be used to update sensor values. This is a very flexible way of accepting sensor values, and makes it easier

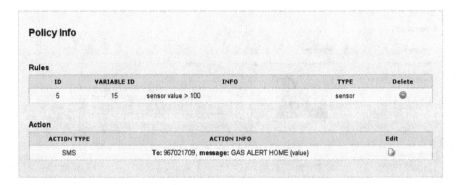

Fig. 7.6 A policy to alert via SMS when there is a gas leak (gas_value > 100)

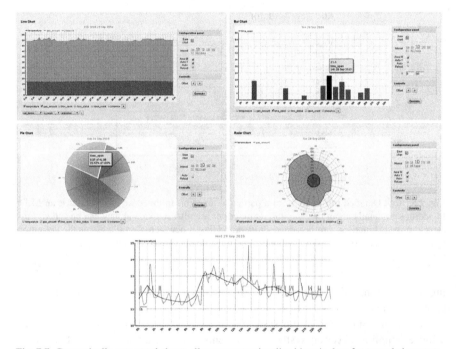

Fig. 7.7 Dynamically generated charts allow users to visualize historic data for recorded sensors

for our system to work with embedded systems that may be incapable of generating XMPP messages. In this case, an HTTP wrapper is used to accept values for a particular sensor: the sensor id, the value, and a pre-shared secret. The wrapper then interprets this input, identifies from which sensor it is generated, and generates an internal XMPP message to update the sensor value. This solution ensures that sensor values can be updated easily, while at the same time the authorization and security model of XMPP is maintained.

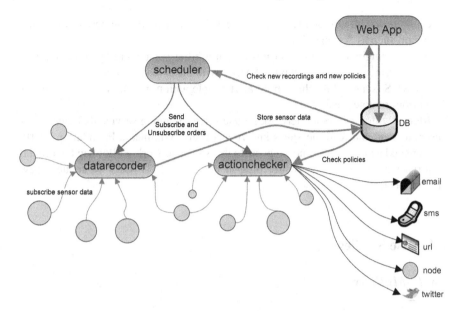

Fig. 7.8 High-level architecture

7.3.3 Plugins

The advantages of using plug-ins are well known, they are easy to deploy, they are efficient, and they increase the extensibility of applications. To achieve this functionality, we used GModule functions, which provide a portable way to dynamically load object files. The system provides a number of plugins that can be triggered as part of policies.

Email. Email is a communication method and is used in almost every notification system. The plugin allows static and dynamic text to be generated and sent to a recipient.

URL. Efficient notifications can take the form of URL calling, a simple and basic notification that can be very useful in communicating between two unknown systems. This plugin relies on the HTTP GET method to call a pre-defined URL with or without parameters. One way in which this plugin can help bring together diverse systems is, for example, by calling a foreign systems' API by accessing a REST API: http://example.com/lights/set/33/off.

Functions. This plug-in enables the publication of events using XMPP nodes. In particular, it allows the publication of commands to actuators, such as "activate", "turn_off", "increase", or any pre-defined command. In sensor gateways, when a message is received, the gateway parses the XML message to get the command or function, and can easily identify if the function contain arguments. After that, the sensor gateway is responsible for calling the local actuator with the right communication protocol. Optionally the sensor gateway may report the new status of the actuator, such as "running" or "active".

SMS. The plugin allows the transmission of arbitrary static and dynamic text to a mobile device capable of receiving SMSs. With the spread of mobile communications, SMS is a good mechanism to alert people with urgency, and to send sensor data from remote areas.

Twitter. Twitter is a social networking and micro blogging service that enables its users to send and read messages known as tweets (Wikimedia Foundation 2010). We created a plug-in for sending posts to this social network. Following the official tutorial we developed the twitter plug-in that uses HTTP GET to create a new twitter post.

7.4 Case Studies

7.4.1 iMailbox

The motivation for this use case was to build a system that notifies the user via SMS whenever new physical mail arrives in the post box. To implement this idea we used an Arduino board with a door sensor. The physical sensors detect the status of the door (open, closed), and also detects when a mail is added to the mailbox.

To detect when a mailbox door is opened, a cheap magnetic door switch was used. This sensor consists of two parts, the magnet and the magnet detector. The magnet was attached to the rotating lock mechanism and the magnetic sensor was glued to mail box, as shown in Fig. 7.9. To detect the presence of mail we used a sensor that acts like a button: when new mail is inserted the metal plates touch and close the circuit.

In the installation, we used an external power supply unit, but a battery or a solar panel can be used. The mail sensor was attached to the box, a few centimeters above mailbox slit. In tests using physical envelopes the sensor detected the insertion of all mail.

Once the hardware was configured, we were able to use our online platform to achieve the desired notification behavior. In the web application we registered a "mail sensor", and we registered two variables for it: *new_mail* (set to 1 when new mail is present) and *door_status* (set to 1 when the door is opened).

Using the appropriate network, sensor and variable IDs, our Arduino board transmitted values using HTTP POST to a server using a simple protocol as follows: message_number#sensor_id#variable_id#variable_value. The server re-broadcasts the received information using XMPP to our system.

Next, a policy was created such that whenever the variable *new_mail* becomes "1" an SMS action is triggered with the message "New mail arrived!". In addition, a notification was created such that whenever the mailbox door was opened a further SMS notification was sent (see Fig. 7.10).

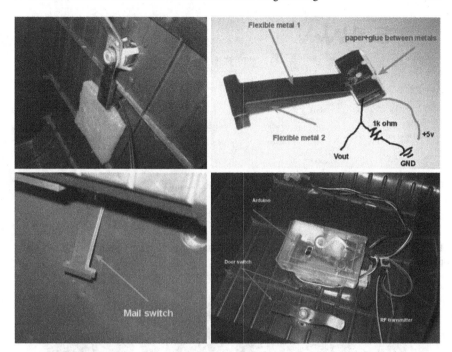

Fig. 7.9 *Top left*: Magnetic door sensor. *Top right*: metal plates for detecting mail. *Bottom left*: metal plates installed in the mailbox. *Bottom right*: final installation

7.4.2 iRefrigerator

The motivation to monitor a refrigerator was to assess the impact of opening the door on energy consumption. To accomplish this, we used a temperature sensor, a photo resistor sensor, a gas sensor to detect butane gas leaks, and a presence sensor to monitor people's presence in the kitchen (see Fig. 7.11).

Every refrigerator has a light which is turned on when the door opens, and is turned off when the door is closed. To detect when the door was open, a photo resistor was used. When the door is closed (no light present) the sensor will report "0" and when the light intensity is more than zero, means the door is open. Along with the light intensity sensor a thermoresitor was attached to measure temperature. The gas sensor, which is highly sensitive to gases, was used to monitor the presence of butane and propane gas in the kitchen. Finally, a Buzzer that emits a sound alert when the gas sensor detects high values was installed. Similar to the iMailbox, we used an Arduino board platform, a RF transmitter module, and the same protocol and procedure for sending sensor values.

The chart in Fig. 7.12 represents the data from four variables within one hour (10 h). The darkest brown line is the refrigerator temperature, the light brown represents the gas sensor data, and the line with magenta color represents humans' presence in that hour. The blue line shows the duration for which the refrigerator

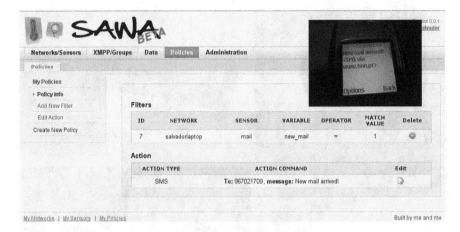

Fig. 7.10 Policy information for the iMailbox case study (*inset*: a received SMS as a result of new physical mail arriving in the mailbox)

Fig. 7.11 iRefrigerator sensors

door was opened, and it is noted that this line only contains 7 data points (ideally is should be rendered as a bar chart, but combining multiple chart types is not technically possible at this point). In addition, a Twitter update was generated once per hour to announce the iRefrigerator's temperature.

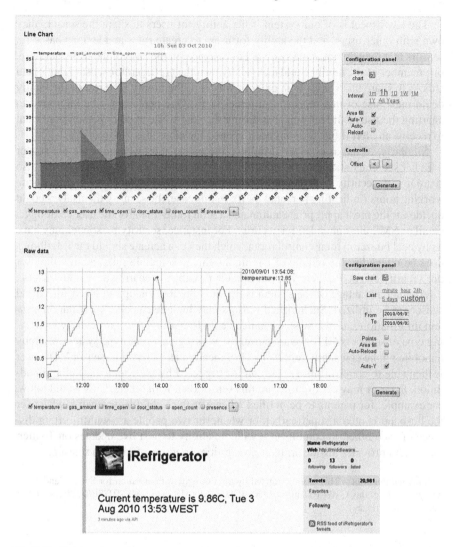

Fig. 7.12 *Top*: one-hour data recorded by the iRefrigerator (*x*-axis: time, *y*-axis: value). *Middle*: high granularity data for the refrigerator temperature (*y*-axis) over time (*x*-axis). *Bottom*: an automated twitter post every hour indicated the iRefrigerator's temperature

7.5 Discussion and Conclusion

This chapter has presented a sensor middleware that allows users to network, record and share sensor data. The chapter has described the system itself, and has presented two case studies where the middleware was used. Both the iMailbox and iRefrigerator case studies exemplify the technical capabilities of our system, however we wish to point out the fact that they also exemplify the potential of the system's sharing capabilities.

The key aspect is of our system is the ability for users to share the sensors they own with other users, and the ability for users to create rules and actions based on sensors that they do not actually own. For instance, in the case of the iRefrigeratore, one member of the family could technically own the "refrigerator sensor", but could choose to share that sensor with other members of the family. The rest of the family could make use of this sensor in different ways. One person may be interested in charting the use of the kitchen area during the day, while another person may want to receive an alert if the door has been opened for more than 300 seconds.

Similarly, in the case of the iMailbox, the owner may wish to share the sensor with her secretary such that she could pick up the mail whenever it arrives, and also share it with security such that they can monitor whether the door is opened outside working hours (indicating potential theft). In this case, the security themselves could decide for the most appropriate automated action rather than for the user creating an email or SMS alert intended for security. For instance, security personnel may have a physical buzzer in their control room which they can actuate should the iMailbox's door be opened in the middle of the night—this is something that neither the user nor security can do on their own but is made possible by sharing access to sensors.

Another advantage of the system is that it is flexible enough to allow for virtual sensors to be utilized. Such virtual sensors may include calendar information, system information such as file space, unread emails, and so on. A particularly interesting type of sensor is GPS: we are currently working on a prototype system whereby a mobile phone constantly reports its GPS location as a "location-sensor". The user is then able to create arbitrary rules online triggered by the phone's location. In addition, the user may choose to share this sensor data with others. This would allow, for example, for parents to be notified whenever their child leaves work, whenever the husband is near a supermarket, or whenever two people are within certain distance of each other. In combination with the ability to post live updates on Twitter, the system provides a wide array of possibilities in terms of location sharing.

Acknowledgements This work is funded by the Portuguese Foundation for Science and Technology (FCT) grants CMU-PT/HuMach/0004/2008 (SINAIS) and CMU-PT/SE/0028/2008 (Web Security and Privacy).

References

1. Barrett, K. May 2009. http://fyi.oreilly.com/2009/05/what-can-you-do-with-xmpp.html.
2. Dickerson, R. F., et al. (2008). MetroNet: case study for collaborative data sharing on the world wide web. In *2008 international conference on information processing in sensor networks (IPSN 2008)* (pp. 557–558).
3. Elahi, B. M., Romer, K., Ostermaier, B., Fahrmair, M., & Kellerer W. (2009). Sensor ranking: A primitive for efficient content-based sensor search. In *Proceedings of the 2009 international conference on information processing in sensor networks*, Washington (pp. 217–228).
4. Fletcher, B. (2006). *XMPP & cross domain collaborative information environment*. PowerPoint Slides. August 2006.
5. Newburry, N. (2008). http://www.frost.com/prod/servlet/market-insight-top.pag?docid=118964127. 22 January 2008.

6. Hammoudeh, M., Newman, R., Mount, S., & Dennett C. (2009). A combined inductive and deductive sense data extraction and visualisation service. In *Proceedings of the 2009 international conference on pervasive services*, London (pp. 159–168).
7. http://xmpp.org/about-xmpp/. January 2010.
8. Kenniche, H., & Ravelomananana, V. (2010). Random geometric graphs as model of wireless sensor networks. In *The 2nd international conference on computer and automation engineering (ICCAE)*, 6 February 2010 (pp. 103–107).
9. Ribeiro, A., Silva, F., Freitas, L., Costa, J., & Frances, C. (2005). SensorBus: a middleware model for wireless sensor networks. In *Proceedings of the 3rd international IFIP/ACM Latin American conference on networking*, Cali, Columbia (pp. 1–9).
10. Rowe, A., et al. (2008). *Sensor Andrew: Large-scale campus-wide* (Technical Report). Carnegie Mellon University, Pittsburgh.
11. XMPP Software Foundation. http://xmpp.org/xsf/press/2003-09-22.shtml. September 2003.

Chapter 8
Mobile Context-Aware Support for Public Transportation Users

Esben von Buchwald, Jakob Eg Larsen, and Roderick Murray-Smith

Abstract We present a fully functional location-aware application prototype named Relevant Service Suggestion System, which runs on an off-the-shelf Nokia 6210 Navigator. The system allows the user to point and probe to find the services needed, using the awareness of the user's location and the measured compass bearing, in addition to a distance range chosen by a physical gesture. The main application tested in this paper is a system to support public transport users in Copenhagen. Users can point at any bus-stop or train station and be given timetables, next departure times, and buy a ticket via SMS direct to their phone. The requirements for text entry are minimal, due to the use of location, bearing and pose sensing.

8.1 Introduction

In this paper we demonstrate how currently available technologies can be combined to make a novel ubiquitous information system for public transport users. We present a method of making public transportation information available by means of a context-aware mobile application on modern off-the-shelf mobile phones, rather than investing in expensive hardware at each bus stop or station. The study was carried out in the greater Copenhagen area in Denmark, where there is a well developed public transportation system including bus, train and metro. Information systems for acquiring public transportation information including bus, train and metro schedules and buying online tickets are available. These systems have also been adapted for mobile devices, but the daily use has been limited, due to the need to provide information about where you are going from and to via laborious text-entry.

E. von Buchwald (✉)
DTU Informatics, Technical University of Denmark, Copenhagen, Denmark

J. Eg Larsen
DTU Informatics, Cognitive Systems Section, Technical University of Denmark, Copenhagen, Denmark

R. Murray-Smith
School of Computing Science, University of Glasgow, Glasgow, Scotland, UK

T. Lovett, E. O'Neill (eds.), *Mobile Context Awareness*,
DOI 10.1007/978-0-85729-625-2_8, © Springer-Verlag London Limited 2012

In this paper we discuss the potential of supporting public transportation use by providing easier access to information (including schedules) and better integration with existing systems for buying tickets through the use of context-aware mobile applications. We present a context-aware mobile application prototype system. The client-server architecture of the system consists of a server aggregating public transportation information from multiple sources and a mobile application utilizing multiple embedded sensors on a mobile phone, presently the Nokia 6210 Navigator. The mobile user interface is a point-at-and-gesture system based on detection of current location (GPS), direction (compass bearing), and allowing gesture-based input (accelerometers). The pilot system has been developed and tested in Copenhagen, utilizing the existing systems for accessing bus, train and metro schedules, location of stops and terminals, as well as the SMS-based system for buying travel tickets. It demonstrates the possibilities of promoting public transportation with relatively small resources and investment in development, implementation and deployment compared to traditional public transportation information systems, such as information displays at a bus stop.

8.2 Related Work

Early experiments in location-aware services tended to use PDAs and external sensors to test the basic concepts of providing appropriate information as a function of location. Tourism services were a common focus, with an early example [2]. Recent work in mobile spatial interaction is outlined in [4]. Non-visual feedback in location-aware systems has included audio feedback, e.g. [5, 6, 10]. Vibrotactile navigation systems include [4]. Many applications involved predominantly visual feedback and touch or keyboard navigation, but some alternatives included interfaces where the pitch control could allow you to project further along the current bearing, as used in [10–12]. This was used in [8, 9] for various explorations of augmented information in the environment. Gestures for playful interaction with game characters is used in the REXplorer system [1].

The latest mobile phones have all the sensors necessary for such interactions, since the Nokia 6210 Navigator, Nokia N8, iPhone 4 and HTC Sensation smartphones, and we have seen a series of new applications and papers relating to this. Mobile augmented reality examples include the Layar [7] project for Android, which allows users to browse the local environment using the camera viewfinder, and it places layers of geotagged data and weblinks on the screen. Much of the recent output has been less visible in the academic literature, but has been disseminated via e.g. the Apple AppStore in the form of applications. The Wikitude API project for Android allowed developers to add their own content to their applications based on the Wikitude API [13]. Many cities' public transport systems have shown rapid improvements in their web sites for supporting users trip-planning, and these have in part been transferred to mobile applications, such as the "London Bus, Tube and Rail Journey Planner", or the one-bus-away [3] app for the iPhone, although these tend to require you to enter which stop you are at, which might not always be clearly marked, or which might require you to walk to the place to find out. The "Nearest Tube" app from Crossair is a prototype mobile augmented reality system which overlays information about how to get to the nearest train station on the iPhone screen as you focus the camera on different areas.

8.3 Usage Scenarios

We sketch two example usage scenarios, which illustrate the ways such a system could be used in practice.

1. Peter is a tourist from Germany coming to Copenhagen for a few days. He is happy to use public transportation, but doesn't speak Danish, and is unfamiliar with Copenhagen. When he lands at the airport he also has no Danish Kroner, but only Euros. On arrival, he points his phone at the railway station in the airport, and enters his destination. The phone tells him when the next train is, how long the trip will take, how to connect to a bus that will take him to his hotel, and how much the ticket would cost. He decides that this is a good trade-off compared to the cost of a taxi, and he buys a ticket on his phone using the Copenhagen traffic system's SMS ticket option. While on the train, he is alerted by his phone a few minutes before arriving at the transfer station, and on coming out into the large main station he easily finds his bus stop using the built in compass. The phone tells him the bus is due in 2 minutes, so he jogs to the stop to ensure he catches the bus. He shows the phone's SMS ticket to the bus driver and boards the bus.
2. Søren lives in Copenhagen and he has to go to a job interview in a part of town he rarely visits. He thinks he could walk there, but after a few minutes he realizes he is running late, and notices a bus stop. Unsure about the bus routes, he points the phone at the bus stop and it tells him which routes go from there. He selects the route which will take him to his destination, and the phone tells him a bus will be arriving in 4 minutes, and will get him there 13 minutes earlier than expected walking speed. This makes sense, so he buys the ticket and waits for the bus.

   The system described in this paper is a first, functioning step to creating such a mobile transport aid, and has the station finding, timetabling and ticket purchasing working on an off-the-shelf mobile phone, using the existing Copenhagen traffic system.

In Fig. 8.1, the flow of a typical usage situation is illustrated, with screenshots from the actual prototype, and shows a user who wants to arrange a trip by train from a station "Peter Bangs Vej".

8.4 System Overview

Our system consists of a mobile client and a server back-end. The mobile application primarily acts as an assistant to find the services relevant for the user in its current context (i.e. nearby bus/trains). It also lets the user interact with the selected services

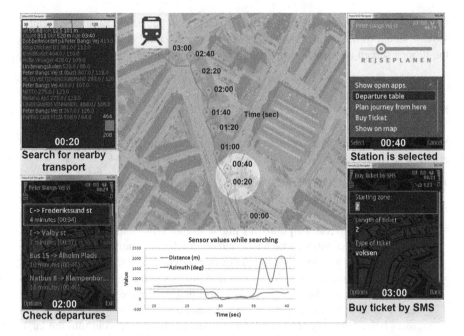

Fig. 8.1 The flow of actions when a user walks towards a train station. In the time sequence 00:20–00:40 seconds the mobile application prototype is used to find the station, through the gesture-based interaction. When the station has been chosen the user checks the departure table, finds the next departure, and buy a ticket through the integrated SMS service

afterwards, enabling the user to see live departure tables from the chosen station, plan a journey from the station to a chosen destination, and buy an SMS ticket for the trip, all through the built in features of the mobile application. To find the relevant services, it couples the known context data acquired from the sensors, with the service data received from the server application, and shows a list of matching services. The presentation of data and the interaction options for a given service is based on the service-specific data provided by the server application, which means that the mobile application is totally independent on specific service providers etc. The mobile application is running on a Nokia 6210 Navigator, and is written in Python for S60.

The server application provides data to the mobile application upon request. It basically acts as an interface between the mobile application and the provider modules, with a database to be used by the provider modules, and data import scripts to import service data from external service providers. Each module has its own customized table of data in the database, and its own API to provide a list of services, interaction options for its services, or call service-specific functions. For the 'Rejseplanen' module used in this paper, there are custom functions for getting live departure tables, train and bus station information (IDs, names, price zones, and geographic positions) and purchasing SMS tickets. The server application is written in PHP and the data about services is stored in a MySQL database.

Fig. 8.2 (a) A user tilts the phone to indicate distance, (b) A user is pointing in the direction of different services

8.5 User Interaction

The system enables the user to select a point of interest (i.e. a bus terminal or train station) from the pool of available services, by simply pointing the phone in the direction of it, and selecting it when suggested by the application, as illustrated in Fig. 8.2. The user can also choose the interval of distance to the desired service, by holding the phone closer to the face or further away from the body. This movement results in a tilting of the phone around the x-axis, which is measured by the accelerometer. When tilted towards the body, it will be vertical, giving a large acceleration value for the y-axis, and when the user tilts the device away from the body, the phone will be placed horizontally, giving only small amounts of acceleration on the y-axis.

8.5.1 Location

We use a window of 1×1 degree to make 2D-plane approximation of the spherical earth surface, which results in a small but insignificant difference of about 0.1 % when calculating the distance to objects within 500 meters, in Denmark. By using this approximation, the calculations for distance and bearing between the current position and relevant services can be simplified. Using this method, we get the length of one degree, called d_{lat} and d_{lon}. The selected area in which to get services, is determined by first calculating some exact point, that the user is pointing at. With the knowledge of position (lon_0, lat_0), bearing ϕ and distance d, a new point (lon_1, lat_1), can be calculated:

$$\Delta x = \cos(\phi) \cdot d$$
$$\Delta y = \sin(\phi) \cdot d$$

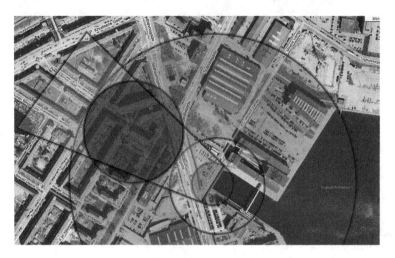

Fig. 8.3 Distance inaccuracy is *larger* than the bearing inaccuracy

$$lon_1 = \frac{lon_0 + \Delta_x}{d_{lon}}$$

$$lat_1 = \frac{lat_0 + \Delta_y}{d_{lat}}$$

Then, a circle is drawn around the calculated position, with a radius based on the reported inaccuracy for either the compass sensor or the chosen distance. If the width of the angle made by compass inaccuracy, at the chosen distance, is smaller than the distance inaccuracy, the circle is limited to only cover the angle scope made by the compass inaccuracy (see Fig. 8.3).

Otherwise, the circle is limited to only cover the area within the chosen distance interval (see Fig. 8.4).

It can be determined whether a given service is within the covered area, by simply calculating its distance to the chosen point, and afterwards filtering out the services outside distance interval or angle scope.

8.5.2 Sensor Data

The system is based on the data acquired from the GPS receiver, accelerometer and digital compass (magnetometer sensor), available in the Nokia 6210 Navigator. The magnetic north azimuth is derived from the data acquired by the 3-axis magnetometer and the accelerometer. When the phone is held in a hand, this results in a significant amount of noise. The majority of the recorded values are within a 2 degree range from the mean, which means that a filtering threshold of at least ±2 degrees needs to be applied to avoid constant flickering of the obtained value. This also affects the inaccuracy, which will increase from the approximately 20 degrees to

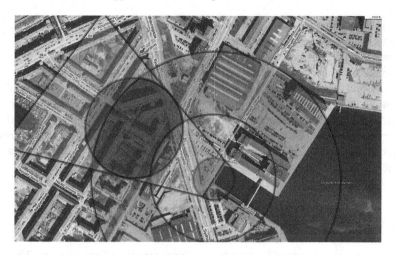

Fig. 8.4 Distance inaccuracy is *smaller* than the bearing inaccuracy

about 24 degrees. In addition, the inaccuracy caused by the magnetic declination is about 0–2 degrees in Denmark, but neglected since it is insignificant compared to the compass inaccuracy itself.

The accelerometer reports an 8-bit signed value representing $\pm 2g$ acceleration for each axis. Also a significant amount of noise is produced when the phone is handheld. Applying a low pass filter makes it stable enough for handheld usage. The Nokia 6210 Navigator offers an integrated GPS receiver with support for network assistance (A-GPS). Sensor data is logged in the mobile application to analyze user behavior and enable usability tests. When the user closes the application, the log files are uploaded to the server, and the user movements can be plotted on a map, or used for simulation.

To demonstrate the system logging feature, Fig. 8.1 also includes a graphical representation of logged data, when the user is walking, searching for services and ends up by pointing at a nearby train station.

8.5.3 Performance and Resource Consumption

The server application can easily handle multiple users simultaneously and returns hundreds of available services. The mobile application works stable and responsive, and delivers the expected results, with exception from failures caused by the phone itself (i.e. unstable network connection, unavailable sensors etc.). When searching (pointing) among 311 services loaded from the server, it provides screen updates at a frequency of 10–12 times per second. Currently the main bottleneck is getting a position fix from the GPS, which may take from seconds to several minutes.

Also, downloading and decoding a large list of services from the server for the neighboring 2 km, takes 15–20 seconds. Such delays reduce the perceived potential for spontaneous use, and optimisation of such issues is an important area. Pre-caching data, and use of newer, more advanced phones with faster network access and processors, is expected to decrease this impact. The power usage when the application is searching among the loaded services (i.e. a user is pointing around) is about 240 mA, and the CPU load is about 85–90 %. When the application is "paused" i.e. the motion sensors and display are off, but GPS is running, it consumes around 90 mA, which allows for a couple of hours usage without fully draining the 950 mA battery of the Nokia 6210 Navigator. The Python interpreter itself takes up about 3 MB of memory, where this application takes up another 2 MB. A list of about 300 services consumes another MB of phone RAM.

8.6 User Feedback

The current user interface is suitable for demonstration of the concept. Thus the system has been informally tested using two persons with no significant technical skills, but who were both experienced mobile phone users. They have been doing tasks, and provided feedback, ending up in an overall user experience discussion. Furthermore, the system has been tested at an internal Nokia workshop where eight participants could define their own tasks and experiment with the system.

In our pilot experiments the test subjects needed some instructions before being able to use the interface, but after the first few minutes, they found the interaction method to work very well, and were able to find the desired services. The current text-based list of services is not optimal for a large numbers of services, and another issue is that the services found are ordered by their distance to the center point of the selected area. This means that the order of the found services currently changes rapidly when the parameters change, i.e. the user slightly moves the hand around. During the workshop, the participants also expressed that it seems more comfortable and less awkward to use a system like this, than the recently publicized camera-assisted mobile augmented reality systems. The main issue with these is that users often feel uncomfortable walking around and "shooting" with their phone, and people on the street might think that photos are taken.

8.7 Discussion

To improve the user interface and user experience, a map-based search method, as used in [3], could augment our current system. It should show a small section of a map, similar to the area covered by the calculation method, and the services could be plotted on this map. The small changes in sensor values would then just result in the map sliding a few pixels left/right, instead of changing the contents of the present text list (see the screenshots in Fig. 8.1). The system could be expanded to a more context-specific approach of processing and presenting the available service data. It could provide everyday commuters with quick access to data about their normal route, and any unusual circumstances that day, or to notify the user to get off at the right bus stop, as implemented in Koozyt [7]. It could help tourists by guiding the user from the current location to the desired destination, by leading the user to the nearest bus/train and showing the suggested journey plan, in addition to offer an electronic ticket for the trip, to the user. The system already knows the location of the user, and its home address, and with a *"Take me home, now!"* system, could provide the necessary instructions to get home as soon as possible.

8.8 Conclusions

We have presented a location-aware application allowing the user to point and probe to find surrounding services, by means of the user's location, the measured compass bearing, and a distance range chosen by a physical gesture. The present version is a fully functioning system supporting public transport users in Copenhagen by allowing users to point at any bus-stop or train station to retrieve timetables, live next departure times, and to buy a ticket via SMS directly from the mobile phone.

Our experiments with the current prototype implementation have provided valuable insights and demonstrated the feasibility and potential of the concept as the application runs on standard off-the-shelf hardware. The generic architecture of our prototype system enables further research and rapid prototyping to be carried out. The results from our experiments carried out in Copenhagen will apply in any other city which makes basic public transportation information and infrastructure available. The system only needs station/stop locations, timetables or live arrival data. We believe that such technology can be developed and deployed with significantly lower resources and provide easy access to context-dependant information and services requiring minimal text entry.

Acknowledgements We would like to thank the participants who took part in our experiments at the workshop and the user experience tests.

References

1. Ballagas, R., Kuntze, A., & Walz, S. P. (2008). Gaming tourism: lessons from evaluating REX-plorer, a pervasive game for tourists. In *LNCS. Pervasive '08: Proc. of the 6th int. conference on pervasive computing* Berlin: Springer.
2. Cheverst, K., Mitchell, K., Davies, N., & Smith, G. (2000). Exploiting context to support social awareness and social navigation. *ACM SIGGROUP Bulletin, 21*(3), 43–48.
3. Ferris, B., Watkins, K., & Borning A. (2010). OneBusAway: results from providing real-time arrival information for public transit. In *Proceedings of CHI*. http://onebusaway.org/.
4. Fröhlich, P., Oulasvirta, A., Baldauf, M., & Nurminen, A. (2011). On the move, wirelessly connected to the world. *Communications of the ACM, 54*(1)
5. Holland, S., Morse, D., & Gedenryd H. (2002). AudioGPS: Spatial audio navigation with a minimal attention interface. *Personal and Ubiquitous Computing, 6,* 4.

6. Jones, M., Jones, S., Bradley, G., Warren, N., Bainbridge, D., & Holmes, G. (2008). Ontrack: Dynamically adapting music playback to support navigation. *Personal and Ubiquitous Computing, 12*(7), 513–525.
7. Koozyt. http://www.koozyt.com.
8. Robinson, S., Eslambolchilar, P., & Jones, M. (2009). Exploring casual point-and-tilt interactions for mobile geo-blogging. *Personal and Ubiquitous Computing.* doi:10.1007/s00779-009-0236-5.
9. Robinson, S., Eslambolchilar, P., & Jones, M. (2009). Sweep-Shake: Finding digital resources in physical environments. In *Proceedings of MobileHCI.* Bonn, September 2009.
10. Strachan, S., Eslambolchilar, P., Murray-Smith, R., Hughes, S., & O'Modhrain, S. (2005). gpsTunes: controlling navigation via audio feedback. In *Proc. MobileHCI '05* (pp. 275–278).
11. Strachan, S., & Murray-Smith, R. (2009). Bearing-based selection in mobile spatial interaction. *Personal and Ubiquitous Computing, 13*(4), 265–280.
12. Strachan, S., & Murray-Smith, R. (2009). Nonvisual, distal tracking of mobile remote agents in geosocial interaction. In *LoCA,* Tokyo.
13. Wikitude API. http://www.wikitude.org.

Chapter 9
Quality Sensitive Web Service Profiling and Discovery: In Support of Mobile and Pervasive Applications

Sherif G. Aly and Ahmed M. Hamza

Abstract Web services present themselves as very appealing components in building mobile and pervasive systems. Some of their usage includes data fusion, data format adaptation, support for privacy, backend computational support for functionalities that are simply not practically achieved using resource limited devices, and even compensation for missing sensors on mobile devices. However, as technology recesses into the background and weaves itself into the fabric of daily lives, providing quality of service guarantees for Web service consumption is extremely necessary. Simply selecting a set of matched services offering the same functional requirements, and that claim their own quality of service guarantees is not enough. In this research, and in support of mobile and pervasive systems requiring Web services, we present a policy-based third party system for dynamically measuring relevant Quality of Service (QoS) metrics of Web services, and maintaining these measurements in a modified UDDI that is sensitive for QoS needs made during subsequent look-up requests. Our third independent and trusted party dynamically acquires QoS relevant measurements from Web services. It adopts a policy-based mechanism as a foundation for the measurement acquisition process between this third party and the Web service provider. The maintained measurements are subsequently used as a primary determinant in service lookup requests made by service consumers. A constraint satisfaction matchmaking and service ranking algorithm satisfying both of the service requestor and provider needs and capabilities is used. Our evaluation of this approach indicates a tolerable overhead associated with the introduction of the third party monitoring process.

9.1 Introduction

Mobile devices continue to be highly characterized by their significant lack of resource availability. Although mobile devices have made huge leaps in their computation and communication abilities, applications continue to challenge mobile devices

S.G. Aly (✉) · A.M. Hamza
Department of Computer Science and Engineering, The American University in Cairo, Cairo, Egypt

T. Lovett, E. O'Neill (eds.), *Mobile Context Awareness*,
DOI 10.1007/978-0-85729-625-2_9, © Springer-Verlag London Limited 2012

with overwhelming needs that significantly deplete power resources, and constrain the abilities of the devices themselves. Service oriented architecture technologies such as Web services, residing on more privileged and resourceful nodes, have posed themselves as very appealing assistive components to such resource-constrained devices. Using this model, application-specific clients interact with functionally specialized interfaces over the Internet [8]. Not only can computation be delegated to such back-end components, but they may also be used to provide necessary sensation that is unavailable on mobile devices. Such great benefit of service oriented architecture technologies has led many contemporary research attempts to enhance the exploitation of the technology in both the industry and academia.

Publish, *Find* and *Bind* are the three major operations that are incorporated in the dynamic behavior of Web services [11]. Service providers publish Web services to a broker (also called the registry or repository in other contexts). Service requestors find the services using the broker, and eventually bind to them. The description of Web services, incorporated in the *publishing* and the *finding* operations, requires a proper specification for the functional and non-functional properties of the service. While the functional properties specification is what a Web service provides, the non-functional properties specification is how a service will operate [2]. Quality of Service (QoS), which is as a subset of non-functional features, is how well a service will be offered. Since its specification is a crucial aspect in distinguishing among Web services offering the same functional requirements, further research contributions are need to support the provision of QoS by Web services.

Three approaches for quality of service guarantees exist:

1. One major already existing solution is to have Web service providers explicitly state their QoS guarantees. However, delegating to the services themselves the specification of their own quality of service guarantees raises a lot of speculation about the credibility of the guarantees.
2. A second solution is to acquire user feedback after service consumption, but the subjectivity of evaluation, bias, as well as the complexity of implementation also undermines this approach [2, 12].
3. A third solution is through active monitoring techniques that could be adopted by third party brokers, or certifiers [2, 12]. Albeit the elevated credibility of such independent monitoring, the monitoring process may itself exercise a significant overhead on the services themselves, and should preferably be implemented in a way that makes the usage of monitoring certifiers or brokers streamlined with customary Web service consumption.

We find the third approach more appealing and further describe the design and evaluation of a third party system that will:

1. Dynamically acquire QoS relevant measurements from Web services after they have been deployed, and are actively servicing consumers.
2. Adopt a policy-based mechanism as a foundation for the measurement acquisition process between this third party and the Web service provider.

3. Maintain the acquired Web service QoS measurements for use as a primary determinant in subsequent service lookup requests made by service consumers, alongside typical lookup based on functional requirements.
4. Adopt a matchmaking and service ranking algorithm to better allocate Web services to consumers.
5. Respond to discovery requests taking into consideration quality of service needs of the consumer and the previously stored Web service QoS measurements.

9.2 Related Work

Numerous research attempts have been conducted in deriving Web service nonfunctional requirements, especially as deals with quality of service. Some of these attempts were either part of large scale projects or proposed as standalone research contributions. The following are the most common and acknowledged ones.

In [2], the authors proposed a QoS model in which functional and nonfunctional requirements such as quality of service were taken into account for service discovery. Two main contributions were added to the classical publish, find, bind model. The first being a QoS certifier with which all Web services supply their functional requirements, as well as their QoS claim. The second being an extension to UDDI's data structure types to contain QoS information to eventually serve applications needing quality of service assurance. In [1], the authors proposed an approach handling dynamic Web service selection in an agent framework along with a QoS ontology. Within this approach, participants collaborate to determine each other's service quality and trustworthiness.

In [15], the concept of a Web service profile along with a service profiling mechanism as well as the architecture of a profiling system was proposed. The framework was used to generate a profile which is an up-to-date description of a subset of nonfunctional characteristics of a service, and allowed for service comparison based on non-functional parameters and selecting the service that best matched the user needs. In [19], a generic information and computation framework for a QoS-based selection mechanism for Web services was proposed. An established QoS ontology between providers and consumers provided a common understanding of QoS parameters and their semantics. The framework used a technique called Similarity Distance Measure [3] in the underlying QoS selection algorithm.

In [11], the authors proposed an open, fair and dynamic QoS computation model for Web services selection. In this model two mechanisms were incorporated. In this approach, active execution monitoring was used to keep track of service execution time. User feedback was also collected to gather further information about the services being used. In [20], a framework was proposed handling quality of service compliance. It offered an HTTP monitoring technique for evaluating the level of conformance of an SLA-enabled Web service provider to a signed SLA, and hence provided a realistic indication of the service delivered.

In [12], an approach that was based on workflow management was proposed. It discussed a QoS model that also supported the ability to automatically compute

QoS based on a specification of component Web services. If any deviation from the desired QoS metrics (initial requirements) was detected, it would register them, automatically notify interested users, and the faulty task would be replaced by an equivalent task to restore the soundness of the system; such replacement can be accomplished by applying dynamic changes to the instances, either manually or automatically.

In [23], the authors introduced an approach to provide an efficient, dynamic, and QoS-aware selection and monitoring of Web services. The prototype of their approach consisted of the following components: a WS-QoS Editor for the specification of QoS properties, a WS-QoS Requirement Manager for retrieving QoS requirements specified by client applications, a Web service broker for an efficient and QoS-aware selection of Web service offers, and a WS-QoS Monitor for checking the compliance of the service offers.

Part of the work introduced in [26] was a measurement architecture that consisted of a *collector and evaluator service* that gathered the *AtomicMetric* values pushed from *measurement handlers*. These handlers acquired values from the client, the provider and intermediate parties. Each *Collector* would then start deriving the *ComplexMetric* values from gathered *AtomicMetric* values and store the received data for calculation. Once it was done with the collection, it generated a measurement service-level objective (SLO). As a final step, this service would indicate whether the service abides by the promised SLO. Further work was done in [13, 14] to describe and discover Web services and to represent QoS related information as in [10, 16].

Table 9.1 summarizes the aforementioned approaches. In this table we used *Yes* if the approach support the property, *No* if not and *N/A* (i.e., not applicable) if the criteria is out of the domain of the approach or if the approach uses another competing property.

From our literature review, we find that existing individual approaches have major drawbacks in the sense that they:

1. Do not profile the Web service under realistic consumption conditions such as in [19].
2. Do not consider a reasonable set of QoS properties. The approach is usually tested against two or three properties leaving the remaining as future work.
3. Some of the approaches do not reach an acceptable level of extensibility as in [20], thus making it very difficult to modify monitoring behavior.
4. Lack a policy-based mechanism to measure each metric as in [1, 15, 20, 23]. Policies are typically needed to schedule the time, frequency, and type of monitoring. For example, monitoring for best case latency behavior cannot typically happen during peak service utilization times. The frequency of certain types of monitoring such as throughput for example may not happen in a way that severely imposes unnecessary overhead upon the service itself.
5. Are not based on a proper description and discovery mechanism (i.e., Quality-based ontology, a description language or any other consistent approach) as in [19, 20].
6. Do not profile composite Web services as in [17, 19, 21].

Table 9.1 Comparison between different approaches of QoS values derivation

| | Certifier based [19] | Agent based [17] | Work-flow mining based [1] | Aggregation based [21] | Monitoring based approaches | | | | |
| | | | | | Active execution [15] | Compliance monitoring based | | | Push method based [26] |
						Sheth et al. [20]	Ali et al. [3]	Tian et al. [23]	
Dynamic profiling	No	Yes	Yes	Yes	Yes	Yes	Yes	No	N/A
Extensible to new metrics	Yes	Yes	Yes	Yes	Yes	N/A	Yes	Yes	Yes
Policy-based mechanism	N/A	N/A	No	Yes	No	No	N/A	No	N/A
QoS description mechanism	No	Yes	Yes	Yes	N/A	No	N/A	Yes	Yes
Profile composite WSs	No	No	Yes	No	Yes	Yes	Yes	Yes	Yes
Client feedback independent	N/A	No	Yes	No	No	Yes	Yes	Yes	No
Seamless (no change in WS logic)	No	No	No	No	No	Yes	No	No	No
Clear description for the profiling	No	Yes	Yes	Yes	Yes	No	Yes	N/A	No
Prioritization and ranking of matched WSs	No	Yes	Yes	Yes	Yes	N/A	Yes	N/A	Yes

7. Exhibit unfairness issues, as they could entirely or partially rely on some of the attributes advertised by the provider or accessed through the provider's interface. Such QoS information whether directly acquired or used to compute other metrics are subject to any overestimation by the provider as in [1, 15, 21, 23, 26]. They may also rely on client's "provider/consumer" feedback. In such case, they could be underestimated by a malicious provider tending to ruin the reputations of its competitors or by an unfair consumer. Moreover, this acquired feedback is static in nature and will not be updated consistently as in [15, 17, 26].

8. Have a tendency to amend in the Web service logic itself as well as the consumer's side, leading them to be expensive and inflexible to implement as in [1, 3, 15, 17, 19, 21, 23, 26].

9. Lack a clear description for the mechanism of the QoS values measurement (either probing or monitoring) as in [20, 26] or the QoS values verification as in [19].

10. Lack a proper mechanism to rank the importance of quality of service metrics to consumers such that services can be properly ordered according to consumer preference [19].

9.3 Proposed System

We introduce our proposed profiling and selection system for the sake of realizing the aforementioned contributions. We will start by describing the architecture of our system, followed by how we extended the classical UDDI to incorporate QoS information. We then describe how we actually profile Web services for QoS properties. Once Web services are profiled, and relevant QoS indicators are stored in the lookup directory, mobile pervasive applications that need Web services for their back-end computational needs, or even for usage as virtual sensors, can now select their needed Web services. The selection will not only rely on functional properties, but also on a reliable specification of the non-functional characteristics of the Web services. In specific, real-time, or near-real-time needs for mobile pervasive applications can be met with a higher degree of reliability.

9.3.1 System Architecture

The approach proposed in this research will cover the four major phases required to quantitatively measure, and consequently understand a system as specified by Menascé et al. in [18]. The four phases mentioned by Menascé et al. are: (1) *Measurements Specification*, (2) *Test Points Specification*, (3) *Data Instrumentation and Collection*, and (4) *Data Analysis and Transformation*. For phase 1, we settled on attributes that are more relevant and momentous to mobile pervasive applications, namely, latency, throughput, reliability, availability, integrity, accuracy, and robustness as the set of QoS attributes to be measured. For phases 2 and 3, we created a third party that will be used as a client to send and receive SOAP messages to Web services to monitor them for the selected QoS properties. For phase 4, a *Q-Profiler* will analyze collected data, map the results into a QoS profile understood by our newly modified UDDI, namely the *Q-UDDI* then send those QoS information to the *Q-UDDI Repository* for storing such information.

To gain the benefits of other successful work, we decided to develop our architecture based on a hybrid of the desirable features in these approaches. As Fig. 9.1 illustrates, the proposed architecture consists of two main packages: *Q-UDDI* containing the *Q-UDDI repository* and the *Q-Profiler* that consists of four components: *Profile Manager, Profiler Repository, Metric/Attribute Profiler* and *Policy Manager.*

- **The Q-UDDI Repository**: Is used to store published Web services using its classical mechanism (save_service) or using our newly extended interface (save_q_service). We subsequently provide a description for why and how the classical UDDI (repository and API) would be extended. This extension is to allow for the following:
  - Publish the Web services that the provider agrees to be profiled.
  - Notify the service Profile Manager with the newly published Web services to be profiled.
  - Store the QoS metrics that will be used in profiling. The current UDDI database in itself does not accommodate such kind of information [25].
  - Find candidate Web services fulfilling functional and QoS requirements.
  - Respond to consumers by a list of candidate Web services ranked according to what is available in the repository and according to the QoS needs indicated by Hafez et al.'s discovery mechanism indicated in [9].
- **The Profile Manager**: Is used for the following:
  - Receive profiling requests for (atomic/composite) Web services along with the parameters used by the profiler to be able to invoke the Web service.
  - Retrieve the policies that will be used in profiling each Web service.
  - Execute each QoS metric profiling activity according to the retrieved policies.
  - Receive the QoS values from each QoS metric profiler.
  - Save QoS values of the profiled services in the Q-UDDI Repository.
- **The Profiler Repository**: Is used to store invocation parameters of Web services, profiling policy and the profiling status of each property of each Web service. The profiling status is an integer number between 0–2. A record holding the value "0" means that the QoS property for the Web service is not profiled yet. A value "1" means that the profiler started profiling this property. A value "2" means that the profiler ended the profiling phase and saved the measured QoS values in the Q-UDDI Repository. Mobile pervasive applications will use such stored QoS values returned by the Q-UDDI repository after a Web service lookup request to make decisions about the most suitable Web service to use.
- **The Metric Profiler**: Is used to invoke the Web service being profiled by sending and receiving SOAP messages, taking the required probes that are appropriate for the metric being measured, and then subsequently passing on the measurements to Profile Manager for further processing before being stored in the Q-UDDI Repository.

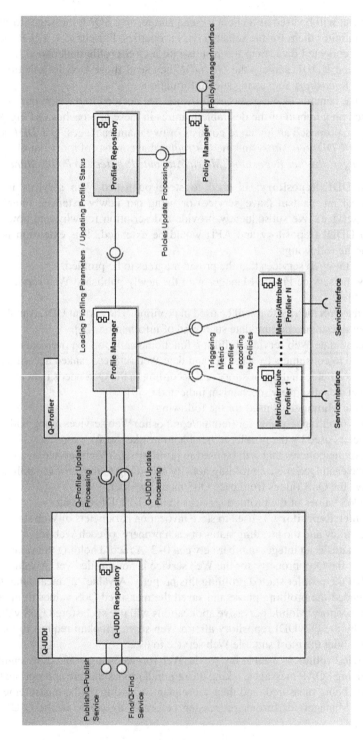

Fig. 9.1 The component architecture of service quality-based profiling and selection

- **The Policy Manager**: Is used to store the policies used to schedule and synchronize the SOAP requests sent from the Metric Profiler to the Web service.

9.3.2 Architecture Information Models

In this section, we describe our extensions to existing information models to accommodate QoS information.

9.3.2.1 Q-UDDI Information Model

The diagram in Fig. 9.2 depicts the relationship between the different core information elements making up the *Q-UDDI* information model. The elements put in bold (i.e., *qosBag* and *qKeyedReference*) are the ones added to the classical UDDI information model [24] to hold the QoS information. This addition consists of the *qosBag* holding the *qkeyedReference* records. Each *qkeyedReference* holds the *keyName* which is used to hold the name of the QoS metric, the *keyValue* used to hold the value measured by the *Q-Profiler*, and *keyMonotonicity* used by the Hafez et al. [9] discovery mechanism to indicate whether smaller values are good or bad, and vice versa.

9.3.2.2 Q-Profiler Information Model

The diagram in Fig. 9.3 illustrates the relationship between the different core information elements making up the *Q-Profiler* information model. It consists of the *tModel* element of the classical UDDI information model [24] added to it the *invocationBag* and the *policiesBag*. The *invocationBag* consists of a set of *keyedReference* records in which each record holds an invocation parameter (e.g., the WS access point, WS method to call, and method parameters to be passed) to be used by the *Metric Profiler* while probing the Web service. The *policiesBag* holds the *qkeyedReferences*. In the *policiesBag* of the *Q-Profiler*, the *qkeyedReference* holds the remaining information elements of the *qkeyedReference* in the *Q-UDDI* which are the *keyPolicy* and the *keyStatus*.

9.3.3 Architecture Usability

Our proposed system will be used assuming that every network has its own Q-Profiler and that every client whether stationary or mobile is querying the Q-Profiler in closest geographic proximity. The following steps will explain the usability of our proposed third entity as Figs. 9.4 and 9.5 illustrate.

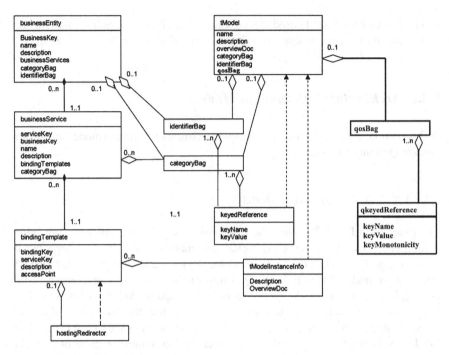

Fig. 9.2 The Q-UDDI information model

1. Each Web service provider starts by publishing its Web services that are going to be profiled in Q-UDDI registries (Fig. 9.4).
2. The Q-UDDI will then forward the key of each published Web service to the Profile Manager to initiate a profiling request to the responsible QoS Metric Profiler for the services with a profiling status equal to "0" (i.e., its probe did not start yet) in the Profiling Repository (Fig. 9.5).
3. According to the policies configured in the Policy Manager (Fig. 9.5), the Metric Profiler will then start sampling those services by sending SOAP requests, and update the Profile Manager with the QoS measurements of the metrics.
4. Once the Profile Manager is done gathering the profile of the "candidate Web service" that are based on probes taken over a prolonged period of time according to predetermined policies, it sends those QoS values to the Q-UDDI.
5. Clients, and more importantly mobile clients, submit their requests to the Q-UDDI asking for Web services that satisfy some functional and QoS properties (Fig. 9.4).
6. The Q-UDDI will try to find the Web services that satisfy the functional requirements and then apply another filtration to satisfy the QoS requirements, this latter filtration is processed using the Hafez et al. mechanism [9] (Fig. 9.4).
7. As in the mechanism proposed by Hafez et al. in [9], these services are then ranked and returned to the Web service requestor (Fig. 9.4). In our case, a mobile client will select, from amongst the returned set of services, a Web service that

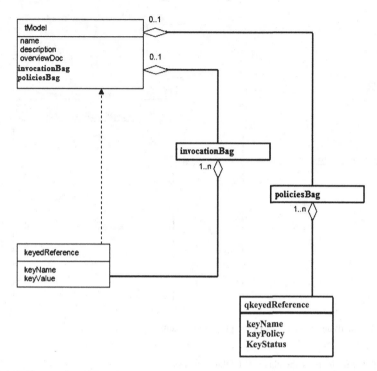

Fig. 9.3 The Q-Profiler information model

it finds most suitable for the required task. It is worthy to note that the entire returned set of Web services abides by the initial functional and non-functional requirements of the client.

9.3.4 UDDI Extensions: Q-UDDI

In our proposed system, a user should be able to use three main additional functionalities that did not use to exist in the classical UDDI (see Table 9.2). Those three activities are:

- **save_q_tModel**: To save a *tModel* with the proper invocation parameters needed by the *Q-Profiler* to profile the Web service binding to this *tModel*.
- **save_q_service**: To bind a Web service to a *tModel* saved using *save_q_tModel*.
- **find_q_service**: To find Web services with some QoS guarantees.

Moreover, any kind of communication in the *Q-UDDI* is realized through SOAP message passing, (e.g., *save_q_tModel*, *Save_q_service* and *find_q_service* are SOAP messages). And therefore, it is relevant enough to analyze the constituents of each of those SOAP messages. Profiled data is stored in the Q-UDDI according to the technique proposed by Blum et al. in [5].

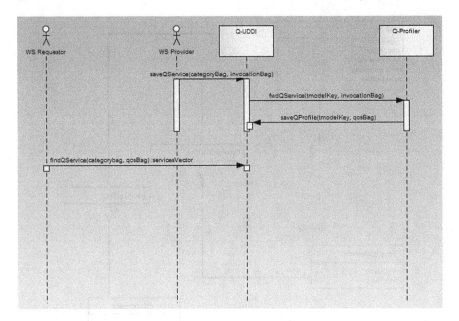

Fig. 9.4 The dynamic behavior of the proposed system

Table 9.2 Summary of the classical UDDI APIs [4]

Inquiry functionalities		Publishing functionalities	
Find	find_business	Save	Save_business
	find_service		Save_service
	find_binding		Save_binding
	find_tModel		Save_tModel
Get Details	get_businessDetail	Delete	delete_business
	get_serviceDetail		delete_service
	get_bindingDetail		delete_binding
	get_tModelDetail		delete_tModel
	get_registeredInfo		Get_registeredInfo
		Security	Get_authToken
			discard_authToken

9.3.4.1 save_q_tModel

In the *save_q_tModel* (Fig. 9.6), the content of the *categoryBag* content is saved normally in the *Q-UDDI Repository*, similar to its usage in classical UDDI, but the content of the *invocationBag* is now forwarded to and saved in the *Q-Profiler Repository*. This is because the *Q-Profiler* is the one performing the probing activities and

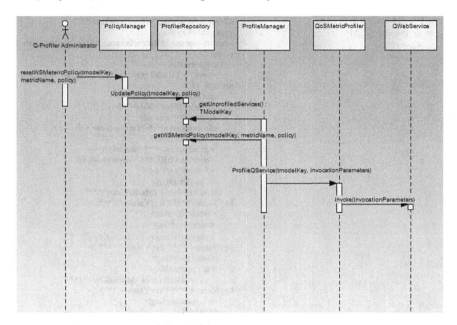

Fig. 9.5 The dynamic behavior of Q-Profiler

there is no point to save such information in the *Q-UDDI* as it is not part of the probing phase.

The following figure illustrates an example of an *invocationBag* after being populated:

Moreover, through the *save_q_tModel*, we provide the *Q-Profiler* with the parameters (e.g., access point, method name to call and the parameters this method takes) that should be used while invoking this service through the *Q-UDDI* interface. This is done by choosing the *save_q_tModel* and entering those values in the *invocationBag* (Fig. 9.7), then binding the service being published later on to this *tModel* through the *save_q_service*. The *invocationBag* structure is exactly the same as that of the *categoryBag* (Fig. 9.8) (i.e., consists of a group of *keyedReferences*, each of which consists of a *tModelKey*, a *keyName*, and a *keyValue*). This structure holds a group of *keyedReferences*, where each *keyedReference* represents an invocation parameter.

The following are examples of the invocation parameters:

- A service access point.
- The service target name space.
- Methods to be called.
- Types of parameters passed to each method to be called.
- Sample values to assign these parameters to.

Fig. 9.6 The schema of the
save_q_tModel SOAP
message

```
<?xml version="1.0" encoding="utf-8"?>
<soapenv:Envelope
xmlns:soapenv="http://schemas.xmlsoap.org/soap/env
elope/">
  <soapenv:Body>
    <save_q_tModel generic="2.0" xmlns="urn:uddi-
org:api_v2">
    <authInfo>***</authInfo>
    <tModel tModelKey="">
    <name>***</name>
    <description>***</description>
    <overviewDoc>
      <description>***</description>
      <overviewURL>***</overviewURL>
    </overviewDoc>
    <identifierBag>
  <keyedReference tModelKey="***"
keyName="***" keyValue="***" />
      </identifierBag>
      <categoryBag>
        <keyedReference tModelKey="***"
keyName="***" keyValue="***" />
      </categoryBag>
      <invocationBag>
        <keyedReference tModelKey="***"
keyName="***" keyValue="***" />
      </invocationBag>
      </tModel>
    </save_q_tModel>
  </soapenv:Body>
</soapenv:Envelope>
```

9.3.4.2 save_q_service

Using the *save_q_service*, the service provider agrees implicitly to profile this Web service "by choosing a *save_q_service* instead of a *save_service*", then binds to the *tModel* that was saved through the *save_q_tModel*. As Fig. 9.9 illustrates, the *save_q_service* has exactly the same entries as these of the *save_service* which is part of the classical UDDI functionalities. Nevertheless, *save_q_service* initializes the *Q-Profiler* with the newly published service (i.e. informing the *Q-Profiler* that there is a service just bound to a certain *tModel* for which the *Q-Profiler* already has received the proper invocation parameters in the *save_q_tModel* step).

9.3.4.3 find_q_service

Using the *find_q_service*, the service requestor (in specific, a mobile client) can look up a Web service satisfying functional and QoS requirements. As in Fig. 9.10, the functional requirements are specified in the *categoryBag* as it used to be in the classical UDDI. However, in *find_q_Service*, we added the *qosBag* to hold the requestor's QoS requested values "or range of values" for each QoS metric/attribute. A *qosBag* (Fig. 9.11) consists of a group of *qkeyedReferences* (Fig. 9.12). It is obvious from these figures that we follow the structures of and the relationship between those of the *categoryBag* and *keyedReference* except that we just added *keyMonotonicity* for

```
<invocationBag>

    <keyedReferencekeyName="acessPoint"

    keyValue="http://www.ecubicle.net/driving.asmx" tModelKey=" 1 "/>

    <keyedReference keyName="targetNamespace"

    keyValue="http://www.ecubicle.net/webservices/" tModelKey="2"/>

    <keyedReference keyName="method" keyValue="GetDirections"
tModelKey="3"/>

    <keyedReference keyName="parameter1" keyValue=" from Address"

    tModelKey="4"/>

    <keyedReference keyName="text1" keyValue="1615 Rhode Island
AreNW,

    Washington, DC 20036, USA" tModelKey="5"/>

    <keyedReference keyName="parameter2" keyValue="toAddress"
tModelKey="6"/>

    <keyedReference keyName="tert2" keyValue="2121 I Street, NW,
Washington, DC

    20052, USA" tModelKey="7"/>

    <keyedReference keyName="parameter3" keyValue="distanceUnit"

    tModelKey="8"/>

    <keyedReference keyName="text3" keyValue="km"
tModelKey="9"/>

    <keyedReference keyName="parameter4"
keyValue=" expresswayEnabled"

        tModelKey="10"/>

    <keyedReference keyName="text4" keyValue="true"
tModelKey="11"/>

</invocationBag>
```

Fig. 9.7 An example of invocationbag

each metric "that is represented by a qkeyedReference". The *keyMonotonicity* is explained in details in the discovery mechanism we borrowed from Hafez et al. [9]. As opposed to the *invocationBag* content, the content of the qkeyedReference here is saved in the *Q-UDDI Repository*, since matchmaking and selection is performed online based upon a client's request.

9.3.5 The Profiling Mechanism

9.3.5.1 Measurement and Derivation of QoS Properties

Many research efforts have tried to gather and classify the QoS attributes. According to the research works conducted in [2], the QoS attributes can be grouped into four classes which are runtime, transaction, security and network related QoS.

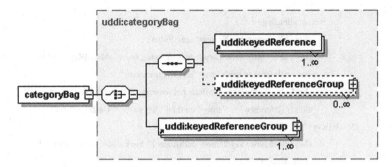

Fig. 9.8 The structure diagram of categoryBag [6]

Fig. 9.9 The schema of the
save_q_service SOAP
message

```
<?xml version="1.0" encoding="utf-8"?>
<soapenv:Envelope
xmlns:soapenv="http://schemas.xmlsoap.org/soap/envelope/
">
  <soapenv:Body>
  <save_q_service generic="2.0" xmlns="urn:uddie-
org:api_v2">
    <authInfo>***</authInfo>
    <businessService businessKey="***" serviceKey="">
    <name>***</name>
      <description>***</description>
      <bindingTemplates>
      <bindingTemplate bindingKey="">
      <accessPointURLType="http">***</accessPoint>
      <tModelInstanceDetails>
        <tModelInstanceInfo tModelKey="***">
        <instanceDetails>
        <overviewDoc>
        <overviewURL>***</overviewURL>
        </overviewDoc>
        </instanceDetails>
        </tModelInstanceInfo>
      </ tModelInstanceDetails>
      </bindingTemplate>
      </bindingTemplates>
      </businessService>
    </save_q_service>
    </soapenv:Body>
    </soapenv:Envelope>
```

Our proposed system should be generic enough to measure a significant subset
from each type in each class. However, due to the fact that we are only introducing a prototype, we will only tackle the QoS attributes that could be inferred upon
manipulation of logs taken from invocation SOAP messages.

Therefore, we restrict the prototype presented in this chapter to measure *Performance (Latency and Throughput)*, *Reliability*, *Availability*, *Integrity*, *Accuracy* and
Robustness.

Table 9.3 puts every QoS attribute definition along with the metrics used to measure it and the mechanism used by the *Q-Profiler* to measure each metric.

Fig. 9.10 The schema of the find_q_service SOAP message

```
<?xml version="1.0" encoding="utf-8"?>
<soapenv:Envelope
xmlns:soapenv="http://schemas.xmlsoap.org/soap/envelope/
">

  <soapenv:Body>
    <find_q_service generic="2.0" xmlns="urn:uddi-
org:api_v2">
      <findQualifiers>
        <findQualifier>***</findQualifier>
      </findQualifiers>
      <name>***</name>
      <identifierBag>
        <keyedReference tModelKey="***" keyName="***"
keyValue="***" />
      </identifierBag>
      <categoryBag>
        <keyedReference tModelKey="***" keyName="***"
keyValue="***" />
      </categoryBag>
      <qosBag>
        <qkeyedReference tModelKey="***" keyName="***"
keyOperator1="***" keyValue1="***"
keyOperator2="***" keyValue2="***" keyWeight
="***"/>
      </qosBag>
    </find_q_service>
  </soapenv:Body>
</soapenv:Envelope>
```

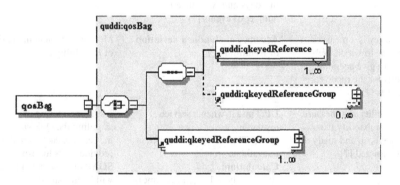

Fig. 9.11 The structure diagram of qosBag

9.3.5.2 Usage of Policies in Web Service Profiling

To schedule our profiler, we simply use Cron, which we found as a very reasonable scheduling tool. The tool, initially developed for Unix, enables its users to schedule any job to execute at certain times or dates. Cron is configured by using a string called the Unix Crontab Entries. Each entry is a string containing a scheduling pattern and task to execute. We are only interested in the scheduling pattern, in which the syntax is as follows. Each pattern consists of five fields separated by blank-spaces and the following is the description of each field in order from left to right [22]:

Table 9.3 The QoS attributes to be measured by the Q-Profiler

Attribute definition	Metric(s) mapping	Measurement mechanism
Performance is a measure of the Web service speed in processing and serving a request [7]	**Throughput** is the number of requests serviced in a specific amount of time [7] **Latency** is the amount of delay experienced by the client starting from the time of a request submission to the time the response information starts to arrive [7]	Sending different number of SOAP requests from a client to a Web service, keeping track of the response time of each trial
Reliability is a measure of how the service performs, in a specific amount of time and the present network conditions, while maintaining the service quality [7]	**Number of failures on a specific amount of time**. That could be mapped to number of: **Dropped deliveries, Duplicate deliveries, Faulty message deliveries, and Out of order deliveries** **Calculation**: Success rate or Reliability $= 1 - (n/(N^*t))$, where n is the number of failures in t days and N is the total number of events [7]	Like that of performance, a number of SOAP requests should be sent to a Web service over a period of t days but this time the number of failures will be our indicative variable to derive *Reliability*
Accuracy is a measure of the level to which Web services give accurate results for the received requests [7]	Accuracy = **standard deviation of Reliability** [7]	Measured upon computation of Reliability [7]
Availability is a measure of the probability that service is up and ready to be consumed [7]	**UP Time** is when a service available **Down Time** is when a service is unavailable **Calculation**: Availability $= 1 - [(\text{down time})/(\text{unit time period measured})] = (\text{up time})/(\text{unit time period measured})$ [7]	While monitoring or sampling the QoS values of the service, each time the provider fails to respond to a SOAP request, down time will be measured

- First field: Minute [0, 59]
- Second field: Hour [0, 23]
- Third field: Day of the month [1, 31]
- Fourth field: Month of the year [1, 12]
- Fifth field: Day of the week ([0, 6] with 0 = Sunday)

Knowing that our system may operate autonomously, the metric profiler lifetime is considered the second parameter used along with scheduling of policies. Once the

Table 9.3   (Continued)

Attribute definition	Metric(s) mapping	Measurement mechanism
Robustness is a measure of how quick a service will recover from a failure and its performance during worst case scenarios including heavy network loads and invalid inputs [7]	**Mean Time Between Failures (MTBF)** which is the amount of time it takes for a failure to occur then recover **Calculation:** $MTBF = MTTF + MTTR$, where **MTTF** is mean time a system takes to fail another time and **MTTR** is the mean time a system takes to recover from the failure [7]	While monitoring, if a system didn't respond to a request with a specific period of time, failure time is logged. Then, the sampler will start sending a finite number of SOAP requests to the service until it is recovered and the recovery time is logged as well. Finally, the service will be monitored till the next failure that will be logged
Reputation is a measure of the trustworthiness of a Web service and mainly based on user experience upon its usage [8]	heuristics using repeated usage [17] of the same service as we are not relying on any client's feedback	While monitoring or sampling the QoS values of the service, repeated usage from one client to the same service will be logged

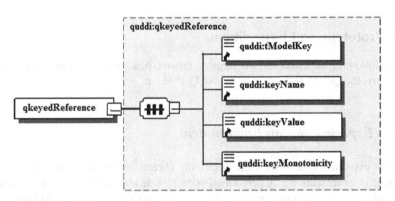

Fig. 9.12   The structure diagram of qkeyedReference

scheduling policies are passed to the metric profiler, the profiler will need to fix a time frame within which it will keep probing the Web service to take the required samples. Since metrics vary in their profiling nature, for each metric we take an average value from the values measured during the profiler lifetime. Thus, for each corresponding profiler, the lifetime should be set moderately in order to exactly cover the proper period needed to measure the metric. This is in order to neither make it too long as it might cause undesirable overheads nor too short as it might lose significant values.

9.3.6 The Discovery Mechanism

Since we have multiple Web service requestors and multiple Web service offers (i.e., profiles in our case), we used the matchmaking algorithm explained in Hafez et al. [9] that relies on a Constraint Satisfaction Optimization Problem (CSOP) solver to match requests with Web services satisfying both functional and QoS requirements and then ranking the Web services.

For the matchmaking phase, we ended up having multiple service offers and multiple service requestors resulting in constraint satisfaction problem where the variables are the QoS offers (i.e., QoS measurements) and the QoS needs resulting in:

- Not matching
- Partially matching
- Better matching
- Exactly matching

For the selection phase, it is about ranking the Web services according to the utility function used in the Hafez et al. approach [9] based on:

- User preferences (i.e., weights specified by the requestor for each QoS property)
- Degree of matching

9.4 Prototype and Experiments

In the following experiments, we measure the overhead introduced by our modified directory, the *Q-UDDI*, as well as by our Q-Profiler.

9.4.1 Experimentation Environment

For our experimentation, we used a "Driving Directions" Web service. Driving directions in general are easily performed using mobile applications. However, as mobile devices roam from one geographic region to another, navigation maps may not be readily available on the client devices themselves. In such case, navigation can be implicitly performed using a back-end Web service. Such opportunistic usage of a Web service needs to be done in a way that does not necessarily involve the user, and more importantly, without the user feeling a significant degradation in quality of service.

To perform our experimentation upon a "Driving Directions" Web service, and to isolate the effect of the network, we installed both the *Q-UDDI* and the *Q-Profiler* on the same node. This is one of the reasons why the absolute overall latency that is imposed by our system is relatively low, as the following experiments show. However, the measured latency values of the *Q-UDDI* and the Web service are only for comparative analysis, and more accurate measurements could be obtained if the *Q-UDDI* and the *Q-Profiler* were running on real hardware servers in the cloud.

Table 9.4 Cases of experimentation with the Q-UDDI latency

Case	Latency	Throughput	Reliability	Availability	Integrity	Accuracy	Robustness
0							
1	X						
2	X	X					
3	X	X	X				
4	X	X	X	X			
5	X	X	X	X	X		
6	X	X	X	X	X	X	
7	X	X	X	X	X	X	X

Fig. 9.13 The Q-UDDI latency

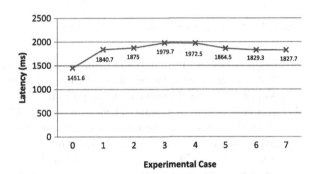

9.4.2 Experiment 1: Q-UDDI Latency

The objective of this experiment is to observe the effect of increasing the number of QoS needs made by service consumers upon the latency of our newly modified directory, namely the Q-UDDI. As a reminder, we profile seven different kinds of QoS metrics, namely latency, throughput, reliability, availability, integrity, accuracy, and robustness. In the experiment, we varied the number of QoS needs made by consumers, starting from no need at all, increasing the needs one by one in no specific preferential order until we reach the maximum we support, which is seven as shown in Table 9.4.

For each of the cases of the aforementioned QoS needs, and after ten runs each, we measured the average latency as the average elapsed time taken by the *Q-UDDI* to reply to consumer discovery requests in milliseconds (Fig. 9.13).

After measuring the *Q-UDDI* latency, we made some observations as follows bearing in mind that experimental case 0 indicates the lack of any QoS needs made by consumers:

1. By observing experimental cases 1 through 7, which reflect the presence of QoS needs, the Q-UDDI latency does not appear correlated to the number of consumer made QoS needs. We did not observe any quasi-linear behavior in the latency as we increased the number of consumer needs.

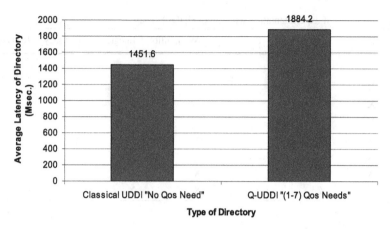

Fig. 9.14 The average latency values of the UDDI and the Q-UDDI directories

2. Comparing cases 1 through 7 again, the maximum observed average latency was 1979.7 ms, and the minimum was 1827.7 ms, indicating a mere 8.31 % difference between the best and worst case latency values.
3. Upon comparing the average latency without any QoS needs (case 0) and the average latencies of all the other cases that indicate the presence of some QoS needs (cases 1–7), and from Fig. 9.14, the difference was a mere 432.6 ms indicating an average 29.8 % overhead when our Q-UDDI was used. This overhead is primarily attributed to the usage of the backtracking search algorithm indicated in Hafez et al. [9] to properly allocate Web services to consumers using a constraint satisfaction approach.

From the above observations, we can safely say that our newly introduced lookup directory, which is sensitive to QoS needs, does not impost a significant overhead upon the Web service lookup process itself. We also conclude that the lookup latency is not correlated with the number of QoS needs made by clients, a very favorable characteristic for any lookup directory of this kind.

9.4.3 Experiment 2: The Effect of Profiling on Web Service Latency

The objective of this experiment is to examine the effect of our own profiling process (conducted by our *Q-Profiler*) upon the latency of the Web service being profiled. We would like to understand the effect of profiling for any QoS property (metric) we support upon the latency of the Web service being profiled. In more specific terms, we would like to understand the effect of profiling for throughput upon the consumption latency, and the effect of profiling reliability upon the consumption latency, and the effect of profiling for availability upon the consumption latency, and so on. We continued to use the "Driving Directions" Web service for experimentation.

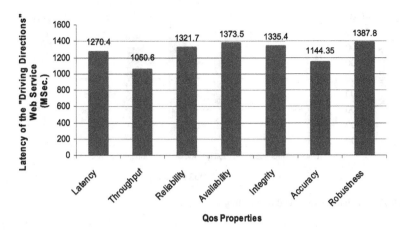

Fig. 9.15 The effect of profiling QoS properties on the Web service latency

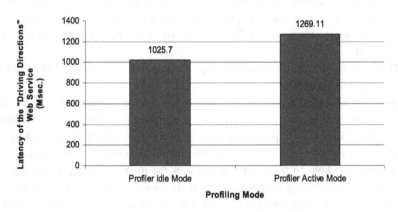

Fig. 9.16 The effect of the profiler idle and active modes on the Web service latency

To measure the Web service latency while the *Q-Profiler* is in the process of profiling for the seven QoS properties, we decided to tackle it as follows: For each of the *seven* QoS metrics we support, we initially activate the *Q-Profiler* to profile for the property in question, then we activate the *Q-Profiler* subcomponent responsible for measuring latency. We take ten measurements each time and average the results. Our results lead us to the results shown in Fig. 9.15. The *X* axis represents each QoS property being profiled and the *Y* axis represents the corresponding latency of the Web service in milliseconds.

To further illustrate the overall effect of the profiler, Fig. 9.16 compares between the "Driving Directions" Web service latency values while the profiler is idle and while it is activated. The value presented in the active mode is the average latency of the Web service as it is being profiled for our seven QoS properties as indicated in Fig. 9.15.

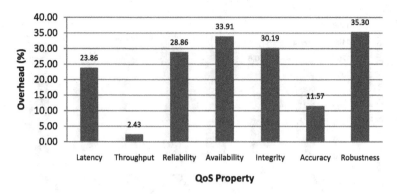

Fig. 9.17 The latency overhead of profiling

The latency overhead that the profiler incurs upon the Web service is indicated in Fig. 9.17. The values indicate the percentage difference between the latency values in Fig. 9.15 and the latency of the Web service while the profiler is idle, as indicated in Fig. 9.16.

There are significant observations one can deduce from the experiment and the charts in the above figures:

As Fig. 9.16 shows, the difference between the average latency value of the Web service while the profiler is idle and while the profiler is active is 243.41 milliseconds. This indicates an approximate 23.7 % overhead on average incurred by our profiler upon the latency of the experimented upon Web service. The overhead can be attributed in bulk to the nature of some of the metrics being profiled for. For example, while profiling for availability, if the Web service fails to respond to a SOAP message the Q-Profiler will send a defined number of consecutive SOAP messages to log the recovery time. Furthermore, while profiling for robustness, if the Web service fails to respond to a SOAP message the Q-Profiler will send a defined number of consecutive SOAP messages to log the recovery time followed by a defined number of consecutive SOAP messages to log the next failure time.

From Fig. 9.17, we can realize that there is a definite overhead that the profiler incurs upon the latency of the Web service being profiled. This overhead varies depending on the type of property being profiled. At its worst, the overhead is 35.3 % of the latency of the Web service, and at its best, the overhead is 2.43 % with a median overhead of 28.86 %. However, it is worthy to note that even though the latency overhead is as such, profiling only happens in accordance to pre-defined policies with the service provider. Providers can plan their capacity taking into consideration the presence of the profiler behaving as such.

As an overall behavior, we therefore conclude that our profiler, namely, the *Q-Profiler* does not have significant effect on the consumed Web service latency.

9.5 Conclusion

In this chapter, we note how important Web services have become, serving as basic building blocks supporting the development of mobile pervasive applications. However, Web services continue to be primarily specified in a functional fashion, with minimal specification of the non-functional characteristics. For this purpose, and in support of building mobile pervasive applications, we introduced a system to perform profiling and selection of published Web services. We dynamically acquired Web service QoS measurements by probing them according to some predetermined and managed policies. We extended the classical UDDI to hold QoS information of profiled Web services, and also provided Web service requestors, such as mobile clients, with an interface to request the services they need with both functional, as well as QoS requirements. We demonstrated that this system could be implemented seamlessly without change in the Web service logic. To evaluate our system, we investigated the latency of the lookup directory as the number of QoS demands made by consumers increased. We also investigated the effect of profiling the Web services for various QoS measurements upon the latency of the Web service that is being profiled. Our evaluation indicates a tolerable overhead associated with the introduction of the third party monitoring process.

References

1. Abramowicz, W., Kaczmarek, M., Kowalkiewicz, M., & Zyskowski, D. (2006). Architecture for service profiling. In *Proceedings of the IEEE services computing workshops, SCW*, 18–22 September 2006 (pp. 121–130). Washington: IEEE Computer Society.
2. Abramowicz, W., Kaczmarek, M., & Zyskowski, D. (2008). Profiling of Web services to measure and verify their non-functional properties. In K. M. Khan (Ed.), *Managing Web service quality: measuring outcomes and effectiveness* (pp. 96–113). Hershey: Idea Group Inc (IGI).
3. Ali, A. S., Rana, O., & Walker, D. W. (2004). WS-QoC: Measuring quality of service compliance. In *Proceedings of the international conference on service oriented computing (IC-SOC04)*, New York, NY, USA.
4. Bellwood, T. (2002). Understanding UDDI IBM developerWorks. http://www.ibm.com/developerworks/webservices/library/ws-featuddi/. 1 July 2002.
5. Blum, A., & Carter, F. (2004). *Representing Web services management information in UDDI* (Ed. Report). January 2004.
6. Booth, D., Haas, H., McCabe, F., Newcomer, E., Champion, M., Ferris, C., & Orchard, D. (Eds.) (2003). *Web services architecture* (World Wide Web Consortium (W3C) Working Draft). 8 August 2003. www.w3.org/TR/2003/WD-ws-arch-20030808.
7. Clement, L., Hately, A., von Riegen. C., & Rogers T. (Eds.). UDDI Spec. Technical Committee Draft, Dated 20041019. http://www.oasis-open.org/committees/uddi-spec/doc/spec/v3/uddi-v3.0.2-20041019.htm. Bellwood, T., Capell, S., Colgrave, J., Dovey, M. J., Fegin, D., Clement, L., Hately, A., Kochman R., Macias, P., Novoty, M., Paolucci, M., von Riegen. C., Sycara, K., Wenzel, P., Rogers., T., & Wu, Z. (contributors).
8. Coulouris, G. F., & Dollimore, J. (1988). *Distributed systems: Concepts and design*. Reading: Addison-Wesley Longman.
9. Hafez, D., Aly, S. G., & Sameh, A. (2009). *Expanding the context-oriented architecture to incorporate QoS*. M.Sc. Thesis. The American University in Cairo.

10. Han, Q., & Venkatasubramanian, N. (2006). Information collection services for QoS-aware mobile applications. *IEEE Transactions on Mobile Computing*, 5(5), 518–535.
11. http://www.ibm.com/developerworks/webservices/library/w-ovr/.
12. Hunaity, M. A. (2008). Towards an efficient quality based Web service discovery framework. In *Proceedings of the 2008 IEEE congress on services—Part I*, 6–11 July 2008 (pp. 261–264). Washington: IEEE Computer Society.
13. Kritikos, K., & Plexousakis, D. (2007). Semantic QoS-based Web service discovery algorithms. In *Proceedings of the fifth European conference on Web services, ECOWS*, 26–28 November 2007 (pp. 181–190). Washington: IEEE Computer Society.
14. Kritikos, K., & Plexousakis, D. QoS-based Web service description and discovery. In *ERCIM news*. http://ercim-news.ercim.eu/qos-based-web-service-description-and-discovery.
15. Liu, Y., Ngu, A. H., & Zeng, L. Z. (2004). QoS computation and policing in dynamic Web service selection. In *Proceedings of the 13th international World Wide Web conference on alternate track papers & amp; posters, WWW Alt. '04*, New York, NY, USA, 19–21 May 2004 (pp. 66–73). New York: ACM.
16. Lo, C., Cheng, D., Lin, P., & Chao, K. (2008). A study on representation of QoS in UDDI for Web services composition. In *Proceedings of the 2008 international conference on complex, intelligent and software intensive systems, CISIS*, 04–07 March 2008 (pp. 423–428). Washington: IEEE Computer Society.
17. Maximilien, E. M., & Singh, M. P. (2004). A framework and ontology for dynamic Web services selection. *IEEE Internet Computing*, 8(5), 84–93.
18. Menascé, D. A., & Almeida, V. (2001). *Capacity planning for Web services: metrics, models, and methods* (1st ed.). New York: Prentice Hall.
19. Ran, S. (2003). A model for Web services discovery with QoS. *ACM SIGecom Exchanges*, 4(1), 1–10.
20. Sheth, A., Cardoso, J., Miller, J., & Kochut, K. (2002). QoS for service-oriented middleware. In *Proceedings of the 6th world conference on systemics cybernetics and informatics (SCI02)*, Orlando, Florida.
21. Taher, L., Basha, R., & El Khatib, H. (2005) QoS information & computation (QoS-IC) framework for QoS-based discovery of Web services. *Upgrade*, VI(4), August 2005.
22. The Open Group Base Specifications Issue 6 IEEE Std 1003.1, 2004 Edition. http://www.opengroup.org/onlinepubs/000095399/utilities/crontab.html.
23. Tian, M., Gramm, A., Ritter, H., & Schiller, J. (2004). Efficient selection and monitoring of QoS-aware Web services with the WS-QoS framework. In *Proceedings of the 2004 IEEE/WIC/ACM international conference on Web intelligence*, 20–24 September 2004 (pp. 152–158). Washington: IEEE Computer Society.
24. UDDI Technical White Paper. http://www.uddi.org/pubs/Iru_UDDI_Technical_White_Paper.pdf. 6 September 2000.
25. Zhou, J., & Niemela, E. (2006). Toward semantic QoS aware Web services: Issues, related studies and experience. In *Proceedings of the 2006 IEEE/WIC/ACM international conference on Web intelligence*, 18–22 December 2006 (pp. 553–557). Washington: IEEE Computer Society.
26. Zhou, C., Chia, L., & Lee, B. (2005). Semantics in service discovery and QoS measurement. *IT Professional*, 7(2), 29–34.

Chapter 10
A Middleware Supporting Adaptive and Context-Aware Mobile Applications

Lincoln David, José Viterbo, Marcelo Malcher, Hubert Fonseca, Gustavo Baptista, and Markus Endler

Abstract Mobile Applications with context awareness features allow mobile users to communicate and share different sorts of context-based information among themselves, such as the current position of other users, geo-referenced data, device speed and others. Although many of such mobile collaboration applications potentially share a good amount of functionality, most of them are developed from scratch, monolithic and tailored to specific mobile platforms, what limits their applicability. This chapter presents a client middleware architecture which supports dynamic deployment and composition of components for context-awareness, common collaboration services, and presents a context oriented language easing the coding of such applications. We also present some prototype context-aware applications implemented on the top of our middleware services, one of which was used to assess the advantages of using our middleware.

L. David (✉) · M. Malcher · H. Fonseca · G. Baptista · M. Endler
Laboratory for Advanced Collaboration (LAC), Pontifícia Universidade Católica do Rio de Janeiro, R. Mq. de S. Vicente, 225, Rio de Janeiro, RJ 22451-900, Brazil
e-mail: lnsilva@inf.puc-rio.br

M. Malcher
e-mail: marcelom@inf.puc-rio.br

H. Fonseca
e-mail: hfonseca@inf.puc-rio.br

G. Baptista
e-mail: gustavolb@inf.puc-rio.br

M. Endler
e-mail: endler@inf.puc-rio.br

J. Viterbo
Instituto de Computação, Universidade Federal Fluminense, R. Passo da Pátria, 156/Bloco E/3° andar, Niterói, RJ 24210-240, Brazil
e-mail: jviterbo@id.uff.br

T. Lovett, E. O'Neill (eds.), *Mobile Context Awareness*,
DOI 10.1007/978-0-85729-625-2_10, © Springer-Verlag London Limited 2012

10.1 Introduction

Mobile and context-aware collaboration allows geographically distributed mobile users to communicate and share different sorts of context- and location-based information among themselves, such as geo-referenced annotations or the current positions of other users. Although many of such applications may share some functionalities related to context-/location-awareness, communication and sharing mechanisms, most of them are developed from scratch. As a consequence, they are monolithic and include platform dependent-code, what limits their applicability and prevents their portability.

Such restraints may be overcome by the use of middleware platforms, which allow the development of applications that are less dependent of the specific features of mobile platforms and device resources/sensors. Therefore, the development process becomes less complex due to the adoption of high-level software structuring and management mechanisms, as well as the reuse of common modules. Hence, major considerations driving the design of middleware platforms for mobile collaboration are built-in support for flexible deployment and composition of services, context-awareness, flexible and asynchronous service interaction model, data sharing and event distribution, and provisioning of context- and location-aware services.

Nevertheless, while current middleware platforms for context-awareness usually emphasize architectural styles and effective mechanisms for context processing and modeling [1], most do not provide the adequate programming level support (e.g. access to context information is simply through APIs). This lack of support causes the resulting context-adaptive application source code to contain several conditionals that are not part of its main logic, i.e., if-else control structures spread all over the code, increasing the complexity of development and maintenance.

In order to address these problems, we have developed—on top of Android— a mobile client middleware that eases the development and maintenance of adaptive, context-aware mobile applications. Our middleware not only supports the composition, dynamic deployment and interaction between application components and context provisioning modules (i.e. small shareable internal components called Context Providers), but also provides a programming-level abstraction that eases the coding of context-aware mobile applications in Java.

This chapter is organized as follows. In the next section we summarize the related work on middleware for mobile context-aware and adaptive applications. In Sect. 10.3, we give an overview of the proposed architecture. Then, in Sect. 10.4, we describe in more detail the main middleware level components that we have implemented. In Sect. 10.5, we explain the programming-level support given by our system. In Sect. 10.6, we give an overview of some of the prototypes that we developed with our middleware. In Sect. 10.7, we present a qualitative evaluation of the advantages of using our middleware. Finally, in the last section, we present our concluding remarks.

10.2 Related Work

From the middleware perspective, research on context-aware software has mostly addressed dynamic adaptation, exploring the architecture styles and the mechanisms that best support dynamic adaptation for specific platforms. Along this line, several middleware systems for context-awareness have been developed in the last decade [1]. However, many of them only support deploy-time configuration of context providing components, and not the download, deployment and activation of these middleware elements during execution time, as it is possible in our middleware (cf. Sect. 10.4). One exception is the work by Preuveneers and Barbers [2], which presents a resource- and context-aware middleware for mobile devices that is component based and self-adaptive. In their system, however, there is no integration with programming-level mechanisms to facilitate the implementation and maintenance of context-aware applications.

ContextPhone [3] also supports the development of context-aware applications for smart phones. It is composed of interconnected modules which provide a set of open-source libraries and components to be executed on mobile phones. The main modules are the sensor module, which acquires raw context data from different sources, like positioning information from a GPS sensor, and the communication module, which implements connectivity and communication with remote services through different protocols, such as GPRS, Bluetooth, SMS and MMS. However, this platform only provides very simple forms of context-awareness and lacks support for dynamic adaptation of the middleware and applications.

From the programming language perspective, the most promising approach is probably Context Oriented Programming (COP). It has been explored in many forms, but the main problem with most works is that they are based on specific programming languages—or require specific compilers—that are not available on mobile platforms. For example, ContextL [4] and AmOS [5] are built on top of CommonLisp, and ContextEmerad [6] is based on the concurrent functional language for real-time systems Emerald, while ContextJ [7] is an extension of Java which requires a specific Java compiler.

There are also works that explore the COP paradigm using a variety of scripting languages, such as ContextR, ContextLua or ContextPy [8], in which the COP concepts of layers and dynamic layer activation have been incorporated into Ruby, Lua and Python languages, respectively. Here, the main problem is that most of these scripting languages either are not available for mobile platforms, or require much run-time resources for these platforms. Appeltauer et al. [9] present a quite complete comparison and evaluation of several variants of COP.

10.3 Proposed Client Architecture

Our client architecture is composed of a middleware layer and a programming layer, as shown in Fig. 10.1. In our approach, a mobile client application is built out of dynamically deployable and composable components (represented as Comp_X in

Fig. 10.1 Client architecture and MD-ECI

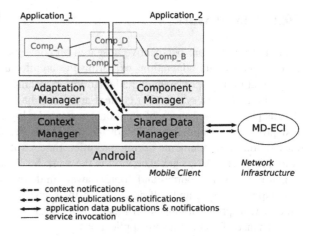

Fig. 10.1), each of them implementing an elementary functionality of the application (e.g. instant messaging, a map annotation service, etc.). The composition, execution, dynamic adaptation and interaction of these components are supported by five middleware-level services presented ahead. In addition, each component may be implemented using a sixth element, our Context Oriented Programming support, so that the components' behavior may be context-aware and dynamically adaptive as well.

1. Component Manager: This service is responsible for the discovery, dynamic deployment and binding of the components used by applications. It also supports queries about all components currently deployed at the device, and their current states (e.g. loaded, deployed, active/inactive).
2. Adaptation Manager: This service is responsible for triggering dynamic adaptations in the applications components, whenever required. For this purpose, it listens to notifications of context changes, monitors the current configuration of components and requests basic operations on components through the Component Manager. The Component and Adaptation Services are elements of the Kaluana [10] component-based system (cf. Sect. 10.4.1).
3. Shared Data Manager: This service provides a uniform API for asynchronous communication among any components, based on a Publish-Subscribe mechanism. A single parameter at the publication operation determines if matchmaking with subscriptions and notifications will be provided only to local subscribers, or also to remote ones. For the latter, SDM relies on MD-ECI.
4. MD-ECI: This service is a SIP-based Publish-Subscribe system [11] that supports remote distribution of notifications of publications—which may be data objects or events—among mobile devices. The main difference between an event and a data object is that the latter is kept in persistent storage at the MD-ECI broker for access by late-joiners, i.e. subscriptions made after the object's publication.
5. Context Manager: This service supports the discovery, deployment and execution of any number of Context Providers. Each of them will collect, process or

distribute context data (e.g. resource states or events, and location or sensor data) from the device's mobile platform.

6. Situation Evaluation Engine (SEE): supports the definition of context situations and its association with ContextJ* [7] programming layers, as means of implementing variant and context-specific, dynamically switchable behavior of software components. These context situations and layers define an appropriate programming language abstraction that supports the dynamic and context-aware switching between application code segments.

We chose Android as the primary mobile platform target for our middleware because it supports Java programming, defines a Service Oriented Architecture and provides a rich set of libraries for sensor probing and control, GUI development and Programming Interfaces to Google services, such as Maps or Calendar. The Android programming model defines four essential types of elements that make up a mobile application: Services, Activities, Broadcast Receivers and Content Providers. Although most of our current middleware implementation depends on Android features, all its constituent services can, in principle, be ported to any other service oriented platform, such as OSGi [12].

10.4 Implemented Middleware Services

In this section we discuss in more detail the basic services of our middleware.

10.4.1 Kaluana

Kaluana [10] is the tier of our middleware that implements the Component and Adaptation Managers. It defines a component model on the top of Android's service-oriented framework. In this model, each component defines a set of provided services, a set of used services, and the names of other components it depends on. Also, any Android service or activity is component-based, i.e. has a descriptor which defines the set of services it requires for execution. When an activity or service is started, the Component Manager uses the Android framework to search for the required services. If it finds a locally loaded component that implements this service, it simply activates the component. Otherwise, it may download and deploy a suitable component from a remote component repository.

The Adaptation Manager is responsible for determining if a component should be added to, activated, deactivated or replaced from a device, and for selecting the candidate components for such adaptation. This selection is based on the current system context (or user location) and according to an execution pre-requisite associated with each component. For example, when the device switches from a GRPS to a WiFi connection (of a specific and trusted SSID), a component for WiFi RSSI-based (indoor) and site-specific location service may be deployed and activated at the device. In order to actually perform such a dynamic adaptation, the Adaptation Manager issues basic activation and binding requests to the Component Manager, which does the activations and re-bindings and then updates its registry.

10.4.2 Shared Data Manager

The Shared Data Manager, or SDM, is an Android service that implements a publish-subscribe mechanism which is used by applications and middleware services to exchange data and events both locally, i.e., for asynchronous interaction with components deployed on the same device, or remotely, with components and applications executing on remote devices. SDM can be used for sharing almost any type of data. For publishing a data or event, an application middleware service only needs to inform the data/event's subject. Optionally, it may inform other properties (attributes), which are used in subscription expressions for filtering. In case of a data publication, it should add a serialized object representing the data itself, e.g. a geo-referenced text, video-clip or audio recording. To receive updates on a specific subject, an application or middleware component must subscribe with the SDM, registering a listener and optionally informing also an expression referring to the data/event properties. Whenever a new publication on this subject happens, the SDM will notify all subscribers of this subject whose expressions match the properties of the published object/event. In order to deliver data/events to subscribers on other devices, SDM implements also a MD-ECI client.

10.4.3 MD-ECI

The MD-ECI is a content-based pub/sub system, with a classic centralized architecture. It is composed by a Java API for event publishers and subscribers called Agents, and a Java API, which represents an event broker called Broker. By using the JAIN SIP [14]—a Java API for the SIP protocol—it provides mechanisms for handling client mobility (dynamic changes of their IP address) and periods of client disconnection. More information about the MD-ECI can be obtained from [11].

10.4.4 Context Management Service

The Context Management Service, or CMS, is an Android service that manages the gathering, processing and distribution of any type of context data. Within CMS, each type of context data/event is de facto obtained or produced by a specific Context Provider (CP). Each CP is a component that can be deployed and activated/deactivated independently by the CMS, depending on whether there is an application component interested in the corresponding context type. CMS also supports the discovery and dynamic download of new CP from a remote repository.

Fig. 10.2 CMS interactions
upon new context
subscription

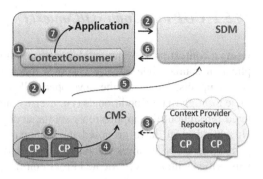

CMS uses SDM to deliver the requested context data object to the subscribers, regardless if they are local or remote. Context subscribers may be application specific components or other CPs, such as those responsible for transforming or aggregating lower-level context data and producing higher-level context information. CMS also provides class ContextConsumer, aimed at hiding from the application the code necessary to interact with SDM and CMS, and thus offering a much simpler interface, referring only to the specific context information needed.

Figure 10.2 illustrates the basic interactions between an application, the CMS and SDM: A ContextConsumer of an application issues a subscription at SDM for some specific type of context information, e.g. battery level, and notifies CMS (steps 1 and 2); Alternatively, the Context-Consumer may also make a synchronous request to obtain the current state of a specific context type (step 2). In either case, CMS searches for any locally deployed CP that can produce the requested context information. If none can be found locally, CMS searches, downloads the corresponding CP from the remote repository and activates it (step 3). Once activated, the CP polls or invokes methods at the Android API of the corresponding Resource Manager, and delivers the polled data to CMS as a ContextInformationObject (step 4). CMS adds some data to this object (e.g. the deviceID and timestamp), and publishes it through SDM (step 5). This object is then delivered to all ContextConsumers with matching subscriptions (step 6), which in turn pass it to the applications for specific handling (step 7). Currently, we are setting up a library of Context Providers for CMS that includes following types of context: Geographic location (GPS), Time, Battery level, Type of wireless connection, WiFi RF signal strength, Accelerometer, etc.

10.5 Programming Level Support

In this section we introduce the Context Oriented Programming paradigm and explain how we extended it to implement SEE, our programming-level middleware support for adaptive and context-aware application programming.

10.5.1 COP and ContextJ/ContextJ*

Using a context provisioning middleware component, such as CMS, the mobile application source code already becomes much less mingled with context-specific code snippets. However, the developer still has to code the adaptation's control logic through many conditionals (i.e. if-else control structures), which remain scattered throughout the application's source code. In order to mitigate this problem, Hirschfeld et al. have proposed the Context-Oriented Programming (COP) [12] paradigm, which is an extension of Object-Oriented Programming and has some similarities with Aspect-Oriented Programming, in that it also supports modularization of cross-cutting concerns. The basic idea underlying COP is to provide means of dynamic activation and composition of behavioural variations, by defining alternative source-code segments that can be switched on and off according to the associated context state. Such a variable behavior can be compared to the polymorphism obtained by class inheritance in Object-Oriented Programming, with the difference that the sub-classes are switched at execution time, according to the corresponding context state.

ContextJ [9] is a Java-based COP programming language which extends Java with only some very few constructs, which makes it very easy to learn for Java programmers. The main new structuring concept in ContextJ is called layer, which is a named first-class entity used to group all the source code fragments related to a same context-specific functionality. In ContextJ, the layers must be switched on/off explicitly using the commands with and without, respectively. Thus, there is still no means of toggling between the layers by an element that is external to the application. In our middleware, we use ContextJ*, which is a pure Java implementation of ContextJ's layers. The main disadvantage of ContextJ* is that the resulting source code becomes slightly more complex than if using ContextJ's layer structures. However, the advantage is that ContextJ* programs can be executed on any JVM without the need of the ContextJ compiler. And this was the main reason for us to use it on our Android-based middleware, for which there is no ContextJ compiler.

10.5.2 Situation Evaluation Engine (SEE)

The Situation Evaluation Engine (SEE) is a Java library that enables the application programmer to define Context Situations (i.e. arbitrary complex conjunctions and disjunctions of expressions on context variables), associate listeners to each situation, and link each context situation with a ContextJ* layer. By doing so, these layers can then be automatically activated/de-activated according to the validity of the corresponding context condition. In order to evaluate each registered context situation, the SEE library works in tandem with CMS, and subscribes to all the context types appearing in any such context situation. Then, whenever a new context update is received from CMS, SEE checks the validity of all the registered Context Situations, and for each one that evaluated as true, it calls the corresponding listener and switches to the corresponding layer. The use of listeners thus makes it possible to implement reactive applications. But even if no listeners are used, the activation of some ContextJ* layers will cause the application to change its behavior according to the current context.

In other words, the SEE works as a mechanism that automatically switches between the alternative implementations of a layered method, without the need to implement ContextJ with clauses. Since every layer is linked with a context situation, the platform guarantees the applications behavioral changes exactly in the way the developer planned, by selecting the correct code segment for each method corresponding to the current context on the execution time.

10.6 Application Prototypes

In this section, we give an overview of four prototype applications that we have developed with our middleware.

10.6.1 TrackService

TrackService is an application used for creating Off-road/Trekking routes/tracks, grading track sections, and sharing this information (i.e. the track log) with other mobile users. The mobile user is able to log his/her route as a sequence of GPS coordinates of his/her mobile device. Figure 10.3 shows three possible screens of TrackService. While the user is walking/driving along a route, he/she is able to evaluate the route according to the difficulty or danger level, giving a grade from 1 to 10 for each route section (cf. Figure's leftmost screen). As he/she gives grades to the sections of the track, a different color is used to represent each difficulty/danger level, ranging from green (e.g. easy) to yellow, and then to purple (e.g. very difficult). The user can also choose if, he/she wants to share his track with others (cf. rightmost screen), and the options are: in real-time, after saving it on the device, or no sharing.

10.6.2 ActiveCal

ActiveCal is a location-aware mobile application used for managing meetings. Users running ActiveCal on their smart phones are be able to schedule a meeting, (through Google Calendar) at a specific place and invite some other ActiveCal users. Thereafter, each invited participant is able to track the other participant's position, estimate how long it will take for each one to arrive at the meeting place, and send alerts to the latecomers. The current version of ActiveCal uses Google Maps API

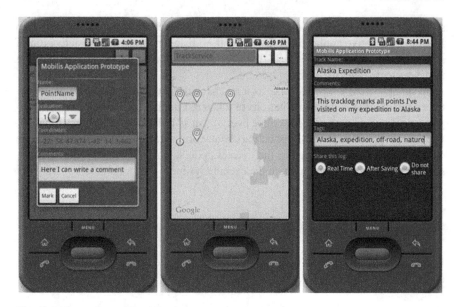

Fig. 10.3 Screenshots of TrackService

and Google Calendar API. The first is necessary for obtaining the distance between two geographic points, the route and the estimated time to reach the destination, while the second provides access to the meeting data, such as date and time, list of participants and meeting place. These pieces of information are collected by specific CMS Context Providers, which combine them to generate a higher-level context information of the sort "Your are late to the meeting at PlaceX". Because of its component based implementation, it is fairy easy to deploy new calendar or route modules for obtaining the meeting data and the position/distance data from other web services than Google Calendar and Maps.

10.6.3 Bus4Blinds

Bus4Blinds is a mobile application that notifies a person—with visual impairment—waiting for a bus of a selected line when it is approaching the place where he/she is waiting. The notification is symmetric, meaning the bus driver is also notified of the presence of the bind passenger at the bus stop. Thus, the application has two client modes, one for the passenger and one for the bus driver. In this prototype we did not implement any special UI for the passenger mode, but of course, it would have special voice- and audio-based functions for entering/modifying the bus line number. Instead, in our prototype implementation, we exercised the on-line sharing of location information. In fact, Bus4Blind uses our middleware services to track the geographic positions of the driver and passenger clients which have matching bus line numbers. These positions are obtained by GPS ContextProviders and shared

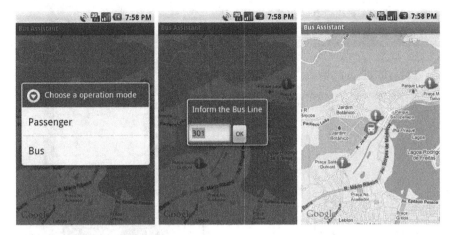

Fig. 10.4   Screenshots of Bus4Blinds

in real-time among each other using SDM. As soon as the distance between the matching clients is less than 30 meters, an audio notification is generated at each client. Figure 10.4 shows three moments of the applications usage: when choosing the client mode (left), when entering the bus line number (middle), and a map-based mode showing the positions of passengers and the bus 301 (right).

10.6.4 Adaptive Mobile Communicator (AMC)

Adaptive Mobile Communicator (AMC) is a simple Instant Messenger for the Android platform (version 2.1, or above) which adapts its user interface depending on the user's movement (Fig. 10.5). It uses periodic GPS data readings to infer whether the user is stationary or moving slowly (i.e. less than 5 km/h) or fast. By default, the messaging interface is entirely textual, as found in all traditional messengers. When moving fast, however, an audio interface is switched on, in addition to the textual interface. This audio interface uses the Android's text-to-speech functionality for output and the Android 2.1's Voice-Enabled-Keyboard [13] to dictate messages instead of typing them. The rationale of this adaptation is the following: when the user is moving fast, s/he may be engaged in another activity (e.g. driving, riding a bike, or climbing on public transportation), which hinders him/her to focus on the textual interface of the messenger.

In AMC, the context "in fast/slow motion" is computed as follows: (i) the device location is requested to the Android platform; (ii) once the location is acquired by GPS, —or any other mechanism, —the Android informs it to the application; (iii) this location may already carry the speed value (depending on the device), but, if not (iv) the application saves this position on a history queue and uses that queue to calculate the average device speed. Figure 10.5 shows AMC's User Interface

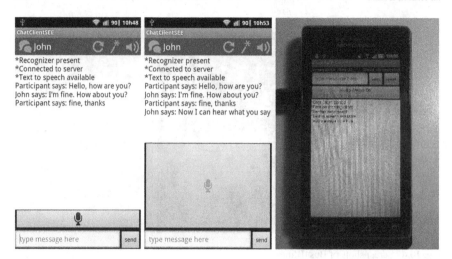

Fig. 10.5 Screenshots of the AMC

with text-based input activated (left), voice-based input activated (middle), and the application executing on a smart phone (right).

10.7 Qualitative Evaluation of the Middleware from the Developer's Perspective

To assess the advantages of using our middleware, we chose the AMC and compared two implementations of the application: one based only on Android, and another using CMS and SEE. The AMC was choose because we think it explores our middleware features in a more advanced way, since it is a context-aware application that also has a adaptive user interface.

Both application implementations share a common core, composed of classes responsible for the user interfaces and for handling communication with a chat server. The MessageHandler class, part of the core, is responsible for showing the text messages received from the other participants. Depending on whether the device is moving fast (e.g. more than 5 km/h), this class will also activate the text to speech feature to synthesize the new message. Due to the requirement to adapt to the context, the implementation of this class is slightly different in each version of the AMC, which will be discussed ahead. The core also contains the RecognitionHandler class, used to de/activate the speech-recognition feature at the same conditions mentioned above.

In the Android-only version, the *MessageHandler* has the method *setAudioOn*, which is used by the class *ContextHandler* to de/activate the text to speech functionality. The *ContextHandler* is only present in this implementation version and includes all the Android code to handle device location updates and calculate its speed. This code is completely platform dependent, and requires specific concepts and knowledge that may not be familiar to most developers. It should be noted that the *ContextHandler* is the element responsible for all the application adaptation, and thus it must have a reference to most classes of the application (including *Message-Handler* and *RecognitionHandler*); which is not a desired class dependency.

In the SEE version, the context-dependent variant functionalities are coded as partial implementations of the *processNewMessage(Message)* method in *Message-Handler* class. For the AMC, we defined a layer *OnMovement* and then did a partial implementation of this method that synthesizes the message received. Then we associated this layer with the Context Situation *OnMovementSituation*, enabling that, every time this situation is evaluated as true, the corresponding partial implementation will be executed.

Every Situation in the SEE is composed of some *SituationRules*, but for the AMC only one *SituationRule* was defined. As shown in the code fragment below, this rule is computed based on the context information this.location.speed. When the application is launched, the SEE automatically starts the CMS to acquire all context information needed and informs subscribes about updates of the corresponding Context Providers. It should be noted that no extra code is necessary to probe or calculate any context information, since, as was show in the previous sections, the platform has appropriate services to catch and deliver this information. Thus, with CMS and SEE the development of the adaptive application is much simplified, since the developer does not need to worry about sensor probing and platform-dependent code: he just need to know the name of the required context information.

```
public class Layers {
    public static final Situation OnMovementSituation = new Situation() {
        protected SituationRule[] defineInitialSituationRules() {
            SituationRule[] rules = new SituationRule[1];
            rules[0] = new SituationRule("this.location.speed") {
                public boolean getValue(String infoVal) {
                    float speed = Float.parseFloat(infoVal);
                    if (speed >= 5) return true;
                    return false;
                }
            };
            return rules;
        }
    };
    public static final SituationLayer OnMovement =
        new SituationLayer(OnMovementSituation);
}
```

Table 10.1 shows some coding complexity metrics used and the values obtained for each version of AMC: Android-only and using our middleware (CMS/SEE). All the values presented in this table concern only the extra code added to the AMC to make it context-aware. The "external classes used" row indicates the number of platform classes needed to be referenced and used by the implementations. Since the SEE version only needs one SituationRule to define the Situation, the value is always 2. The Android-only version must use the platform specifics to probe sensors, etc. The "new methods" row represents the number of new methods that must be implemented for the platform API interfaces. SEE only dictates that every behavior-variant method must presents a partial implementation version for each adaptation. The number of "external constants" represents the number of constants,

Table 10.1 Implementation comparison

	Android only	CMS/SEE
External classes used	8	always 2
New methods	8	1
External constants	5	1
Concepts to learn	7	2
New lines of code	167	59
Development time	48 h	18 h
Testing time	12 h	2 h

like error codes, the application must handle. SEE only returns an error when the information is not available. The "concepts to learn" row represents the number of platform concepts needed to familiarize. In our example, the Android-only version needs: Looper, Listener, Android Services, Android Bundles, GPS activation, GPS configuration; however with SEE we just need Situation and SituationRule. The remaining rows are self-explanatory.

Since AMC requires data from only one sensor (GPS), the values in the left column are relatively low. Of course, this number would increase with the number of sensors required (e.g. accelerometer with GPS), and according to the complexity of the algorithms required for computing high-level context information from the raw sensor data.

While developing the AMC we noticed that the speech recognition function of Android's library is not very accurate, so more complex sentences in English are not correctly recognized. This, of course, makes the application not usable as we hypothesized in our scenario. On the other hand, the text-to-speech function worked satisfactorily well, and all received messages could be understood. For these reasons, we were not able to evaluate the usefulness of adaptive UI by users in a concrete scenario yet.

10.8 Conclusion

In this chapter, we have shown how our middleware can support the Context-Oriented Programming paradigm by extending ContextJ* with automatic layer activation. This represents a significant improvement in comparison with other middleware approaches discussed in this chapter. We have also shown that our middleware makes it easier for developers to create their context-aware applications, as opposed to using platform-specific libraries.

A noteworthy limitation of our study is that both versions of the application used in our evaluation were implemented by the same team that developed the middleware, which could have introduced bias in the results or in the selection of the metrics used in the evaluation. Further studies are needed in which we only briefly instruct programmers on the middleware, to gather additional metrics on the learning curve, and also some subjective data to help to uncover needs or opportunities for refinement. We are also aware of the scalability problems of our remote context distribution approach and aim at developing a context sharing architecture based on scalable self-managed Publish/Subscribe platform. Additional work is underway to further evaluate our middleware. We are also planning the development of additional adaptive applications to assess the applicability of the middleware, i.e., the range of applications and situations to which it can be applied.

The work presented here was done in the scope of the Project ContextNet, which aims at devising and implementing middleware services for efficient and scalable sharing and reasoning of context information from mobile users. Our initial efforts were targeted on developing some basic middleware mechanisms and services, featuring dynamic deployment of components, extensible context-awareness, uniform interface for sharing data, asynchronous communication support (among local and remote components), and providing programming-level abstractions to ease the implementation of applications.

However, there are still many things to be improved, specially with regard to coping with scalability problems. In our view, context information collected from the user's mobile devices will be made available and correlated/combined with data of social networks, so as to derive higher-level information about activities and events of groups of people. Our current research focus on deriving a comprehensive representation of context and situations, developing reasoning approaches and mechanisms for inferring higher-level information and implementing scalable identification and matchmaking mechanisms.

Acknowledgements   This work was partially funded by BMBF/CNPq grant 490817/2006-8.

References

1. Miraoui, M., Tadj, C., & ben Amar, C. (2008). Architectural survey of context-aware systems in pervasive computing environment. *Ubiquitous Computing and Communication Journal* 3, no. 3.
2. Preuveneers, D., & Berbers, Y. (2007). Towards context-aware and resource-driven self-adaptation for mobile handheld applications. In *Proceedings of the 2007 ACM symposium on applied computing*.
3. Raento, M., Oulasvirta, A., Petit, R., & Toivonen, H. (2005). ContextPhone: A prototyping platform for context-aware mobile applications. *IEEE Pervasive Computing*, 4(2), 51–59.
4. Costanza, P. (2008). Context-oriented programming in contextl: state of the art. In *LISP50: Celebrating the 50th anniversary of Lisp*, New York: ACM, 15 pp.
5. González, S., Mens, K., & Cádiz, A. (2008). Context-oriented programming with the ambient object system. *Journal of Universal Computer Science*, 14(20), 3307–3332.
6. Ghezzi, C., Pradella, M., & Salvaneschi, G. (2010). Programming language support to context-aware adaptation: a case-study with Erlang. In *Proceedings of the 2010 ICSE workshop on software engineering for adaptive and self-managing systems (SEAMS '10)* (pp. 59–68). New York: ACM.
7. Appeltauer, M., Hirschfeld, R., Haupt, M., & Masuhara, H. (2009). ContextJ: Context-oriented programming with Java. In *Proceedings of the JSST annual conference 2009, 2D-1*, Shimane University, Matsue, Shimane, Japan, 16 September 2009.

8. Hasso-Plattner-Institute Potsdam. http://www.swa.hpi.uni-potsdam.de/cop/. Last visit: February 2011.
9. Appeltauer, M., Hirschfeld, R., Haupt, M., Lincke, J., & Perscheid, M. (2009). A comparison of context-oriented programming languages. In *COP'09: International workshop on context-oriented programming*. New York: ACM, 16 pp.
10. Fonseca, H. (2009). *A component-based middleware for dynamic adaptation on the Android platform*. M.Sc. Thesis, Department of Informatics, PUC-Rio.
11. MD-ECI (2009). http://www.lac.inf.puc-rio.br/moca/mdeci/mdeci.htm.
12. Hirschfeld, R., Costanza, P., & Nierstrasz, O. (2008). Context-oriented programming. *Journal of Object Technology, 7*(3), 125–151.
13. Android Developers, Speech Input. http://developer.android.com/resources/articles/speech-input.html. Last visit February 2011.
14. NIST SIP: http://snad.ncsl.nist.gov/proj/iptel. Visit July 2011.

Index

T. Lovett, E. O'Neill (eds.), *Mobile Context Awareness*,
DOI 10.1007/978-0-85729-625-2, © Springer-Verlag London Limited 2012